ACCOUNTABILITY

IN
ACTION

A Blueprint for Learning Organizations

Douglas B. Reeves, Ph.D.

**LEAD+
LEARN
PRESS**

LEAD+
LEARN
PRESS

Lead + Learn Press
317 Inverness Way South, Suite 150
Englewood, CO 80112
Phone (800) 844-6599 or (303) 504-9312 • Fax (303) 504-9417
www.LeadandLearn.com

Edited by Cynthia A. Barnes, Ph.D. and Allison Wedell Schumacher, M.F.A.

Library of Congress Cataloging-in-Publication Data

Reeves, Douglas B., 1953-
    Accountability in action : a blueprint for learning organizations / Douglas B. Reeves.--
2nd ed.
        p. cm.
    Includes bibliographical references and index.
        ISBN 978-0-9747343-1-6(pbk.)
        1. Educational accountability--Handbooks, manuals, etc. I. Title

    LB2806.22 .R45 2004
    379.1'58--dc22   2004047649

Printed in the United States of America

10 09 08 07 06 05   10 9 8 7 6 5 4 3 2

Dedication

Je pren de vous mes graces plus parfaits:
Vous m'inspirez, et dedans moy vous faites,
Si je fay bien, tout le bien que je fais.

Ronsard
Morne de corps, et plus morne d'espris

Onde s'alcun bel frutto
Nasce di me, da voi vie prima il seme:
Io per me son quasi un terreno asciutto
Colto da voi, e'l pregio é voistro in tutto.

Petrarch
Perché la vita é breve

About the Author

Dr. Douglas Reeves is chairman and founder of The Leadership and Learning Center (formerly Center for Performance Assessment), an international organization dedicated to improving student achievement and educational equity. Through its long-term relationships with school systems, the Center helps educators and school leaders to improve student achievement through practical and constructive approaches to standards, assesment, and accountability.

Dr. Reeves is a frequent keynote speaker in the U.S. and abroad for education, government, and business organizations and is a faculty member of leadership programs sponsored by the Harvard Graduate School of Education. In addition to his numerous publications, Dr. Reeves work can be seen in national journals, magazines, and newspapers. Doug has twice been selected for the Harvard Distinguished Authors Series and he recently won the Parents' Choice Award for his writing for children and parents.

Beyond his work in large-scale assessment and research, Doug has devoted many years to classroom teaching with students ranging from elementary school to doctoral candidates. Doug's family includes four children ranging from elementary school through college, all of whom have attended public schools. His wife, Shelley Sackett, is an attorney, mediator, and school board member. He lives near Boston and can be reached at dreeves@LeadandLearn.com.

Acknowledgments

My obligations are the debts of the student to his teachers, and, thus, far more significant than the thanks briefly offered here.

My thinking on the issues of accountability and assessment has been guided by a number of thoughtful practitioners, leaders, and thinkers. Dr. Joyce Bales, Superintendent, Pueblo School District No. 60, and Dean of Education at the University of Southern Colorado, is a model of the intersection of intellect and determination. Dr. Stan Scheer of the Littleton Public Schools is the only superintendent I know who regularly puts himself on the substitute teacher list and thus walks the talk of educational leadership in an extraordinary way. Perhaps because he spends so much time listening to students and teachers, he has been able to begin and end his leadership of school systems with the same focused priorities. Other school leaders to whom I am particularly indebted include Dr. Rudy Castruita, San Diego County; Dr. Woody Cummins, State of Arkansas; Dr. Rick DuFour, Adlai Stevenson School District; Mr. Carmen Granto, Niagara Falls Public Schools; Mr. Bill Habermehl, Orange County; Dr. Bob Hetzel, Cairo American College; Mr. Robert Jasna, Milwaukee Public Schools (retired); Hon. Shirley Holloway, State of Alaska (retired); Dr. Vickie Markavitch, Penn-Harris-Madison School Corporation; Dr. John Oldani, Rockwood School District; Dr. Dennis Peterson, Princeton City Schools; Dr. Robert Reeves (no relation), Poway School District; Hon. Ray Simon, State of Arkansas; Dr. Terry Thompson, Wayne Township, Indiana; Dr. Bill Walz, Hoonah City Schools; and Dr. Chris Wright, River View Gardens, Missouri. For the many other leaders, board members, parents and teachers who are omitted on this list of acknowledgments but who have generously shared their ideas and insights, I offer my deep thanks.

The Honorable William F. Burns taught leadership by example long before it was the title of a book. The reason that children in the latter part of the 20th century can learn in a safe environment rather than "duck and cover" as they did in the 1950's is due in no small part to the courage and vision of General Burns. He is one of many authentic American heroes whose examples are followed more frequently than their names are honored. Ms. Barbara Horton is a resilient leader who mixes passion with calm determination. When Ms. Horton speaks, she moves her listeners to action. Dr. Deanna Housfeld is walking evidence that leadership and management are not mutually exclusive. She creates organization amidst chaos, making adults whine while children benefit. Dr. Jeff Howard, president of The Efficacy Institute, is a visionary thinker and leader whose ideas I steal without remorse. But most of all, he is my friend. Professor Audrey Kleinsasser taught me more than most people have forgotten about educational research and analysis. Perhaps the key to her brilliance is the fact that she was a teacher before becoming a professor. There might be a lesson there. Dr. Jay McTighe, Director of the Maryland Assessment Consortium, proves that the person behind the assessment curtain need not be the great and powerful Wizard of Oz, but might be someone who cares deeply about kids and how they learn. Professor Alan Moore says that if you torture statistics long enough, you can make them say anything. He also showed me by example that time and effort trump glibness and eloquence any day of the week. Dr. Bob Marzano and Dr. Grant Wiggins wrote the books on standards and assessments, respectively. Anyone who speaks on those subjects today stands on their shoulders. Dr. Mike Schmoker has lived Harry Truman's statement, "People get mad because I give 'em hell; I just tell the truth and they think it's hell." Mike's focus on results should embarrass those who substitute rhetoric and zeal for evidence. Ms. Karen Young transforms vision into reality. Her energy, vision, and determination make the theory that is too easy to espouse become the reality that is so difficult to implement.

Andy Reeves is the sort of smart person who asks, "How do you play this game?" before taking all of your money. His personal support is the reason my colleagues and I can attempt to help millions of kids. Julie Reeves' editorial advice ranges from the details of proofreading to a gift for transforming impenetrable prose into sentences that make sense. Her mother, Laura Anderson Johnson, was a teacher and superintendent when the leadership gifts of few women were recognized. My father, Jean Reeves, wrote prose that demonstrated the difference between vision and sight. His father, Sherman Vester Reeves, had to put his test scores on the teaching license he received in 1907. Brooks, Alex, Julia, James and Shelley let me be a part of their lives even when traveling 300,000 miles in a year and without saying (aloud, at least) that there have been long stretches when I have been a better consultant than a dad.

My colleagues at The Leadership and Learning Center (formerly Center for Performance Assessment) offer a stimulating and challenging environment in which to think, write, and speak about educational issues. In particular, I am indebted to Dr. Cynthia Barnes and Mrs. Allison Wedell Schumacher, M.F.A.,for their insightful editing and challenging dialogs.

I am also indebted to Larry Ainsworth, Eileen Allison, Greg Atkins, Laura Besser, Ken Bingenheimer, Cheryl Bonnell, Nan Caldwell, Lisa Carbon, Jan Christinson, Donna Davis, Mia Dellanini, Sarah Denker, Cheryl Dunkle, Anne Fenske, Tony Flach, Todd Gilmore, Robin Hoey, Liz Hunt, Mary Kate Karr-Petras, Michelle LePatner, Matt Minney, Peggy Morales, David Nagel, Peg Portscheller, Stacy Scott, Earl Shore, Cathy Shulkin, Jill Unzicker, Mike White, Stephen White, and Nan Woodson.

My books and articles usually provoke some controversy, and I doubt that the present volume will be an exception. As a matter a fact, *I* don't agree with everything I've written, and a bit of reflection on the words that follow will inevitably produce more than one *mea culpa*. Nevertheless, I accept responsibility for the errors of commission, the phrases that only a statistician would love, and the jargon that, despite my best efforts, might have crept into these pages. I am, in brief, accountable to readers. Their decisions to implement or ignore the principles and recommendations in this book will be the greatest reward or punishment any author can expect.

Contents

Introduction

When *Accountability in Action* was first published, No Child Left Behind was a line in a few campaign speeches. Fewer than half the states had established academic content standards, and the term "accountability" typically referred to a set of test scores that were locally determined and reported. Despite the typical association of educational accountability with a list of test scores, *Accountability in Action* proposed the somewhat radical thesis that educational accountability must be *more* than a set of test scores. The book included both research and practical experience that suggested that educational leaders must consider not only scores, but also the "antecedents of excellence," those measurable indicators of teaching, curriculum, leadership, parent involvement, and other factors that are associated with student achievement.

Accountability After No Child Left Behind

Today, all fifty states have academic content standards and some form of testing based on those standards. The No Child Left Behind Act represents the most sweeping federal education legislation in more than three decades. Although the Act remains controversial on many counts and is certain to be a campaign issue in the 2004 elections, the fact remains that more than 90 percent of members of Congress from both political parties voted for the law in 2001. Most observers expect that the law will be modified in the years ahead, particularly with respect to the methods by which special education students are assessed and to the calculation of "adequate yearly progress" in some student populations. But whatever changes may be made to the law, the four essential elements of No Child Left Behind—standards, accountability, testing, and choice—are very likely to remain.

While the original attempt by some in Congress to include federally funded school vouchers was defeated in committee, charter schools continue to grow, fueled by an increasing demand by parents and teachers for greater choice and fewer regulations. Most critics of the No Child Left Behind Act, including members of Congress who have come to regret their vote in favor of the Act, are quick to add that they support the concept of the Act, but regret that Congress did not fully fund it. Others find fault with the initial series of administrative regulations with which the U.S. Department of Education implemented the Act or disagree with the vastly different ways in which state departments of education have interpreted the Act. At the end of the day, however, the consensus remains the same: states will have academic standards, tests based upon those standards, and accountability systems that are comprehensive and public. Just as was the case six years ago, the majority of policy makers appear to equate accountability with test scores.

Beyond Test Scores

Therefore, it is now more essential than ever for educators, school leaders, school board members, parents, and everyone else with an interest in education to make this declaration: Accountability is more than test scores. Some might argue that the notion of a constructive accountability system that considers the antecedents of excellence is no longer possible. We are in a test-driven world where students' test scores are carefully measured and displayed in headlines, but we too seldom give the same systematic attention to the actions of teachers, school leaders, and policy makers.

Practical experience and a growing body of evidence suggest that we need not give up hope. School systems that have used the accountability system described in the following pages have received national recognition for their improvements in student achievement and their successes in narrowing the equity gap in schools. Foundations and other funding sources are increasingly requiring schools to provide more than a set of test scores, but rather to produce a body of evidence that links specific professional practices to improved student achievement. Federal and state requirements for educational research have become more and more stringent, calling for a consideration of multiple variables and comparison groups. Researchers investigating alternative programs have discovered that brand-name labels are not helpful, as the programs are sometimes effective and sometimes not. They have learned that the presence or absence of a brand name is not a useful indicator; instead, a measurement of the degree to which programs are implemented yields insight into effective educational policy. These are challenges that one-dimensional accountability systems cannot address. Only a comprehensive accountability system that considers system-wide indicators—test scores, school-based variables, instruction, curriculum, leadership, and the many other factors affecting student achievement—and narrative descriptions of school environment will meet the complex demands of stakeholders.

Since the publication of the first edition of *Accountability in Action*, I have elaborated on the structure of effective accountability systems in other writings. Readers who prefer a brief overview to the subject might consider *Holistic Accountability: Serving Students, Schools, and Community* (Corwin Press, 2001) and *Accountability for Learning: How Teachers and School Leaders Can Take Charge* (ASCD, 2004). A consistent theme throughout my writing and thinking about accountability is that no child in any school will be more accountable than the adults. When accountability systems have greater consequences for fourth graders and high school students than they do for superintendents, principals, teachers, and board members, I cringe. It does not have to be that way. There are courageous school boards that have established accountability indicators for themselves, and there are remarkable superintendents who hold themselves and their central office colleagues to the same level of public accountability that affects every student, teacher, and principal[1]. When accountability is broadly distributed and its burdens

---

[1] To read more about exemplary educational leadership, please consider two additional books by Dr. Reeves and available from The Leadership and Learning Center: *The Daily Disciplines of Leadership: How to Improve Student Achievement, Staff Motivation, and Personal Organization* and *The Leader's Guide to Standards: A Blueprint for Educational Equity and Excellence* (Jossey-Bass, 2002).

fairly shared, the central outcome of accountability is not ranking or humiliating, but rather a relentless search for effective practice and practical solutions. When accountability systems include the actions of adults, then the focus of the entire organization shifts to a constructive approach to improving professional practices of teachers and leaders.

Data-Driven Decision Making

One dominant feature of schools in the era of accountability is a relentless focus on data. Surely, facts are good things, and no one wants to confess to being less than "data-driven" in the current parlance. Facts, particularly when they stem from test scores, are interesting and sometimes necessary, but are always insufficient when making sound educational decisions. It's a fact that many Americans could stand to lose a few pounds. It's not at all clear that the fad diets and drugs associated with weight loss will enhance our health. Similarly, it's a fact that many American school children could stand to improve their skills in literacy and math. It's not at all clear that the fad staff-development diets and educational drugs associated with dramatic claims of test score improvements will truly improve American education. If the "data" in data-driven decision making merely says that "things are bad, and you will be fired if you don't improve," then the decisions that ensue may be, indeed, based on data, but they will not necessarily be wise or productive. If, by contrast, the data considered by educators and school leaders includes not only test scores, but also a host of system-wide and school-based indicators related to curriculum, teaching, and leadership, then the ensuing decisions will not be the educational equivalent of a fad diet, but rather a thoughtful mix of improvements in the professional practices associated with student achievement. For example, one consistent finding of comprehensive accountability research has been this: the classroom variable associated with improved test scores is neither frantic test preparation nor mindless drilling on low-level skills, but rather an increase in nonfiction writing, editing, rewriting, and collaborative scoring by teachers. This is, to be sure, less dramatic than the breathless announcements of the latest educational cure, but it is far more effective, long-lasting, and sound.

In A World without Accountability

What if the No Child Left Behind Act is repealed the day that you read these words? What if your state repeals its standards and testing program? You could, I suppose, return this volume to your bookstore for a refund. But my greatest hope is that you will find that when we do accountability right, it is not merely to comply with a federal or state mandate, but to respond to a moral imperative. We consider the interactions among student and adult variables not to assure compliance with authority, but to improve teaching and learning. That would be a worthy goal irrespective of the present or future role of federal and state governments in education. Accountability, in the end, is not a device for rating students and schools, but rather a system for improving the quality of life for every student and, as a result, for us all. We do not, after all, get to choose whether or not to have an accountability system. We can only choose whether it is a system that is destructive and limited to test scores, or whether it is constructive, comprehensive, and dedicated to the interests of children and the society in which they live.

Douglas Reeves
Swampscott, Massachusetts
February 2004

PART

Accountability: The Key to Sustained Reform

I

PART

CHAPTER

Fads and Fantasies: Why Educational Reform Fails

As I stand before thousands of teachers, educational leaders, and board members every year, I ask the veterans of twenty-five years or more in education to stand and accept the thanks of the rest of the audience. As the applause dies down, I then ask these veterans, "How many educational fads have you seen come and go during your careers?" The answer is never less than twenty-five. The focus of this chapter—indeed of the entire book—is that evidence must be substituted for uncritical enthusiastic and evangelical zeal as we analyze educational information. The dogged pursuit of evidence will not allow us to move from cynicism to certainty, for certainty appears to be the province of those true believers who dare not let data interfere with prejudice. Our goal is not perfect certainty, but simply an analysis of the weight of evidence. Systematic accountability leads us away from the inspiring anecdote or horrifying story toward a decidedly less exciting, but ultimately more satisfying, review of the evidence.

The cynicism surrounding educational reform initiatives is palpable not only among teachers and administrators, but also among the general public. The failure of public education is not a hypothesis, but a certainty, at least in the eyes of those who believe that rhetorical condemnation of public education and evidence of its failure are the same thing.

Simultaneous Success and Failure

One can hardly be blamed for cynicism in any evaluation of American education. The parade of innovations littering the educational landscape is distinguished more by expense in time, energy, and emotion than by results. Yet amidst all the debris of fact-free debates and rhetorical smugness, there is striking evidence of success in a number of schools (Berliner and Biddle, 1996; Darling-Hammond, 1997; Bracey, 1999; Schmoker, 1999).

Schools today educate more students, with more challenges, to a higher level of learning than at any time in the past 100 years. At the same time, our schools produce record numbers of students who are ready for neither jobs nor additional schooling. These students cannot read, write, or compute well. They appear to have graduated from high school with the conviction that self-esteem and a modicum of effort, or at least the appearance of effort, are all that are required for praise and acceptance by teachers and school leaders.

How can the same system provide simultaneous success and failure? A number of causes are at the heart of this paradox. The growth of the educational system, the complexity of the challenges, and the institutional failures of teacher education programs have all combined to yield high numbers of students who have spent time in schools with few apparent beneficial results. At the same time, this complex array of factors has produced a record number of high school students who are succeeding as network engineers, database designers, digital graphic artists, programmers, and other demanding professions. The fact that the same school systems—indeed the same school buildings—sometimes house both our failures and our successes make it difficult to analyze what works and what doesn't.

Causes and Effects

Why do some students raised in poverty attend ancient schools led by poorly paid teachers working under very difficult conditions, yet leave the school system ready to pursue rigorous courses of study at universities or technical schools? Why do some students raised in wealthy homes attend schools with well-paid teachers working in sparkling schools, yet leave that system not only unable to read and write well, but lacking the ability to know just how poor their academic skills really are?

No simple answers will suffice here, save one essential observation: *Educational analysis* is *multivariate*. In other words, those who claim that a change in one variable "causes" a change in another variable have usually not scratched the surface of the issue at hand. For example, many claim that the "cause" of poor student achievement is poverty. It is easy, after all, to find a relationship or statistical correlation between high poverty and low student achievement. The conclusion that the former causes the latter is wrong, not because poverty is unimportant, but because there is never a single cause of either poor or excellent student achievement.

To illustrate the importance of the multivariate nature of educational analysis, consider the case of student demographics and achievement. It is an article of faith—seldom if ever challenged—among educators, administrators, and the legions of those presuming to give advice on the subject, that demographics and achievement are inextricably linked. Poverty, ethnicity, location, language—these are all immutable factors, baggage with which a student comes to school on the first day.

Whenever I advocate methods for high student achievement, I am invariably accosted by teachers and administrators who angrily contend that parents, not teachers and schools, are to blame for poor achievement. Expecting schools to alter in six hours what parents do or fail to do in the other 18 hours of the day is folly, they emphatically claim.

Such a hypothesis calls for testing. Unfortunately, the "testing" of such claims is very bad politics, akin to trying to test gravity. Why, it's just *obvious* that poverty leads to low student achievement, isn't it? Fortunately, not every researcher and teacher is willing to bow to the "obvious," and the present hypothesis allows us to investigate a common claim: The economic status of a student is directly proportional to the academic achievement of that student.

In the bi-variate world of "this cause, therefore that effect," such a claim can be quickly and easily supported.

Figure 1.1

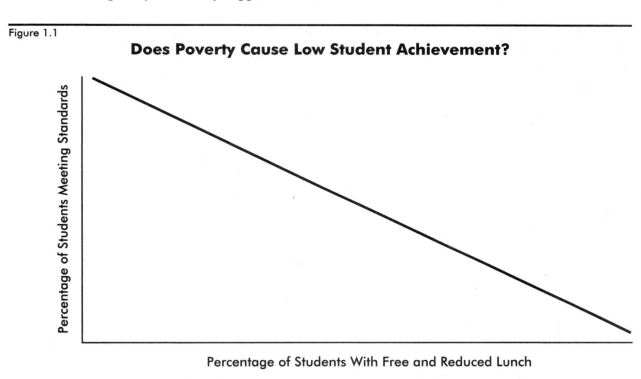

Does Poverty Cause Low Student Achievement?

As Figure 1.1 indicates, the higher the percentage of students eligible for free and reduced lunch (a figure commonly substituted for the percentage of low-income students), the lower the level of academic achievement. That settles it: poverty causes low student achievement, and the hypothesis above has been confirmed.

Not so fast! What *else* influences student achievement? What about the dynamics that happen inside the classroom? Let's ask the fundamental question of education: Do teaching, instruction, and schools really matter?

Linda Darling-Hammond (1997, 1998) and Ronald Ferguson (1991) have assembled some of the most impressive evidence on the multivariate nature of educational analysis. Their conclusions: Of course, demographic variables matter, but they do not matter nearly as much as we have thought. When researchers also consider other variables, such as whether or not students have teachers who are certified in the subject they are teaching, a not-so-funny thing happens. The power of demographic variables as predictors of academic success is drastically reduced. In fact, whether or not a student has a teacher certified in the subject being taught accounts for more than twice the variance in student achievement as all demographic variables combined (Education Trust, 1998). As Figure 1.2 illustrates, the root relationship between poverty and low achievement may not be poverty at all, but rather the work that researchers appropriately call a "confounding" variable: teacher quality. In this example, a school system displayed the typical relationship between high poverty and low achievement. In the same system, the more likely a student was to participate in free and reduced lunch program, the less likely that student was to have a teacher with an advanced degree. An important qualifier must be stated: the mere presence of an advanced degree does not automatically indicate higher quality teacher. Moreover, the presence of an advanced degree is probably a surrogate for many things: time in the profession, commitment to teaching as a career, and participation in multiple professional development opportunities. Those caveats notwithstanding, it is clear that, in this district at least, the relationship between high poverty and low achievement does not tell the whole story, because students who are poor routinely receive teachers who have fewer professional qualifications. Kati Haycock and the Education Trust (1998,1999) have conducted a number of studies and syntheses of studies that demonstrate conclusively that teaching quality is a critical variable in understanding student performance. These can be found at www.edtrust.org.

Figure 1.2

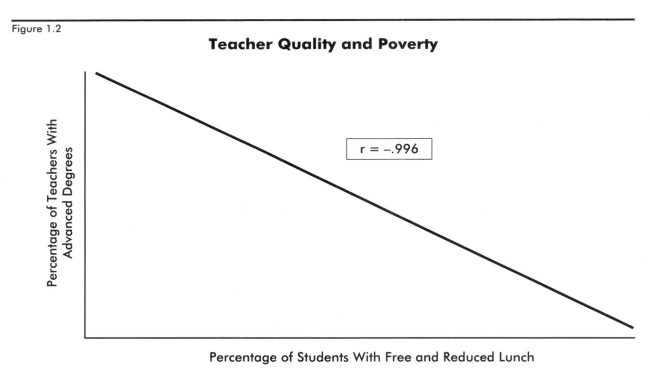

Teacher Quality and Poverty

r = −.996

Percentage of Teachers With Advanced Degrees

Percentage of Students With Free and Reduced Lunch

If this is so obvious, why do so many national studies (and, for that matter, so many local policy makers, leaders, and teachers) persist in the bivariate fallacy of poverty "explaining" poor performance? One possible explanation is that it is easier to blame the student victims than to assign responsibility to the adults in the system. A less threatening but equally discouraging explanation is that it is simply easier to resort to facile answers and quick fixes rather than engage in the more challenging analysis of causes of student achievement and effects of public policies.

Beyond the Quick Fix

Tenuous reforms are based on untenable research, facile conclusions, and faulty logic. Some of the public skepticism about education may be based on political agendas and distrust of any governmental entity. But much of the distrust of educational reforms is founded in the failure of reform efforts to meet the simple criteria advocated here: resistance to fads, recognition of the complexity of multiple variables, and the inclusion of both causes and effects in the reform model. While these criteria may not ensure civil discourse among education critics and defenders, they may lead to a playing field characterized more by reason than by rhetoric.

Questions for Discussion

1. Brainstorm a brief list of "reform" initiatives that your district has undertaken over the past ten years.

2. Which initiatives improved student achievement? How do you know?

3. Which "reform" initiatives are still underway? Why have these continued while some others have been discontinued?

4. What causes high and low student achievement in your district? How do you know? How could you find out? How are these causes of student achievement measured now? If they are not measured, how can you measure these causes in the future?

5. How do you define "achievement" in your schools? What sort of student achievement is omitted from this definition? If some important elements of achievement are not measured now, how can you measure those elements of achievement in the future?

Reform History of Our School System

Reform Initiative Name and Date	Impact on Student Achievement

Definitions of Student Achievement

Elements of Student Achievement	How We Measure It

Causes of Student Achievement

Causes of Student Achievement	How We Measure It

Effective Accountability: Clear Answers for Common Sense Questions

George Orwell (1949) helped generations of students learn the meaning of the term "double-speak." Few practitioners of the art of double-speak have studied the concept as assiduously or applied it with as much vigor as attackers and defenders of public education. Both the strident tone of the debate between these two camps and the obscurity of the arguments employed by the debaters cause many observers to throw up their hands in dismay.

Parents and policy makers have a more direct agenda. In terms of educational accountability, they express the issues very clearly:

- "How's my kid doing?"

- "Are the schools succeeding or failing?"

- "What works best to help students learn?"

- "Do test scores prove the effectiveness of educational programs?"

These are serious questions, and effective accountability systems must address them with clarity and candor. An accountability system that fails to address these common sense questions does not deserve the support and confidence of citizens or policy makers. Simple questions, however, do not necessarily lead to simple (or, more appropriately, simplistic) answers. So it is with educational accountability. These simple questions require complex responses, which will be explored in this chapter. It covers the best ways to make numbers and statistics yield information that is useful for improving the performance of students and schools, and sets common sense questions in a practical context with an example, in the form of a case study, of how administrators should look at a new program to determine its effectiveness.

"How's *My* Kid Doing?"

A question about the performance of a specific child implies that an effective accountability system will be based on information about individual students rather than groups or classes of students. In other words, an accountability system that can supply information about the progress of a specific child must be based on a series of individual student achievement records. If these records are flawed, then the entire house of accountability is built upon a shaky foundation.

One of the most important developments in educational accountability has been the "value-added" methodology developed by Professor William Sanders and his colleagues at the University of Tennessee (1999). The core of the system is a "student-to-student" comparison. While such a comparison makes common sense, it is rare. By far the majority of state and local accountability systems compare one year's class of students to the previous year's class of students—a comparison that involves almost entirely different individual students. Such group comparisons never address the fundamental question, "How is *my* kid doing?" Rather, parents and teachers are given the curious information that their 8th grade students are better or worse than last year's 8th grade students. Group comparisons tell us nothing about the progress and educational needs of individual students.

This has serious implications for accountability systems that claim to evaluate educational quality, but ignore information about classroom teaching and learning. An accountability system that contains test scores alone, without the context of additional accountability information about teaching practices and curricula, is incomplete. A school district that bases its accountability system on test scores alone is analogous to a physician who evaluates physical health based upon indicators such as body temperature or blood pressure, but ignores the other medical indicators that any reasonable physician would regard as essential to a competent diagnosis. In the most bizarre cases, accountability systems not only fail to evaluate substantial parts of the school curriculum, but actually encourage behaviors contrary to those endorsed by the designers of the accountability system.

Consider the case of student writing. Most states, with the resounding approval of boards, legislators, and the public, have established standards for writing. These standards typically require students to express themselves coherently in expository and persuasive writing. Students must also use standard conventions of English grammar, punctuation, and spelling. In order to do this, students must use the writing process (including outlines, rough drafts, and editing) and draft multiple revisions in order to incorporate teacher feedback and make their final written product worthy of the demands for rigor established by state writing standards.

It is axiomatic that standards implementation would require a test congruent with those standards. Simple logic and fairness demand such congruence. Unfortunately, the same logic and fairness seem to elude those legislators and education officials who establish writing standards, but endorse tests incompatible with the standards they have been designed to measure. The standard requires teachers and students to use the writing process; the test uses a single writing prompt followed by a single response. The standard requires teachers to focus on the value of effective written communication; the test requires students to correct spelling and grammar errors in a passage and complete a multiple-choice question—without writing a single sentence.

If parents or stakeholders want an honest and accurate response to the question of "How's my kid doing?" then school systems and districts must use tests or other assessments that will yield the information needed to answer this question. In other words, children need to be assessed to make sure they meet the standard, and only this information will determine how they're "doing." The most virulent critic of public education would not attend an athletic event and, desiring to know the outcome, settle for a description of the weather and field conditions. "What the heck happened during the GAME?" the critic would demand. In the context of the classroom, parents and students must learn about the process and results of teaching and learning.

If the education "game" is to be taken at least as seriously as many people take their weekend athletic events, then it is reasonable to expect that the data used to evaluate the result should be related to the issue at hand: student and school performance. Thus if we want to know how well students write, then we must ask them to write. If we want to know whether they can use the scientific method, then we should ask them to design an experiment and draw inferences from a set of data. If we wish to know whether students understand mathematics, we should ask them to use mathematics to solve real problems.

When policy makers persist in requiring students to perform irrelevant tasks in the name of educational accountability, they could find equal justification in requiring students to run the hundred-yard dash or achieve a certain level of accuracy as they throw a basketball at the hoop. Neither of these activities relates to education, they might reason, but what the heck? They are easy to measure, and they allow us to publish results that validate our thesis.

Students, policy makers, and citizens deserve better. Effective assessment is the foundation of effective accountability. More specifically, it is what Grant Wiggins has called "educative assessment" (1998). If the foundation of an accountability system does not provide students with an opportunity to improve achievement, then the fundamental purpose of accountability has been ill served. Moreover, if individual records of standards-based assessment are not kept, parents and policy makers have no way of gleaning an accurate answer to the question, "How's my kid doing?"

"Are the Schools Succeeding or Failing?"

The second question raised in the name of common sense is built upon the first. Schools succeed only where students succeed. *Thus, assessments of schools, such as accreditation or typical accountability reports, are only as effective as their evaluation of students.* If the evaluation of a school is based upon process alone—the efforts of teachers and administrators—we have a process akin to the experience of a sports player who eagerly awaits entry into the game. The coach offers direction, and the player responds, "I'll try, Coach." The player is then sent back to the bench after the coach explains, "The person in the game is already trying." Failing schools are full of administrators, teachers, and students who are "trying." Accountability systems that look only at process and effort will reward a fixation on meetings, plans, and strategies while ignoring results. Every initiative, including those that I have advocated—high standards, effective assessments, and rigorous accountability—is only effective when it is built upon a foundation that soundly evaluates student achievement. Dr. Mike Schmoker (1998, 1999) is a leading advocate of the focus on results. He has endured heaps of abuse from those who find process a perfectly suitable substitute for student achievement. While a focus on results is important, the "results" which effective accountability systems must consider extend far beyond test scores alone. This is not merely a debate over "process versus results." In fact, a comprehensive accountability system must focus both on measurable elements of the process (specific instructional, assessment, and engagement strategies) and on results (indicators of student achievement). Only with such a comprehensive view can we gain some insight into what the adults in the system can do to influence results achieved by the students.

Although the evaluation of students is the foundation of a sound accountability system, an effective accountability system must base its examination of student achievement on more than test scores. Indeed, the fallacy of reporting school-wide success or failure based on single test scores has been widely documented (Bracey, 1999). Teaching and learning are multiple interactive processes, the results of which are much too complex to be captured by a single score. Accountability systems that depend solely on test scores offer predetermined results: students who are capable test takers will make a school look like a success; students who are not capable test takers will give their school the label of failure. In neither case do the organization, leadership, teaching, and educational practices of the school receive a meaningful evaluation.

Instead, effective evaluation of the success of a school can only be measured with multiple information sources over an extended period of time. There must be several indicators that measure the performance not only of students, but also of the adult decision makers. Such an analysis includes a consideration of resources, teaching methods, and student support. Without a consideration of all of these factors, we are left with the ludicrous notion of evaluating the performance of an entire institution based on the test scores of one group of eight-year-olds during one stress-filled, springtime afternoon.

Effective and comprehensive accountability systems distinguish between student achievement and school achievement, without losing sight of the fact that the latter is integrally related to the former. For example, state and district test scores might provide some indicators of student achievement. But these results are only meaningful indicators of school achievement when they are placed in the context of the specific educational strategies used by the schools. The structure of such a comprehensive system (see Part II) acknowledges both the distinction and the importance of both questions.

"What Works Best to Help Students Learn?"

The third common sense question addresses the heart of an effective accountability system. The question of program effectiveness is far more complex than the recitation of test scores representative of most accountability systems. Such a "box score" approach is the educational equivalent of giving the ranking of teams at the end of the season without shedding any light on the strategies that led teams to succeed or fail. For the disinterested observer who wishes only the most cursory overview, the final rankings may suffice. But those interested in the game would want much more. Those who were owners of the teams would demand far more information. Those people whose futures depended upon the success of their team would demand a continuous analysis, not only of scores, but also of the individual elements of strategies and programs that lead to success.

In the context of school accountability, stakeholders need to know which programs succeeded and which ones failed. In a field littered with "reforms" and "new ideas," some rational method of evaluation other than popularity, enthusiasm, or cost must be used. An accountability system that shows policy makers how intervention strategies correlate with student results can go a long way toward providing such essential program evaluation information.

Some of the best practitioners of such systematic evaluation are Robert Slavin and his colleagues at Johns Hopkins University. In his recent book, *Show Me the Evidence!* (1998), Slavin and his colleagues provide examples of how accountability information can be used to monitor program effectiveness. Perhaps the most astonishing aspect of the book is how few programs have been subject to long-term systematic accountability and analysis.

In sports, media commentators are expected to report not only scores, but they must also demonstrate a thorough understanding of the nuances of the game. They routinely debate the meaning of various statistics. The television commentator or sports journalist who simply writes, "Those with winning records are better teams than those with losing records" would soon be out of a job. When it comes to sports, we expect thorough and detailed analysis of all the relevant data. Moreover, we expect the best commentators to look beyond the data and provide insights based on observation, description, and qualitative understandings that extend beyond numerical explanations. Though the athletic analogy may seem clumsy, I will celebrate the day when analysis of educational accountability data is taken as seriously by the media and the public as analysis of last weekend's sports games. When that day comes, we all may finally know what works best to help students learn. The following example may help to clarify the question.

Case Study: The Whiz-Bang Math Phonics Program

"You've got trouble," Professor Harold Hill, the noted educational consultant and vice-president of marketing for the Whiz-Bang Math Phonics Corporation, intoned. In breathless tones, he explained to the school board that when his program of "math phonics" had been introduced in a neighboring state, student test scores had increased (I originally wrote this to be a parody, and then read in a Midwestern newspaper of a prospective school board member's pledge to bring "math phonics" into the classrooms of the district. Truth is stranger than fiction!). Without a dissenting vote, the board adopted the program and agreed to listen to the proposal by the same company for musical training and character education at its next meeting. Let us consider some questions the board might have asked of the good professor before accepting his claims.

First, they might have asked to examine the data selectively. This means, for example, that we should be extremely skeptical of any data set that is identified as "all students." We might start by limiting our examination of the data only to those students who were present in the school and the particular classroom where the Whiz-Bang Math Phonics program took place. We might further improve the quality of our research by identifying several comparison groups of students who had similar demographic and educational characteristics, but who did not have the benefit of Whiz-Bang training. The question is not "Did the scores of the students in the Whiz-Bang group improve?" but rather, "Did the scores of the students in the Whiz-Bang group improve significantly more than the scores of the students who did not have this training?"

Second, they might examine the extent to which the Whiz-Bang program was actually implemented. The landscape of school reform is littered (as are faculty lounges and school libraries) with programs that evaporated with the morning dew the day after the charismatic speaker addressed the assembled school staff. The research question is not simply, "Did teachers in the Whiz-Bang program have better test scores?" but rather, "Did the Whiz-Bang program advocate greater use of specific and measurable teaching practices, and were they used to lead to greater student achievement?" If this question is not addressed, we are left with what can best be described as "Federal Express" analysis. While there is no doubt that the program (or product or training) was delivered to the faculty, there is no way of knowing if the package was opened and used. (For a more detailed exploration of using accountability systems to evaluate professional development programs, please see Chapter 6.)

These are not exceptional research burdens for any administrator or policy maker to consider before making important (and costly) decisions. Nevertheless, when I have suggested such relatively simple analytical procedures to educators or journalists, I am confronted with the rejoinder that such analysis is excessively complicated. It is interesting that our sports columnists persevere where educators fear to tread. They handle such concepts as "mobility" and even "data dis-aggregation—the systematic analysis of sub-sets of data"—with relative ease.

Consider the case of the Florida Marlins, who won the World Series in 1997. Their 1998 season was miserable. The most casual observer of the game would not make a comparison between the two years and claim that the coaches (teachers) had failed, but would note that a substantial number of the starting players on the championship team were not playing for the Marlins in 1998. Depending on one's point of view, the armchair analyst might conclude that the Marlins' owner was greedy, stupid, or shrewd. However, few thoughtful observers would demand remedial training for the coaches, suggest that they take a coaching test, or conclude that the entire system of baseball is fundamentally flawed and should be replaced with a voucher system.

A comprehensive evaluation of what works best to help students learn must go far beyond mere test scores and include analyses of both how the data reported should be interpreted as well as information about the context in which these results were derived.

Do Test Scores Prove the Effectiveness of Educational Programs?

"Test Scores Increase," blares the headline. This is quite predictable, two or three years into a new testing program, as students and teachers become more familiar with new tests and as curriculum and instruction in schools more carefully anticipate the content of the test (Gardner, 1998). Rather than attribute the increase to familiarity, instruction, and curriculum focus, the advocates of any program that coincided with the increase in test scores trip over one another to take credit for the increase. "We implemented Character Education and our scores increased," declare the advocates of such programs. "We bought five million dollars' worth of new computers and our scores increased," the Director of Technology for the same school system will proudly claim. "Ever since we went to a block schedule, our scores increased," claim the advocates of that particular change. However sincere their advocacy, such claims miss the point. In classical logic studies the error was called "*post hoc, ergo propter hoc*"—after this, therefore because of this.

The assumption that two coincident events are cause and effect can lead to some remarkable claims. The number of churches (or sports bars) increased, the membership in the Boy Scouts (or Rotary Clubs or Satanic Covens) increased, and the scores on our student achievement tests increased. To which of these "causes" shall we attribute the improvement in student achievement? A reasoned response to the question does not come from mere association of coincident events, but a comparison of two groups of students who are, in virtually every respect, similar with the exception of the presence or absence of the educational program being evaluated. Moreover, the analysis must focus on those students who were actually present during the administration of the program. The typical litany of test scores include not only children who were present for the new curriculum or other program being evaluated, but also children who were present for mere days before the administration of the tests. In some states, the test scores also include children who have developmental disabilities and students for whom English is not their native language. When facile analyses of test scores fail to take into account these and other important variables, one knows little more than that test scores changed from one year to the next. Any inferences about the causes for those changes are speculative.

A true analysis of "causes" is profoundly difficult outside of long-term, double blind, clinical studies. Generations of researchers have been trained to recite the maxim that "correlation is not causation." For the reasons noted above, such skepticism of correlation is well founded. Mere association of an educational program with a change in test scores is not a sufficient basis on which to draw conclusions. This does not mean, however, that correlations or associations are without value. Consider the case of smoking and cancer. Medical researchers do not always know what caused a particular cell to become cancerous. For years, the tobacco companies were fond of saying that "correlation is not causation" in defense of their product. After all, they reasoned (quite correctly), the cancer you have might have been caused by solar radiation, by something in your diet, or by your genetic predisposition. You cannot definitely say that tobacco *caused* your particular cancer. Nevertheless, the striking consistency of correlation between smoking and cancer led most observers to conclude that, as the warnings say, "smoking is hazardous to your health."

Giving Numbers Proper Form and Context

Presenting numbers in proper form and context plays a key role in making sure that accountability systems accurately evaluate program effectiveness. Numbers carry authority, even when they lack meaning or context. This is particularly true when the numbers are expressed with decimal points and presented in rank order. Although every beginning student of statistics must learn the error of a "distinction without a difference," the public is regularly treated to a ranking of schools that looks like this:

Rank	School	Math	Reading
1	Merriweather	78.46	69.37
2	Clark	76.24	69.48
3	Lewis	69.37	70.36
4	Jefferson	68.39	46.39
5	Washington	47.39	32.98

Based on a cursory examination of this table, some readers might observe that the difference between Merriweather and Clark Schools appears to be slight. Perhaps an exploration of the standard deviation of the math and reading scores would allow us to explore whether the differences among the schools were "significant" (that is, unlikely to be due to random variation). Surely, however, we can at least draw inferences about the difference between Merriweather and Washington, the highest and lowest scoring schools.

Not so fast! As presented, the data tell us nothing about the number of students tested, the number of students excluded from testing, or the characteristics of the students whose scores appear in the report. Without this information, we know only that the scores are distinct from one another. We do not know if they are different in a meaningful way, nor do we know anything about the educational leadership, instructional practices, or learning environment of these schools. Only with appropriate form and context can we begin to address these issues.

Form and context include, at a minimum, answers to the following questions:

1. Who was tested? This includes complete numbers, including total number of students, number of students tested, number of students excluded from testing, number of students unaccounted for, number of students tested with adaptations, number of students with limited English proficiency, number of students with learning disabilities, number of students who were tested who were also in the classroom throughout the entire year.

2. How representative is the average score of the average student? This includes the range of scores and the standard deviation for the unit that is being compared. In other words, one cannot use the standard deviation for the scores of all students in the nation (typically a lower number) in order to contend that small differences are meaningful when comparing classes, schools, or districts.

3. What other student achievement data are available, and how do they compare to the data being presented? If reading grades are high, but test scores are low, what are we to make of this? Perhaps teachers are just easy graders. Perhaps teachers are hard graders, but they are evaluating a curriculum that is different from the test. Perhaps teachers are neither easy nor hard, but the form of tests that teachers use to determine grades is different from the form of tests that is now being reported in the media.

With schools, as with sports teams, the final score is always reported. In sports, however, the owners, players, and analysts do not merely note the final score. They also conduct comprehensive evaluations of their teams. They try to use accountability information to improve their teams in the future.

The perspectives of taxpayers, parents, teachers, students, and other educational stakeholders find their counterparts in the roles of owners, players, coaches, and analysts, and it is not unreasonable that we provide careful attention to form and context—perhaps with as much care as they devote to sports statistics. However, the sports analogy is not literal, because the taxpayers are no more owners than the parents and students. Irrespective of the roles they play, all participants in the accountability process are well served by the accuracy and context advocated in these pages.

About Standard Deviation, Scores, and Differences Among Students:

This book is intended for a lay audience, and thus I will confine statistical and technical terminology to a minimum. Standard deviation is one of several measures of variation used by researchers. Another common term is "standard error of measurement." Both terms give us some insight into whether the variation between two different numbers is meaningful. The variation to which we refer is the difference between the individual numbers (for example, test scores) and the average number (for example, the average score of a group of students). If the standard deviation is very large relative to individual scores, then it is unlikely that the difference between individual scores is very important. For example, if the standard deviation on a test is 12 points, then one is on shaky ground to assert that the student who received a 140 is smarter, better, or more suitable for college or a particular career than a student who received a score of 130. Both of those scores may be different, but the standard deviation tells us that the scores are not "significantly" different from one another. Even if the second student scored 128, we cannot necessarily say that the first student was "significantly" better. We can only say that it is unlikely that the difference in the scores is due to random variation. This flies in the face of conventional wisdom that in a meritocracy, a 140 is "better" than a 139. Alas for the parents of the child with the 140, this is simply not the case, any more than the .334 hitter is "better" than the .333 hitter. Where this error of a "distinction without a difference" is most pernicious is in the selection of valedictorians based on grade point averages where one student is regarded as "better" than another because of a single class out of a four year curriculum in which one received an A– and the other a B+.

In educational accountability, numbers are an important part of the story, but they tell only *part* of the story. The qualitative dimension of accountability—descriptions, narratives, and observations about culture and climate—creates a lens through which the quantitative data must be viewed. What is the qualitative context of the quantitative data? What are the successes, failures, tragedies, and triumphs of this school that help to explain the story behind the numbers? While no principal in America needs one more report to write, a one-page synopsis of a school's qualitative dimension would add greater context to its test scores. Without such a qualitative context, we are left with the sterility of data that, even when presented with abundant statistical complexity, can leave us wondering, "What *really* happened in that school?" Without the qualitative dimension, our understanding of the "score" is limited, incomplete, and possibly inaccurate. The qualitative dimension is further discussed in Chapter 15 and Appendix B.

What sort of qualitative information should be included? Information about the school climate and environment, the triumphs and tragedies of the school year, and descriptions of any significant changes in programs, personnel, or performance can all be expressed in narrative form. Such narrative information is not a substitute for quantitative data, but rather, gives citizens and policy makers a context in which to interpret numerical results.

Other Common Sense Questions

The essentials of form and context do not end with a mass of data. How do we reconcile apparently conflicting statistics? How do we draw inferences when one part of the team appears to be strong while another appears to be weak? What about the "big play" that appears to create striking distortions in the data? What about the intangibles of the game that cannot be described with a number? These questions are routinely addressed as we consider the fortunes of our favorite team, but the same questions are rarely considered as we review student test scores.

These common sense questions, routinely raised in analyses of sports games, have their analog in educational accountability. How do we reconcile apparently conflicting test data? How do we draw inferences when one school appears to be strong while another appears to be weak? Are the tests in different forms? Do some textbooks, lessons, and activities prepare our students better than others?

Let's take one case in point. Two different mathematics tests were administered to the same group of students, but, on one test, students have significantly lower scores than on the other. What gives? Upon further investigation, we find that the first math test was a multiple-choice test that emphasized calculation skills; the second test required students to explain their answers in writing. The first test emphasized number recognition, minimal reading and no writing; the second test was loaded with reading-intensive story problems and required written responses. The first test allowed students to guess at the correct answer, and about one-fourth of those guesses was correct; the second test allowed no guessing. The first test was a nationally used, norm-referenced test designed to address a very broad range of problems, including some problems that were below grade level and some that were above grade level. The second test was locally designed based on a consensus about end-of-grade proficiencies.

The differences are stark and of critical importance. Of course the scores are different! Why didn't test administrators explain it that way in the first place? Let's think about the last time that we saw a ranking of schools, states, or countries by test scores. Did we see—or even search for—an explanation of the rankings?

Other factors also account for discrepancies in test data. What about the "big play" that appears to create striking distortions in the data? Test-preparation organizations, such as Stanley Kaplan, Princeton Review, PrepMaster and others, routinely claim that their courses can make significant improvements in student test scores. Princeton Review guarantees a 100-point increase on the SAT-1 (the Scholastic Assessment Test), a test for which study and preparation are folly, according to many secondary school faculties. Test preparation programs, however, can have the "big play" effect, camouflaging the impact of a wretched curriculum, poisoned learning environment, and inadequate teaching. Hey, the score is all that matters, right?

Along with the "big play," what about the intangibles of the educational "game" that cannot be described with a number? Despite the myriad statistics that sports commentators offer, they are quick to point out the qualitative dimensions of team success and failure. Qualitative factors describe the environment, culture, and spirit of a team. We listen attentively to these descriptions, because they help provide context for the raw numbers.

Conclusion

An effective accountability system must answer at least four common sense questions: one about individual student achievement; a second about school performance; a third about ways to help students learn; and a fourth about determining educational effectiveness. In order to provide useful information about student achievement, an accountability system must be based on clear standards that have been communicated to students, parents, teachers, and other district stakeholders. Both quantitative and qualitative indicators that measure whether or not these standards have been met must become integral parts of the accountability system. School performance must be based on much more than test scores. Though it is likely to include test data, school performance information must also include how these numbers should be interpreted and the context from which test scores arose.

The questions from parents and the public might be answered as follows:

- "How's my kid doing?"

"James meets all of the standards for reading, creative writing, and social studies. He has yet to become proficient in informative writing and mathematics. With additional work in the areas outlined on the attached detailed report, he should be able to meet all of our academic standards by the end of the current school year."

- "Are the schools succeeding or failing?"

"All but two of our schools are meeting or exceeding the requirements of our accountability system, both with regard to their progress and their achievement of academic standards. Miller School has made substantial progress, but still does not meet district academic standards, and the district has taken steps to expand our most effective programs in that school and discontinue those programs that have been ineffective for Miller's students.

"Washington School has demonstrated neither progress nor achievement for two consecutive years. The experience of other schools in our district with similar characteristics to Washington's student population make it clear that the students are capable of better performance, but that our programs in this school have failed to help students achieve their potential. Our accountability system information tells us that some classrooms at Washington have been remarkably effective, and thus, the district has taken steps to use this information to expand the use of proven best practices in teaching and learning at Washington."

- "What works best to help students learn?"

"Our accountability system information helped identify several programs that have been remarkably effective. The use of block scheduling in our high school has been associated with reduced disciplinary incidents and dropout rates for two consecutive years. The use of a new reading program in the primary grades of some elementary schools has been associated with a significant increase in student achievement for students of all economic, ethnic, and linguistic groups. The pilot program for a new middle school mathematics curriculum has not been associated with improved achievement, and thus, the pilot program will be discontinued, and we will test other alternatives before making a recommendation for district-wide adoption of a new math program."

- "Do test scores prove the effectiveness of educational programs?"

"Not necessarily. Before we can determine whether or not the new writing program for James's school will work, we intend to arrange for two groups of students to have identical curricula and environments. The only difference between the two will be that one has the new reading program and the other does not. Only after this has been established can we test the students and decide whether to continue the program."

Questions for Discussion

1. What are the essential questions that your stakeholders are asking? What do they need to know about students, schools, and policies?

2. How are the answers to these questions developed now?

3. Who are the stakeholders with whom you share information about your educational system?

4. What information do you currently give to stakeholders who want to know how your children and schools are doing?

5. If you wish to tell the "whole story" of your educational system, what additional information is necessary to share with stakeholders?

Questions from Stakeholders for Educational Accountability

Questions from Stakeholders	Sources of Information Now Used to Answer These Questions

Stakeholders

Stakeholders	Information Needs of These Stakeholders

Review the "Stakeholder Questions" in Worksheet 2.1. What additional information is necessary from your new accountability system to meet stakeholder needs?

Stakeholders Questions	Additional Information Necessary to Meet Stakeholders's Needs

3

CHAPTER

Communication: The Essence of Effective Accountability

If educational accountability is to reach its potential, then we must not reduce it to a simplistic set of box scores and headlines. Communication about accountability should be continuous and proactive. Rather than waiting for stakeholders and policy makers to demand accountability, school leaders should embrace the concept by providing information about school successes and challenges throughout the year.

Effective communication about accountability should include answers to the four common sense questions raised in Chapter 2 by addressing the performance of individual students, effectiveness of the entire system, best teaching methods, and the successes and failures of individual programs. The communication surrounding educational accountability has frequently lurched to one of two extremes: attacks by critics, who refuse to recognize success where it occurs; and defensiveness by administrators and educators, who refuse to recognize that their favorite programs may be ineffectual.

The framework for the communications plan of an effective accountability system is provided in Appendix B and described at length in Part II. In brief, effective communication must include information about students, programs, and schools, and this information must be delivered in stakeholder-friendly contexts and terms.

Student Communication

Students should never have to wander aimlessly through their educational journeys, wondering what they need to do in order to please the teacher. Although the "teacher as master evaluator" has a long tradition in our schools, this approach leads students to reach inappropriate conclusions and waste a great deal of time. Early on, students begin the process of learning that it is "what Ms. Jones wants," rather than an objective standard, which determines their success. Students who are compliant and used to picking up signals about adult wishes will succeed; others will fail.

But accountability cannot depend upon guesswork. As a matter of fairness and good educational practice, students deserve to have their work evaluated against an objective standard (Reeves, 1997); Chapter 18 of this book elaborates upon the case for standards-based education. In the most effective schools, students are never surprised by their grades and have daily access to records about their progress. Their daily work is focused on meeting clearly established targets, and they learn to make frequent mid-course corrections in order to achieve those targets. Without the accurate analysis of student work, we can hardly claim to have effective accountability.

Parent Communication: What's in a Grade?

Parents traditionally depend on three sources of information for assessments of their children's school success: examination of schoolwork, scrutiny of report cards, and notices of academic sanctions from schools. These sources of information are often, respectively, uninformative, misleading, and late.

Homework reviews are often distinguished more by quantity than quality in the elementary grades, where children take home "parent packets" and portfolios for inspection. Teachers assume that parents have inspected these packets, a dubious assumption since many student papers never successfully make their way from school to home. A group of symbols, numbers, and letters—inconsistently applied—are supposed to help children and parents understand academic progress. What do the smiling faces, grades, and numbers mean?

Some teachers and students talk about effort, some about proficiency, and most students talk about doing "what the teacher wants." Unclear messages about progress create a guessing game for students and parents alike. To make matters worse, parent reviews of homework become scanty or even non-existent at the high school level. This leaves parents with the next two options for communication: report cards and threatening messages from schools.

Report cards often range from the superficial to those of Byzantine complexity. The compilation of a student's performance into a single letter grade invites superficiality and leaves parents wondering what a "C" in mathematics really means. Should the parent and child spend time reviewing flash cards, solving problems, or looking in the backpack for missing homework?

At the other extreme, teachers spend hours tracking student progress in extraordinary detail by monitoring the status of hundreds of learning objectives. Such a cumbersome system offers the illusion of sophistication. However, it is based on the questionable premise that once an objective has been "covered" by the teacher and regurgitated by the student, it has been learned.

An effective report card would invite reflection by parents, address specific methods that can improve student performance, and recognize a broad continuum of learning, rather than imply that learning consists of a checklist of narrowly focused knowledge (Marzano and Kendall, 1996; Wiggins, 1998). To be sure, content knowledge is important, even necessary. But it is not sufficient. Telling parents that students have "covered" rules of grammar does not tell parents that students can use those rules to write effective essays. Telling parents that students have "covered" multiplication does not tell parents that students can use it to solve mathematical problems.

When report cards fail, the third method of communication with parents is the threatening letter, typically an announcement that a child is in serious academic trouble. These letters sometimes offer redemption and intervention, such as second chances, additional warnings, special programs, and summer school. More often than not, however, these letters threaten consequences, such as the repetition of a grade level, as if doing the same thing over again will yield different results.

There is nothing wrong with correspondence that, at last, communicates with parents about the serious academic challenges their children face. Timing is the problem; typically, the letters come far too late for parents or their children to do anything about poor performance. Ask teachers whether they are surprised about the students who receive failing grades or "D's" (the coward's "F," often given in lieu of the failing grades that teachers are reluctant to assign). Invariably, the answer is, "I saw this coming for many months. In fact, this student wasn't prepared to begin this class." I accept these representations by the teachers but must wonder why it took four to eight months to share those observations with parents. It is no surprise that parents, who find out so late about their children's failures, leap to the conclusion that the schools themselves are failing.

Better Parent Communication: Beyond the Report Card

A great deal of school communication with parents is incomplete, ineffective, and late. It need not be that way. Parents need the same information that policy makers demand: information about individual students, information about the school generally, and information about specific programs. An effective accountability program includes comprehensive communication with parents and the public. Such a comprehensive approach includes:

- **Daily access to information about student proficiency.**

  At the very least, teachers should have "telephone office hours" during which parents know that they can place a call to a teacher in order to discuss student progress. Although these telephone hours might be as little as 20 minutes before and after school, designated office hours can significantly reduce time spent playing telephone tag.

A growing number of schools have made significant investments in technology, but fail to make maximum use of this investment to improve communication about their accountability results. Voice mail, web sites, and e-mail offer opportunities to provide parents with immediate access to student information ranging from daily homework assignments to the details of progress by individual students. Electronic technology does not require extensive bookkeeping by the teacher. In a comprehensive accountability system, a teacher can make an entry regarding student progress one time, and many users can retrieve that single entry in multiple formats. In the traditional system, entries are made multiple times (grade books, parent reports, district and school reports) for infrequent retrieval by limited audiences in restricted formats.

- **Student information in meaningful form and context.**

The typical reporting of student test scores fails to give meaningful information to parents, students, and teachers. In the physician's office, we need to know more than "you're an 82"—we must know what that number means and, if it implies poor health, what we can do about it. In the context of educational information, we have the same need for meaningful form and context. Contrast these two reports to parents. The first report is typical:

> "Your daughter received a score of 82 on the state mathematics examination and therefore is ready for the fourth grade. If you would like to discuss this information, please make an appointment to see the counselor or teacher."

The second report is based on the identical state test, but someone took the time to make the results meaningful:

> "Jennifer received a score of 82 on the state math examination. Although this is only one indication of her math ability, there are some interesting results that may assist you in helping your child academically. First, Jennifer's calculation score was much higher than her problem-solving score. This suggests that she needs more opportunities to apply math in the real world, and parents can be particularly helpful in pointing out math applications around the home. Second, the problem-solving section of the math test requires excellent reading skills. It is possible that one reason for Jennifer's lower problem-solving score was that her reading comprehension and vocabulary need improvement. You can help in these areas by asking Jennifer to read aloud at home and by quizzing her on new and unfamiliar words. Third, additional review and practice can help Jennifer improve. When you see a homework assignment with an incorrect answer, you can help Jennifer by encouraging her to redo and correct the problem. I would be happy to discuss your child's progress with you at any time."

It's the same test—just better communication.

- **Clear comparisons of the present status of student work to a standard, not to a moving average or "norm."**

  Assessment has three typical purposes: auditing (used by policy makers to occasionally monitor student progress), sorting (used to allocate scarce resources), and the improvement of student learning. Only the last purpose should be the central focus of classroom assessment and school accountability. Although a significant number of parents may pressure schools for evaluation systems that focus on sorting, that purpose ill serves teacher-student-parent interaction. Achievement comes from a focus on clear standards, not from the inappropriate complacency that results from short-term victories over classmates. Norm-referenced information, such as "percentiles" or "stanines" or other comparative scores, never give a direct answer to the question, "Is this student competent to perform a particular objective?" Comparative scores only tell whether the student is better or worse than another student on some measurement. Parents, teachers, and the public deserve more meaningful information.

Why Average Test Scores Are Misleading

Average test scores mislead the public in a variety of ways. Reporting average test scores of all students tends to punish the virtuous and reward the guilty. Consider the case of two schools, both of which have established successful academic programs. In fact, the programs, their implementation, and their success are nearly identical. Both schools test statewide and the results appear in newspapers. When the box scores were published this year, however, the first school appears to be a striking success, while the second seems an abject failure.

The political reaction is swift and sure. Candidates for the upcoming school board election seize the opportunity to denounce the failure and promise that, under their careful guidance, heads will roll if things do not improve. The incumbent board members also seize their chances. They denounce the deplorable results of the second school, but quickly take credit for the success of the first. The superintendent, after a stormy meeting with her cabinet about inconsistencies in district results, is approached by the research director. The research director suggests that the data are more complicated than the media report. The first school tested substantially fewer students than the second school. "We can't look like we're making excuses," comes the superintendent's swift reply, and the discussion ends.

The rest of the story is clear and demoralizing. Other principals in the district quickly learn their lessons well. What lessons are these? Not that good performance is rewarded and that bad performance is punished. On the contrary, principals of both schools in the example provided fine academic leadership for their schools.

Both, in fact, provided nearly identical leadership, academic programs, and levels of success.

The first principal—the principal of the school labeled a "success"—however, had learned a vital lesson in a previous job: educational accountability systems do not reflect student achievement, but are really political reactions to numbers. As is the case in many schools, the first principal excluded the test scores of students who didn't speak English well, who were developmentally delayed and cognitively impaired, who had poor test taking skills, and who were well below grade level in reading and mathematics.

The principal of the first school—the one labeled a "success"—didn't cheat; he simply followed the clear rules of the game. A clever combination of parental demands for test exceptions (on forms conveniently provided by the school) and Individualized Educational Plans and the resultant exclusions (provided with the best of intentions) led to a different "average" test score than the second school reported. The excellent average test scores of this school masked a significant number of students who were ill prepared for the challenges of future grades.

The principal of the second school—the school labeled a "failure"—believed that some testing, even of students who faced special challenges or of students who had only recently enrolled in the school, might offer some good diagnostic information. Besides, she reasoned, surely the superintendent, school board members, and community would understand that average test scores included all of these distortions of the data, wouldn't they?

Conclusion

School stakeholders certainly need clear, accurate, comprehensive information about student, program, and school results. Students need frequent feedback about their performance as compared with clear, objective standards—not as compared with the performance of their peers. Students should not have to guess what individual teachers want from them in order to be successful, but should know exactly what they must do in order to achieve at high levels. Parents must also receive timely information about their children's performance. In addition to letter grades, numbers, or other scores, schools must make an effort to decode this data so that parents readily understand what their children can and cannot do and how they, as parents, can help their children succeed. Effective accountability systems will supply teachers and others with the information they need to communicate frequently and with care about the progress of individual students, programs, schools, and school systems.

Questions for Discussion

Use these questions and Worksheet 3.1 to analyze your communication system. You may notice that information about student achievement is communicated to different audiences in strikingly different ways.

1. What is the primary method used to communicate student achievement to parents and students?

2. Get five samples of completed report cards (names omitted) from different schools in your system. What similarities and differences do you notice in how achievement information is communicated to students and parents?

3. Without changing your present report card system, what action could your school or district take to improve the quality and frequency of feedback given to students about their work?

4. Aside from report cards, what other kinds of feedback do parents receive about the work of children in your school or district? How frequently do parents receive this feedback?

5. What opportunities do teachers and building leaders have to review student achievement? What sources of data do they use? How are these data sources similar to or different from the academic achievement information shared with parents and students?

6. What information is shared with policy makers and the community about student achievement? How is that information similar to or different from academic information shared with parents and students?

Analysis of Communication of Student Achievement

AUDIENCE

Achievement Area	Students	Parents	Teachers	Administrators	Community	Policy-Makers	Others
Classroom academic performance							
District test scores							
State test scores							
Behavior							
Attendance							
Other indicators:							

CHAPTER

Popularity vs. Effectiveness: Accountability as a Decision-Making Tool

The purpose of accountability is to improve student achievement. In order to accomplish this purpose, an effective accountability system must do far more than keep score. It must inform the decision-making process by helping policy makers, educational leaders, teachers, and students use information from the accountability system. Such information does not enter a vacuum, but must compete with pseudo-information that abounds in education and policy discussions. Competition between these information sources sometimes requires decision-makers to choose between popularity and effectiveness.

Fact-Free Debates

Information about the popularity of an educational idea ranges from rumor ("Hey, I don't know much about it, but they say that this program is great ...") to the illusion of substance ("Our organizational climate survey indicates that 63.5 percent of parents endorse this program ..."). While these two statements may differ in the elegance of their presentation, they share the same fatal flaw: they measure the wrong thing for the wrong purpose.

While rumors are easy to ridicule, they are more difficult to control and isolate than errant statistics. Three telephone calls to a superintendent or board member quickly become, "I'm getting a lot of calls on this." A petition hastily circulated around one parent/teacher meeting leads to the technically correct allegation that "Hundreds of parents feel this way."

While school leaders frequently regard themselves as rational decision-makers, I am frequently surprised at the number of school systems and other large organizations that appear to be governed based on incomplete, poorly articulated, and sloppy information. Governance by rumor, mood, and whim quickly replace the ideal of rational decision-making. It is, in the well-turned phrase of a particularly cynical university president, a "fact-free debate."

The Myth of "Organizational Climate"

A number of school leaders make sincere efforts to replace rumor with facts, pursuing the notion that their commitment to "customer service" requires frequent surveys of stakeholders. Districts without adequate textbooks and teacher compensation devote tens of thousands of dollars to studies of "organizational climate" and produce results that would not pass muster in an introductory research class. In many instances, surveys are sent to parents through the least reliable transmission medium of the late 20th century: a child's backpack.

Responses come back, sometimes by the hundreds or thousands. Advocates of these surveys will occasionally crow about a response rate in the high teens, far better than most mail surveys, which garner return rates of only a few percent. If the objective of such expensive exercises is obtaining reliable, representative information, then one should take little comfort in such statistical shenanigans. The best that can be said of such surveys is that they represent the responses of those few parents who methodically searched their children's backpacks. In brief, such surveys yield elegant charts and impressive numbers, but no one knows what the charts and numbers represent, or how accurately they represent it.

The only thing we can say with confidence is that the charts and numbers are unlikely to represent the parents whose attitudes are supposedly being measured. In the first place, it is dubious to assume that "customer service" is a surrogate for sound educational policy. But even if such an assumption were true, surveys that are poorly designed and executed are of little value.

What of the much more rare, but more sophisticated, organizational climate surveys? These include stratified random samples, carefully controlled research protocols, scientifically designed survey items, a mix of closed and open-ended questions, and sufficiently large sample sizes from which reasonable generalizations about the respondents can be made. In brief, the survey design is methodologically sound.

Unfortunately, the premises underlying such surveys are flawed in many cases. Organizational climate surveys begin with two assumptions. The first is that "climate" is the sum of people's opinions, as revealed in surveys. The second is that happy, satisfied employees, students, and parents are indicative of good organizational climate.

While students, parents, and employees are important stakeholders in educational enterprises, it is also fair to note that in a number of poorly functioning school systems, it is the responsibility of leaders to make their stakeholders distinctly uncomfortable. Calling attention to inadequate practices, poor training, and the subsequent need for more work is rarely a prescription for popularity. Canceling school activities that are offered more for popularity than effectiveness will probably not yield great survey results, but such bold moves may be essential for improving educational effectiveness and achieving long-term goals.

The organizational climate and customer service surveys used by many systems are worse than the absence of accountability because they create counter-productive accountability data. Consider the case of a school leader who has a winning football team and deplorable mathematics achievement. The scenario is particularly complicated if the beloved football coach is also the inadequate math teacher. The premise that transient popularity, a more accurate synonym for high-sounding "organizational climate," is the goal of educational leaders is deadly. It is a prescription for cowardice and failure when bold, visionary, courageous, and unpopular decisions are needed.

Pitfalls in Data Analysis: A Case Study

How can a comprehensive accountability system be used for effective decision-making? The first step is to insure that the accountability system includes not only test scores, but also information on programs and initiatives in each building. For example, consider the following school data in Figure 4.1.

We have asked a number of people, including college deans, professors, and educational consultants, to review this relatively simple data set. We asked them to respond to this situation:

> "The Pleasant Valley Board of Education would like you to present an analysis of your findings. Unfortunately, we can only give you ten minutes to make your presentation, and that includes inevitable interruptions by the board members. They would like you to consider these issues: (1) What are the strengths and weaknesses of academic achievement in our system? (2) What programs are working best for us, and which programs should be discontinued? (3) How do demographic variables affect student performance? (4) What other observations and recommendations do you have for us?

Take a moment to consider these questions. What programs do you regard as most effective? What recommendations would you offer to the school board? Organize your thoughts using Worksheet 4.2.

Although reasonable people may differ about their assessments of these programs, two things are abundantly clear from this case study. First, we would never be able to consider making decisions about program effectiveness if the accountability system did not specifically include programmatic information. Schools across the nation spend billions of dollars on such programs and invest much energy and anxiety in the publication of "report cards." Rarely, however, do they link the two, reporting which programs are associated with which report card data.

That is left to researchers who, not infrequently, provide reports of extraordinary complexity that, when all is said and done, come to one of two conclusions. The first

Figure 4.1

Pleasant Valley School District Assessment Data

School	%FRL	%ESL	Gr 5 W	CAT-5 Math	Cal PS	St Math	SS	Program
Angelou High School	24	4	3.9	65	67	92	86	IB
Kennedy High School	67	28	2.1	67	33	42	24	None
Clemens Middle School	18	3	3.5	62	51	47	49	WBMP
Hemmingway Middle School	92	14	3.5	41	1	46	49	WPA
Jefferson Middle School	37	9	2.2	55	49	39	29	EFF
Thoreau Middle School	69	21	1.7	19	21	18	21	WBMP
Alexander Elementary School	92	23	4	32	39	47	76	SFA
Bronfman Elementary School	24	2	4.2	96	61	57	91	WBMP
Emerson Elementary School	88	24	4.2	67	82	89	92	WPA
Pierce Elementary School	31	0	4.1	82	56	61	71	EFF
Westside Elementary School	82	16	1.9	24	19	14	19	SFA
Plato Elementary School	37	6	3.8	67	42	41	61	SFA
Socrates Elementary School	86	3	2.1	26	18	17	16	WBMP
Whitman Elementary School	45	18	3.7	49	82	75	89	WPA

LEGEND:

FRL — Free and Reduced Lunch Eligibility—Students from Poverty-Level Homes

ESL — English as a Second Language

Gr 5 W — Grade 5 Writing Test—State Writing Assessment—5 = highest; 1 = lowest

CAT-5 Math — California Achievement Test Mathematics—Cal = Calculation; PS = Problem Solving—Numbers indicate Percentile

St Math — State Math Test—Percentage at or above the "Proficient" Level—This test requires students to write the solutions to math problems and requires both calculation and problem-solving abilities.

SS — State Social Studies Examination—Percentage at or above the "Proficient" Level—This test requires students to write the responses to geography, economics, history, and civics questions.

Program — These codes refer to special educational programs in use by each school. These codes are:

- IB = International Baccalaureate
- WBMP = WhizBang Math Phonics, a proprietary training program guaranteed to improve math achievement
- WPA = Weekly Performance Assessment, a school-directed program in which teachers administer a variety of teacher-created assessments that require written student responses
- EFF = Efficacy Institute, a national program designed to improve the belief system of teachers and create higher expectations by school leaders and teachers for their students
- SFA = Success For All, a national program that emphasizes basic reading skills

and most frequent conclusion is, "Given the complexity of all the intervening variables and after running this particular series of research grants for all they are worth, we really haven't the slightest idea about whether these programs are effective. Nevertheless, we trust that you will find the following multivariate analysis of variance (MANOVA) quite entertaining." The second response offers greater clarity, with a definitive and emphatic conclusion that the program under investigation works splendidly. Alas, the research conducted appears to be funded and controlled by the distributors of the program being evaluated.

Effective accountability systems must offer clear information on programs, including not only the identification of the programs used, but also a determination of the extent to which they are used. For example, it is not sufficient for an accountability indicator to say, as the rather superficial Pleasant Valley analysis suggests, that a program is merely present. The indicators must include implementation information. Not "We used WhizBang Math Phonics," but "Two hours each week were devoted to skill development using the WhizBang Workbooks with these students, and this represented a 140 percent increase from the previous year's efforts in this program." Only with this level of detail can policy makers determine if their investment has been worthwhile.

The principal advantage of using accountability systems for program analysis is the value it provides to decision-makers in the allocation of scarce resources. There is another, subtler, virtue in this element of accountability systems. The analysis of test scores alone may leave us quite comfortable when the "units" being evaluated are eight-year-old children. It is their performance that is under the microscope, not ours.

Perhaps we might be bold enough to assert that teachers and principals have something to do with that performance, but even that effort is quickly challenged. The inclusion of program data, however, suggests that the decision-makers who select and implement educational programs have some responsibility for the success and failure of schools. It is a threatening and revolutionary notion that accountability is for grown-ups, too. Legislators, parents, and legions of consultants cavalierly enjoin students to work harder and smarter. Comprehensive accountability that includes program analysis forces us to follow our own advice.

Beyond Program Popularity: Asking the Tough Questions

In school systems, two areas are frequently the beneficiaries of huge expenditures, but they have minimal accountability. These areas are technology and staff development. In some cases, administrators frequently equate expenditure with implementation. This is tantamount to evaluating whether or not someone has understood a book by determining whether the mail carrier placed the book in the correct mailbox. It was, to be sure, delivered. But what happened after delivery remains a mystery.

I have personally witnessed great satisfaction by administrators over their use of educational technology, while they remained in blissful ignorance of the fact that more than one million dollars worth of computers remained in boxes for more than a year in their schools. Even more common is the spectacle of staff development that is similarly delivered—the words leave the mouth of the speaker within the hearing of the faculty—and administrators believe that the message has been delivered. The message was certainly delivered; it was just never received. Chapter 6 offers three keys to the evaluation of professional development. A splendid analysis of multi-level evaluation of staff development has been offered by Guskey (1999). Alas, his "Level 1"—essentially the popularity of the program with participants—is far removed from "Level 5"—the impact of the program on student achievement. If every seminar, program, and junket that consume staff development dollars had to pass the "Guskey Test" then I suspect many of the seminars that are more distinguished by superficial inspiration than substance would go the way of the Dodo bird.

While the difference between popularity and effectiveness may appear to be a clear line of demarcation in theory, it is profoundly difficult in the real world of educational leaders who report to elected school boards. In the context of electoral politics, popularity *is* effectiveness. "Parents love it, kids love it, and *we* love it. What's the problem?" asks the irate board member. "The problem, Sir, is that it did not improve student achievement as it claimed," replies the superintendent, as she once again prepares her resume.

Conclusion

Accountability systems establish the ground rules for these discussions. I have attended many board meetings in which the strongly held opinions of audience members appeared to receive far more attention than the "mere facts" offered by the school administration. Nevertheless, I have not heard a single citizen representative on an Accountability Task Force suggest that popularity or conformity with public opinion should be an educational accountability indicator. If rational indicators of educational performance are to carry the day in the policy battle, comprehensive accountability systems will be the chariots on which they will ride.

Questions for Discussion

1. What evaluation instruments that focus on popularity are in use in your district now? How important is popularity as a rationale for sustaining programs in your district?

2. Review Figure 4.1 and the Pleasant Valley simulation. If that were all the information you had on these schools, what inferences would you draw? What additional information would you need in order to make better-informed decisions? Use Worksheet 4.2.

Popularity and Effectiveness as Program Evaluation Tools

Use this worksheet to identify your existing accountability and evaluation mechanisms.

Program	Popularity Indicators	Effectiveness Indicators
Student curriculum and learning opportunities		
Teacher and administrator professional development		
Technology in classrooms		

Pleasant Valley Simulation

Question	Response	Additional Information Needed
1. What are the strengths and weaknesses of academic achievement in our system?		
2. What programs are working best for us, and which programs should be discontinued?		
3. How do demographic variables affect student performance?		
4. What other observations and recommendations do you have for us?		

5

CHAPTER

Complexity in Learning: Accountability as a Teaching Tool

Effective accountability systems inform sound educational practice. Why, then, is it so difficult to find examples of accountability systems that can legitimately be said to have value as teaching tools? Why, for that matter, is it such an alien notion that teachers and students are primary audiences for the results of accountability information? After all, the time-honored tradition of educational policy is that accountability is something "done to" students and teachers. Effective accountability systems, on the other hand, are "done for" teachers and students: to enhance their interaction and to improve student learning.

The Tools of Teaching

Perhaps the notion that there are such things as "tools of teaching" is insulting to some. Some educators have sternly told me, "Teaching is an art, not a science." Some argue that any attempt to provide clear expectations for teaching and learning crosses the boundary from standards to standardization (Ohanian, 1999). Other advocates maintain that it is futile and insulting for anyone to attempt to articulate the practices that can be used for effective teaching and learning. Perhaps other professionals would observe that there is a certain art to the practice of medicine or law, but few would argue that there are not well-defined techniques that physicians and attorneys use to pursue their art. With teachers, as with these other professions, we can identify specific components of the art of effective education. No professionals have all of the necessary tools upon the completion of their schooling, but they continually acquire new skills, update their knowledge, and refine their abilities.

The tools of teaching can be broadly grouped into the following elements: information, curriculum, assessment, and communication. Effective accountability systems provide information for each of these elements. If an accountability system seeks to include inordinate amounts of data about each of these elements, however, it becomes cumbersome and unusable. At the same time, when a system tracks only test scores, it fails to account for the context in which those scores occurred. In this

I

PART

case, an accountability system contains too little data. Neither of these extremes will improve student learning.

Information

First, the teacher needs information so that he or she can create order out of typically chaotic school curricula. Before plowing through curricula and textbooks, teachers must have a clear idea of strengths and challenges for a particular group of students. Are they weak in measurement and problem solving but strong in geometry? Are their creative writing skills stronger than their informative writing abilities? Without this sort of diagnostic information, curriculum becomes a frenzied race to the finish line. Students have been buried, teachers have "covered," and the link to meaningful accountability remains obscure.

There is a better way. We can begin by sharing the information that is already available and then acknowledge that the standardized tests show only a part of the necessary information for a diagnostic approach to instruction. Many accountability systems include detailed information about how students have fared in their mastery of mathematics and literacy. Extraordinary effort is expended to deliver this information (replete with comprehensive analyses, charts, tables, and graphs) to a variety of audiences. The audiences for this detailed analysis of a student's progress include the superintendent, board, media, policy makers, and a host of interest groups—every interest group, it may seem, except the teacher, the parents, and the child. To the extent that information is shared with the teacher, it is typically about students who are, by the time the analysis is presented, in a different classroom under the tutelage of a different instructor.

If a sound curriculum plan for the fourth-grade is to be established, then the teacher needs specific information about the extent to which each student demonstrates proficiency on key academic content standards. Teacher-made materials, observations, performance assessments, or other evaluative tools can be used to assess student progress. Student progress data can be recorded on a "Standards Achievement Report."

A "Standards Achievement Report" is the heart of an accountability system that provides not only comprehensive data to board members, but also uses the same information to provide essential information to students, parents, and teachers in subsequent years. Figure 5.1 illustrates the student report, which identifies the specific level of achievement for individual students. Students, parents, and future teachers would find such a report invaluable. Figure 5.2 illustrates the Standards Achievement Report for Schools. It reports in plain language the percentage of students who are proficient or better on each key academic content standard.

There is nothing magic about this format of a standards achievement report. Schools throughout the nation have used similar forms to better communicate about student

Figure 5.1

Standards Achievement Report

Student Name: _____ Grade Level: _____

Language Arts	4 Exemplary (Date)	3 Proficient (Date)	2 Progressing* (Date)	1 Does Not Meet* (Date)
1. Write and speak for a variety of purposes and for diverse audiences.				
2. Write and speak using conventional grammar, usage, sentence structure, punctuation, capitalization, and spelling.				
3. Read and understand a variety of materials.				
4. Apply thinking skills to reading, writing, speaking, listening, and viewing.				
5. Read to locate, select, and make use of relevant information from a variety of media, reference, and technological sources.				
6. Read and recognize literature as an expression of human experience.				

Teacher Comments:

* Plan for Meeting Standards:

Parent Comments:

Figure 5.2

Standards Achievement Report for Schools

Elizabeth Elementary School
Quarterly Standards Proficiency Report

Standard 2: Communicate effectively, using written, verbal, and artistic forms, and appreciate the creative expression of others.

Classroom		Percent of Students					
Grade	Teacher	Exemplary	Proficient	Progressing	Not Meeting Standard	Not Attempted	Comments
1	Mrs. Blackwell	10	85	5			
	Ms. Williams		70	15	15		
2	Mr. Jillian	5	88	2	5		
	Mrs. Gonzales		92	3	5		
3	Mrs. Davis		90	10			
	Dr. Barnes	15	75	5	5		
4	Mrs. Young		65	10	25		
	Ms. Whited	3	92	5			
	Ms. Sinks	5	90	5			
5	Mr. Lang	8	74	8	5	5	
	Mrs. Lambert		68	20	12		

Percentage of Students Meeting Standards

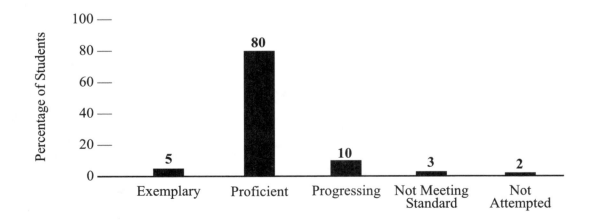

achievement and to help teachers receive more comprehensive information than is provided by a test score. All effective standards achievement reports have these common characteristics:

- **Focus**. They are *not* a recitation of every element and objective from standards and curriculum documents, but represent a focus on a few elements that educators have agreed are most important.

- **Clarity of Language**. They avoid educational jargon and express expectations of student performance in terms that are understood by students and parents.

- **Multi-year Perspective**. They do not focus on achievement during a single grade or class, but on a continuum of progress covering several years. One excellent model is the Middle School Proficiencies now in use by the Milwaukee Public Schools. This district identified the core proficiencies that students need to be ready for their 9th grade year. Information about student progress on these proficiencies allows teachers and counselors to modify curriculum and instruction to meet the needs of students. Has this approach paid off? After two years of using the Middle School Proficiencies, 8th grade achievement was the highest it has been in five years (Milwaukee Public Schools, 1999).

Curriculum and Teaching

The second essential element of teaching tools is curriculum—the sum of learning objectives, scope and sequence, textbooks, and a host of other teaching materials. The fundamental flaw in most educational analysis is the presumed equivalence between the delivery of information and student learning. Only when curricular resources are clearly identified and the extent of their use is documented can one draw any inferences about the relationship between curriculum and learning. In schools around the world, curricula come and go, yet Ms. McGillicutty continues her month-long units linking one holiday to the next, and Mr. Fieldman diverges from the curriculum at hand to explore his political obsessions, vacations, or other fancies of the day. Does this mean that accountability becomes classroom micro-management and monitoring of hourly activities? Certainly not. But if we are unwilling to include curriculum and teaching within the scope of educational accountability, we are left with test scores and student work as the sole foci of accountability, ignoring the vitally important impact of teaching and curriculum.

How can teaching and curriculum be measured in the context of an accountability system? The Taylorist "time on task" analyses of the past two decades can become exercises in minutiae. What can be quickly and unobtrusively measured, however, are the assessment practices of the teacher. Rather than ask teachers to record "how much time you spent teaching writing"—a question that surely can mean vastly different things to different teachers—the accountability system can ask, "how many times did students complete a writing assessment that was based on the district scoring rubric and what percentage of students were proficient or better?" Some teachers will complete such an assessment twice a year and others will do so twice a week. The accountability system should not engage in micro-management, but should respect and encourage classroom assessment as an integral part of the educational process. Without such an emphasis on classroom assessment, we are left with the typical emphasis on isolated state and district standardized test scores.

Accountability in Action: Real-Time Data to Inform Instruction

In Riverview Gardens, Missouri, schools have chosen to focus on writing as an integral part of their district accountability system. Once a month, teachers use the state writing rubric to determine the percentage of students who are "proficient" or better in informative writing. The timing of the assessment and the nature of the writing prompt vary widely from teacher to teacher, from month to month. But everyone shares a common focus on writing. Without micromanagement of curriculum or teaching practice, the stakeholders in this system know that students have a common commitment to excellence in writing and know that students are getting better every month. They also know if a teacher steadfastly refuses to assess writing. This system doesn't ask teachers to turn in lesson plans, track "time on task" or otherwise engage in Orwellian monitoring techniques—it simply asks for two numbers each month: how frequently did you assess writing and what percentage of them are proficient? To be sure, this is more information than teachers usually provide to administrators, but it is a far cry from the micro-management than many educators reasonably oppose.

Teachers who give students clear expectations and offer frequent opportunities for students to meet those expectations have nothing to fear from an analysis of classroom assessment practices. Indeed, this approach is far more respectful of the role of teachers in educational accountability than the mere reliance on test scores. Those few teachers who routinely waste immense amounts of time on pet projects and evaluate students only as the deadline for report cards draws near will, appropriately, have their practices exposed.

Focusing on teacher assessment practices requires less paperwork and time tracking by teachers, but may nevertheless be regarded by some people as too invasive. The traditional notion of "close the door and let me teach" is supported by a number of professional associations and union collective bargaining agreements that specifically limit the amount of time classroom observation can be conducted. It is strange that the very people who complain most about the use of test scores for accountability also resist the creative use of alternatives, such as an analysis of teacher assessment practices. The only hope for a more comprehensive and fair approach to accountability is the elevation of classroom teaching and assessment practices to the point that they receive the same respect and visibility as standardized test scores.

The foregoing paragraph may contain the most controversial and objectionable words of this book for many teachers, as their experiences with programs from

"Mastery Learning" to innumerable "time on task" studies have left them feeling like devalued factory workers. Hence, it is imperative that we pause to address their legitimate concerns and respond to the reasonable question, "What's in this for me?" Teachers whom I have encountered want to be as effective as possible both in the use of their time and in the achievement of their students. Most accountability systems, however, give them only fragmentary data about the effects of their efforts, with little insight into the causes.

Physicians would never settle for such inadequate information. They demand a host of information, not only about the test results of their patients, but also about the specific antecedents to those results. Physicians routinely request information about patient dietary and exercise habits, previous medical interventions and medications, and other tests that were previously completed. Physicians do not regard this information as intrusive; rather, they understand how integral such comprehensive views of causes and effects are to complete analyses of their professional practices. Indeed, physicians need this information in order to change their own strategies, communicate better with their patients, and otherwise improve the health of those whose care has been entrusted to them.

The same is true of teachers. Student behavior, curriculum practice, time allocation, and other test results must all be taken into account if teaching professionals are to use the results of accountability systems to improve student learning. Thus, teachers are an essential audience for accountability systems, not merely drones who feed data into a system for analysis by others. Teachers must receive feedback immediately and in a comprehensive manner. Moreover, they must have direct input into the accountability system so that they can use results during the year to focus, re-focus, expand, and contract their curricular emphases in order to achieve the best results for the students in their care.

Assessment

The third element of accountability for learning is assessment. Too frequently, the assessment component of accountability systems is limited to district and state test scores. A comprehensive accountability system, however, will systematically gather information about teacher assessment of student performance. This is vital for two reasons. First, teachers can provide important "early warning indicators" so that the accountability system is used throughout the year to identify students who need additional help and classrooms that need additional resources.

Teacher assessment gives a more comprehensive view of student performance than a single test score. Assessment information provided by teachers also allows stakeholders to understand the improvement of students and schools during the school year. Teacher assessment is a vital component of an accountability system for a second reason. Frequently, there are disparities between the results of state and district tests and teacher evaluations of student progress.

Newspapers bring to our attention the most flagrant cases of illiterate students who graduated from high school with "C's" and "D's," as well as those students who maintained a "B" average in high school, but require remedial classes in college. This should not be so shocking, however, when one considers the number of fourth-graders who have received unending streams of smiling faces (and their letter-grade equivalents) on their class work, but whose test performance is poor.

What accounts for this divergence, and why should it be part of a comprehensive accountability system? Three explanations are possible for the difference between teacher assessment and test results: (1) Teacher assessments and state/district tests are evaluating entirely different learning; (2) Teacher assessments and other tests are strikingly different in format; or (3) Assessments take place at different times, and hence, the conditions under which the student performs are quite different. Perhaps it is a combination of all three of these. Interestingly, these three explanations are rarely cited by the media or the host of public education critics. "The teachers are too soft, but the state tests are rigorous," are among the most frequent contentions (Hirsch, 1996; Sykes, 1995). Alternative voices point to the strikingly different criteria for achievement used in state and district tests than are used in classrooms and, for that matter, in international comparisons (Bracey, 1999). Another reason for the divergence between teacher information and test data is a difference in metric. Percentile scores, grades, and proficiency indicators may be based on wildly different criteria, where one state's "proficient" is another district's "advanced" and is yet another state's "basic" level of performance.

An accountability report that includes both teacher evaluation information and independent test data should be simple and coherent. It should look something like the information presented in Figure 5.3:

Figure 5.3

Comprehensive Accountability Plan—Teacher Assessment and Test Data

	Percentage of Students "Proficient" or Higher	
Standard	Teacher Evaluation	District Test Results
Math 2.4 Scale and Ratio	Fall—35% Spring—78%	Spring—84%
English 3.5 Informative Writing	Fall—64% Spring—92%	Spring—42%

Most accountability systems would have only the right-hand column, with some meager satisfaction about the math scores and gnashing of teeth about the informative writing scores. Consternation and sincere frowns have rarely been effective substitutes for educational strategies. The math teachers deserve high praise in this example. While we clearly need to have another 16 percent of students achieve proficiency on the "scale and ratio" standards on the district test, teacher evaluation scores in the spring show an extraordinary improvement over fall scores. In addition, the level of agreement between the district test and the math teachers' analysis indicates that this sample district and school are on the right track.

The informative writing scores are another matter. What would an analysis of the right-hand column alone suggest? Perhaps the results would lead to a front-page headline, followed by more English classes, more writing classes, and a few patronizing and demoralizing lectures to the English faculty. While such approaches may honor the tradition of teacher bashing, they miss the point. The English teachers could quadruple their "time on task" without result. The teachers are clearly measuring something entirely different than the district test. A focus on the right-hand column of Figure 5.3 says, "Use more of the same instructional practices, but expect higher test scores." A focus on the entire table allows educational leaders to use accountability data to make meaningful interventions—in this case, on the manner in which informative writing is evaluated—and provide constructive solutions to a serious problem.

Communication

The final teaching tool is communication. This includes far more than the traditional report card. It includes a systematic, continuous method of analyzing the extent to which students are proficient on key academic standards. The audience for communication about student performance includes not only parents and students, but also teachers in subsequent years, specialists who might be called upon to provide special assistance, and stakeholders in the educational system.

What should be communicated? Surely every element of student assessment would create an overwhelming amount of data, and the resultant accountability system would be buried under its own weight. A process of discernment—selection of data most representative of student performance—is essential. Teachers use such discernment every time they make a report card. They include some elements of student performance and exclude others, as they seek to provide the most accurate possible communication about student proficiency in each report card.

Leaders should use the same commitment to discernment as they construct an accountability system. While schools may have fifty or more initiatives and goals, there are probably only five or six that need be included in the accountability system. While there may be hundreds of standards, benchmarks, and learning objectives, only a handful need to be included in comprehensive accountability systems. The processes described in this chapter will assist in this process of discernment. They should make clear what curricular elements and teacher assessments are most effective and which ones can be discarded.

Conclusion

The art and science of teaching cannot be described in a single volume; a single chapter is certainly inadequate. For the lifelong commitment that the profession of teaching requires, four of the recurring themes will be information, curriculum, assessment, and communication. Any teacher of any subject at any level must return to these essential elements. While my professional career has focused on assessment, the reader would be ill served if I fail to acknowledge the importance of the other three. The best standards-based performance assessments (Reeves, 1997) are of little value unless they begin with solid information about the students in our classroom, with curriculum that carefully distinguishes the core from the periphery, and with effective means of communicating the results of our efforts to students, parents, and other stakeholders. Accountability systems that fail to recognize the importance of teaching (and the consequent obligation of the accountability system to serve the informational needs of teachers) will fail to achieve their primary objective: the improvement of student learning.

Questions for Discussion

1. What information do teachers have from your accountability system now? How is this information used to influence curriculum and instruction? Is the information given to teachers related to the students in their classes *right now*?

2. What is the level of detail provided to teachers from your present accountability system? What data do teachers receive about the strengths and weaknesses of their students in individual curriculum areas? What information do teachers receive other than from standardized test scores?

3. How are classroom assessments used in your present accountability system? What are the similarities and differences between district and state tests and those used in the classroom?

4. How are your accountability measurements communicated to students and the public now? How are these messages similar or different from the messages communicated by classroom assessments?

5. What do you know about different assessment practices at the classroom level? How are you certain that every student in your district has an equal opportunity to classroom assessment that is frequent, fair, clear, rigorous, and related to your state and district standards?

Accountability Information Available to Teachers

Accountability Information	Source	Impact on Curriculum and Instruction

Accountability Communication

Accountability Information	Source	Impact on Curriculum and Instruction

Accountability as a Professional Development Tool

Although significant amounts of time and resources are devoted to professional development in most school systems, the link between those expenditures and accountability is often tenuous at best. This chapter outlines a mechanism for improving the strength of the connection between accountability and the professional education of teachers, administrators, and board members.

Educators should set the standard for excellence in professional development. The relationship between what we value and what we learn should be transparent. The link between our investment of resources and the research supporting those investments should be strong. The relationship between our daily professional lives and our professional education should be seamless. Unfortunately, the chasm between what we know we "should" do and what is actually done in many school systems is enormous. Although many excellent efforts have been made to articulate standards for staff development (see especially the work of Guskey, 1999), there are three criteria at the heart of the matter. These criteria are *integrity*—the relationship of our values to our learning; *efficacy*—the pursuit of those practices that make a positive difference for students; and *diligence*—the application of what we have learned. When these criteria are applied to staff development, there is the opportunity for a significant impact on student performance. If any one of these criteria is missing, however, the enterprise is doomed to failure.

Integrity: Linking Values to Learning

"Integrity" is an emotionally charged word. The implication that a staff development program might lack integrity can instantly transform a disagreement into a brawl. Nevertheless, a breach of integrity is precisely the terminology that applies to those situations in which the practice of a system so profoundly contradicts its values. Consider the case of the school system that claimed to value student learning, diversity, and opportunity for all students. These values were little more than Orwellian double-speak when compared to the actual practices of assessment anarchy, one-dimensional teaching strategies, and routine long-term tracking. Professional development time, energy, and resources reinforced the double-speak, as programs were evaluated not based on their promotion of the values of the system, but on their popularity with the staff. Integrity can be a distinctly uncomfortable and unpopular policy. The pursuit of integrity requires a comparison of our present activities to our goals, the welcoming of dissatisfaction, and the painful removal of layers of obsolete and potentially harmful practice before new layers of successful pedagogy can take hold.

How do you know if your professional development program has integrity? On the surface, a simple comparison of values to practices is a good place to start. We value collaboration, but we only use professional programs in which a speaker lectures to people who have scant time to collaborate. We value a focus on student needs, but we do not bring student work to staff development programs. We value equity, but we use staff development programs to validate decisions to sort and select students based on their prior learning rather than on the difference we could make in their lives. We value the professional challenge of new and promising practices, but we evaluate staff development programs based solely on their popularity—and hence their reinforcement of the comfort zone of the vast majority of participants. Twice in the past week I have heard school leaders remark with dismay how a deeply thoughtful author and consultant had "made people mad" by his frank confrontation of the difference between their values and their practices. In both cases, the leaders reacted not with appreciation for the difficulty of confronting uncomfortable issues, but with a resolution to never use that consultant again. In sum, they chose comfort and self-satisfaction over integrity. The message sent to a teacher or administrator who might notice the difference between values and actions is unmistakable: survival means reinforcing the status quo, not confronting frailties.

Integrity must also be at the heart of the accountability system. Does it measure what we value? If we value excellence and equity, with challenging learning opportunities for all students, then we dare not have an accountability system that monitors only the variables measured on a single test. If we value communication skills including writing and speaking, then we must not measure performance based only on the responses to multiple-choice tests. If we value competence in teaching as part of an accountability system, then we must not measure our efforts toward professional competence based solely on participation and popularity of staff development programs.

Efficacy: Making a Difference

Professional development must have efficacy—the power to make a meaningful difference in the lives of the students we serve. Efficacy is not a mystery. A substantial body of research (Slavin, 1996, 1997, 1998; Darling-Hammond, 1997; Schmoker, 1999) supports particular practices in teaching, assessment, classroom organization, and curriculum, all of which are linked to improved student achievement. This is more than the bland assertion that a program is "research-based" and "data-driven," the bywords of the day. It requires a deep and thoughtful inquiry into the research and thoughtful challenges of prevailing hypotheses. At its core, efficacy requires that we accept the principle that truth, reason, and impact on student learning, rather than personal taste, will determine the acceptability of professional development enterprises.

Incredibly, the elevation of reason over personal taste is not something that can easily be assumed. In many school systems, the notion of academic freedom has been twisted to render efficacy a matter of personal taste. Academic freedom appropriately protects the interests of teachers exploring new ideas and uncomfortable hypotheses, including unpopular ones, in the classroom. It does not protect debilitating and destructive practice. Can you imagine the school nurse positing the notion that academic freedom liberates him from the dreary practice of vaccination? Can you imagine the fate of the basketball coach who claims that academic freedom releases her from the obligation of practice? In those areas where we have formed a societal consensus, such as public health and basketball, there are common standards of practice supported by substantial bodies of research and general agreement among professionals. In those areas that get undervalued, such as writing, reading, and mathematics, research and potential consensus fade into oblivion, replaced by the fad of the moment.

Diligence: The Application of Learning

Even if a professional development program has both integrity and efficacy, it remains impotent if it does not adhere to the principle of diligence—the application of lessons learned to the classroom. I recently studied a school system in which all teachers had participated in a professional development program on six-trait writing. Such a program certainly had integrity, as it was linked to the values of this system. The focus on writing was efficacious, as a significant body of research supports the link between improved writing and student achievement. Why, then, did a significant number of students demonstrate a decline in writing ability over the next year? The answer, it turned out, was a result of the violation of the principle of diligence. Only 34 percent of the teachers in the district actually implemented six-trait writing in the classroom.

Diligence is not about good intentions nor about inspiration nor about popularity. It is about action. When former Illinois senator and presidential nominee Adlai Stevenson was introducing John Kennedy to the Democratic National Convention in 1960, he said of the people in ancient times "When Demosthenes spoke, the people said, 'how well he speaks.' But when Cicero spoke, the people said, 'let us march.'" This is the heart of the matter. Professional development that tickles the ears with inspiring anecdotes and funny stories has become *de riguer* at national conferences. Programs that rest on data and practice and, least popular of all, that expect the participants to work rather than to be entertained, are the only ones that can aspire to transform rhetoric into action.

Integrity, efficacy, and diligence—this is not the path to easy accolades, but the path leading to hard work, extraordinary challenge, inevitable frustration, and ultimate results. In this path the professional educator will not find the cheap satisfaction that stems from the sycophant on stage, but the enduring satisfaction that comes only from having made a difference in the lives of those we serve.

Conclusion: Linking Professional Development to Accountability

Once these three essential criteria have been met, the link to accountability should be strong, provided that the accountability system itself is based on integrity, efficacy, and diligence. In working with hundreds of school districts and thousands of schools, I frequently ask to see a copy of the staff development calendar for the coming year. Not infrequently, such a calendar does not exist or has gaping holes such as a date with "site-based staff development" filled in where a coherent subject and direction might be expected. Even in those instances where the subject is clear, the random flittering from one popular subject to another is the predominant theme of these calendars. When I have asked the question, "Can we at least agree that the subjects of staff development should focus on improved student learning?" I have received reactions ranging from blank stares to outright opposition.

A comprehensive accountability system can help professional development efforts achieve their potential. First, the accountability system itself should monitor not only the delivery of professional development but also its application. In other words, the accountability report should not say, "84 percent of our teachers were trained in six-trait writing during a half-day program," but rather "84 percent of our students participated in eight or more writing assessments using the six-trait format learned by our teachers during a professional development program. As a direct result of this emphasis, the number of students who are proficient or better in writing increased by 22 percent."

In other words, it is not the delivery, participation, or popularity of staff development that gives it meaning. A comprehensive accountability system links professional development to application and effectiveness—the things that matter for students.

For More Information ...

These web sites offer excellent resources for standards-based professional development:

National Staff Development Council
(Dennis Sparks)
www.nsdc.org

The Education Trust
(Kati Haycock)
www.edtrust.org

The Leadership and Learning Center
(Douglas Reeves)
www.LeadandLearn.com

Mid-Continent Educational Research Lab
(Robert Marzano)
www.mccrel.org

Assessment Training Institute
(Rick Stiggins)
www.assessmentinst.com

Grant Wiggins & Associates, Assessment, and School Structure
(Grant Wiggins)
www.grantwiggins.org

Questions for Discussion

1. Find the staff development calendar for your district. If you knew nothing else about your district's plans and goals, what would you imagine are the objectives of a school system with your staff development calendar?

2. How do you evaluate staff development now? Get a copy of the evaluation forms that you use. What does that form imply is necessary for staff development to be successful?

3. Compare your district's learning needs to the staff development calendar. Where are the clear matches? Where are the mismatches? Are there undefined opportunities for staff development that can be used to address the mismatches?

Linking Learning Objectives With Professional Development

District Learning Objectives	Professional Development Programs Linked to These Learning Objectives

Professional Development Programs
Not Matched to District Learning Needs

Name of Program and Scheduled Date	Objective of Program	Recommendation for Modification, Cancellation, or Continuation of Program

CHAPTER

Lonely at the Bottom: Accountability as a Leadership Tool

Today's educational leaders face challenges that defy logic and rationality. Advocates and critics alike expect these leaders to be masters of human motivation and experts in multiple academic subjects. Forced to be stern with argumentative adults and disruptive students, school leaders must demonstrate infinite patience with bewildered children and battle-weary staff members (Goodlad, 1994). Everything from poor math scores to teen pregnancy to drug abuse is blamed on the "failing" educational system. Tasked with managing diverse staffs, improving student achievement, and allocating diminishing resources, educational leaders face daily responsibilities that border on the impossible.

A typical week in a school leader's life might read something like this. Monday morning begins with a few angry telephone calls from parents upset about the lost football game on Saturday afternoon. Next, a local politician drops by to demand an explanation for why this year's increased budget allocation from the state has not yet resulted in higher test scores. A parent, scheduled for a 9:00 a.m. appointment, threatens to sue the schools because the new district standards are too high. After scheduling a deposition for another lawsuit, the school leader then faces a frustrated business group. The business leaders report that they cannot find qualified job applicants because the district's standards are too low. At the end of their 70-hour workweek, school leaders open the Sunday newspaper, only to be bombarded by charts and tables outlining the alleged failures of the schools. It is in this environment that the school leader listens to someone suggest that educational accountability is a good thing.

The School Leader as Architect

Amidst the stress of leading schools toward excellence, some leaders find themselves leaning toward one of two extremes. The first is the presumption that their work is all-powerful: "I speak, and the schools literally transform themselves overnight." At the other extreme are the leaders who, frustrated and dejected after a few days like the one described above, conclude, "Whatever I do matters little. Students and children will do whatever they are going to do regardless of what I do or say. I can't fire teachers, I can't motivate students, and I can't change parents. I'm just a glorified caretaker."

For a more reasoned view, consider the job of an architect. She is designing a magnificent building. Some attorneys will lease the 28th floor, financiers will be on the 32nd floor, a telecommunications center will be housed on the 14th floor, and a fledgling group of entrepreneurs will get the 30th floor.

This architect, like the school leader, can also take one of two positions. She can decide that an ideal building design will help the lawyer write a better brief and motivate the entrepreneur to create the first digital wheel. On the other hand, the architect can design a cold, lifeless box of a building and sigh, "It doesn't really matter what I do. The real action takes place inside the walls, and my contribution to the equation is wholly superficial and irrelevant. I might as well be the cab driver who brings them here, for once they are here, my influence is negligible."

In fact, the architect has a very definite influence on her building's tenants—their productivity, creativity, and results. The lighting, convenience, view, comfort, and efficiency of the building will significantly affect the tenants, even if the tenants rarely stop to think about how the architectural design influences their work.

The best architects spend time watching and learning from those who will use the spaces they design. These architects watch how lawyers work and use space, observe the interactions among software engineers, and consider the influence of the environment on creative business leaders. Though the architect does not do the work of these professionals, she will design the space in which they have to operate. The best architects know that the results of their work extend far beyond blueprints for engineers and instructions for construction crews. Good architects know that their designs will have direct and profound influence on the work and lives of some very important human beings.

School leaders must choose to be the architects of learning spaces. They must do more than assume that teachers alone are responsible for students once they enter the schoolhouse door. Educational leaders design the system in which learning takes place. How can they design productive, supportive learning spaces? By using feedback from a comprehensive accountability system. Just as it is not the architect's responsibility to write legal briefs or design software, the school leader cannot get side-tracked by trying to micromanage classrooms. Just as the architect must consider the needs of attorneys and computer engineers, the school leader must systematically investigate which design elements help school professionals and students perform more effectively.

How do architects learn these essential elements of design? They receive continuous feedback from clients. They observe the relationship between what the architect controls—space, light, traffic flow—and the needs of clients.

How do school leaders learn the essential elements of design? They receive continuous feedback from a comprehensive accountability system. They learn, for example, that a school schedule that facilitates collaboration among teachers leads to greater consistency in the application and assessment of standards. The school leader did not create the collaboration, but created the system in which collaboration can occur. Leaders learn that teacher feedback is more useful in a system that permits and encourages the continuous improvement of student work rather than the use of "one-shot" tests. With this knowledge, effective leaders can encourage teachers to abandon traditional final examinations and other single-effort assessments in favor of multiple methods of assessing student performance. Students no longer ignore carefully crafted suggestions for improvement, but use teacher feedback to revise and improve each assignment.

With comprehensive accountability data, effective school leaders learn what the antecedents of excellence are. The architect cannot design the ideal space for an attorney by merely knowing the courtroom win-loss record of the lawyer. The architect must understand how the attorney prepared for those courtroom victories and the role that space, light, and environment played in those preparations. Similarly, the school leader cannot design ideal learning space by analyzing volumes of test data. The school leader must, instead, understand the people, climate, programs, and services that led to those test scores.

Is the architect analogy inappropriate? The only response for one committed to comprehensive accountability is, "Let the data speak." Consider the evidence in Figures 7.1 and 7.2. These charts show the relationship between attendance and academic achievement in a large urban school system. The "R-squared" indicates the square of the regression coefficient. In plain language, this is the amount of variation in student achievement explained by variation in attendance. Thus, an R^2 of .67 means that about two-thirds of the variation in academic achievement is explained by student attendance. The school leader may not be able to influence the daily math and English curricula nor all of the teaching methods employed in the classroom. But the school leader can surely influence the extent to which the building is either a desirable or dreadful place for a student to spend his or her day.

Figure 7.1 and 7.2

Attendance Significantly Affects
Achievement in High Schools

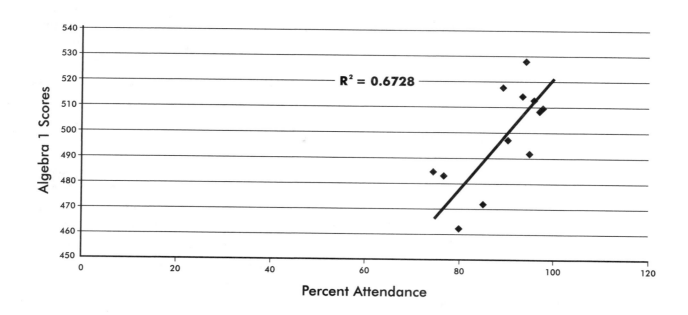

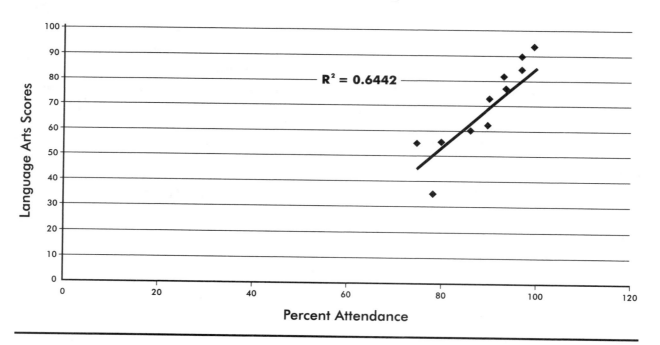

Action Steps for School Leaders

The evidence concerning how principals influence student achievement is overwhelming (Goodlad, 1994). Too frequently, principals are held accountable for student achievement, but the specific action steps they take to improve student performance are not identified. The following is a list of how accountability information and leadership practices can be used together for powerful effects on educational achievement.

Principal Scoring of Writing Assignments

Ms. Flora Flagg is the principal of LaFollette Elementary School in Milwaukee. Her students received low test scores for several years, so Ms. Flagg took decisive action. Every week she developed a writing prompt, and every week she personally graded the student papers written in response to her prompt. In one school year, her students rose from the 34th percentile to the 74th percentile on a national writing assessment.

Walking A Mile in the Teacher's Shoes

Dr. Stan Scheer, now a school superintendent, places himself on the substitute teacher roster and spends long hours in classrooms for 20 days every year. He reports that he receives better information about student achievement, teacher morale, curriculum issues, and a host of other critical educational matters during the hours that he spends with real students than he does from reading hundreds of pages of reports.

Principal Monitors Student Portfolios

Ms. Estelle Sprewer, principal and former director of exceptional education for a major urban school system, personally reviewed the contents of three student portfolios every month at Victory Elementary School. Her personal involvement in evaluating student work led to significant increases in the quality and quantity of the contents of student portfolios.

Principal Intervenes for Under-Achieving Students

Mr. Bill Andrikopolous has established creative programs to assist middle school students who need intensive intervention. His school-within-a-school program gives students not only academic essentials, but also guidance on behavior, organization, time management, and other critical skills linked to student success.

Principal Recognizes Student Achievement

Mr. William Torbert transformed the principal's recognition of outstanding scholarship from the typical "lunch with the principal" (same cafeteria, different table) to a high-profile event. Students on the Principal's Honor Roll were whisked to an elegant lunch with him in six stretch limousines. "I know that it was showy," Mr. Torbert confesses, "but I had to do something to get their attention, and this surely did it."

Principal Builds Credibility with the Business Community

Dr. Gene Bottoms is senior vice president of the Southern Regional Education Board. He is making the link between high school technology programs and businesses in Atlanta. Many of them are now so effective and credible that major employers, such as Bell South, waive their normal pre-employment screening tests for graduates of the program.

Principal Identifies Students in Need

Ms. Diane Neicheril personally monitors the reading performance of every student in her school. Because the students she serves come from an area of high poverty and high mobility, student progress is monitored constantly. She and teachers assess, focus, and re-focus their intervention efforts on a weekly basis in order to meet the most pressing needs of their students.

This is only a partial list of how school leadership can create optimal learning space, but it makes an important point. Each of these school leaders took actions that were visible, measurable, and replicable. They took accountability out of the realm of theory and made it real. More importantly, they made it clear that accountability is not an abstract notion that is applied to students and teachers alone. Accountability is an essential element of effective educational leadership and, ultimately, school success.

Like effective architects who design optimal space for their clients, these school leaders embrace accountability, lead by example, and use the information from their accountability systems to improve the focus of their teachers, the performance of their students, and the quality of their leadership.

Questions for Discussion

1. Think of the school leaders in your system who are most effective in improving student achievement. What specific practices make those leaders effective?

2. What information do these most effective leaders gather and analyze? How is this information different from the information used by other leaders who are not as effective?

Effective Leadership Practices and Supporting Information

Leaders Most Effective in Improving Student Achievement	Specific Leadership Practices	Information Gathered and Analyzed by These Leaders to Support Those Practices

II
PART

Accountability System Design

Step 1: Establish an Accountability Task Force

Developing a comprehensive accountability system is a labor-intensive process. The first step in undertaking this work is the establishment of an Accountability Task Force. The Task Force will have primary responsibility for coordination and oversight as the accountability system is developed and implemented. Because Task Force members will have a number of difficult, time-consuming responsibilities, it is important to make this clear to potential Task Force participants before they agree to join. Members should be willing to serve for a minimum of six two-hour meetings during the design phase of their work, and then participate in quarterly meetings thereafter. Terms of service are typically two years.

The Task Force reports to the superintendent who, in turn, reports to the board. The political dynamics of some school systems are such that the Accountability Task Force reports directly to the board of education. In chartering the Accountability Task Force, the board must make these reporting relationships clear.

Why a Task Force?

Leaders want to collaborate; they also know that they will be held responsible for the implementation of vision and achievement of the mission of their school system. While they want to honor the need for collaboration among many stakeholders, leaders and policy makers frequently find excuses to make the development of the accountability a private endeavor. I have worked in some school systems where the superintendent says, "Look, I've attended a seminar on accountability systems—why can't I just write the system and submit it to the board?" The answer to this question lies not in any particular affection I have for committees and Task Forces, but rather with the essential issue of ownership. Who owns the accountability system, anyway? If accountability is the exclusive creation of the superintendent and board, then other stakeholders—teachers, administrators, parents, students, and the community—can be expected to show little enthusiasm for it. "Here they go again," the excluded stakeholders will sigh, as they watch one more initiative come and go. The reasons for excluding stakeholders from the accountability process are rarely pernicious. Well-intentioned, thoughtful, and (usually) collaborative school leaders have explained their reluctance to engage a broadly based Accountability Task Force with explanations such as the following:

- "This is really about testing and assessment, and that's too technical a field for most lay people."

- "We can't allow parents and business representatives on the Accountability Task Force to act as if they are supervising principals and teachers."

- "We have site-based decision-making, and a community Task Force that designs an accountability system will take away the authority of the site councils."

- "The goals of the district should be set by the board and superintendent—not by the stakeholders."

- "If we bring all the stakeholders together, they will never be able to agree to anything."

- "If I let the teacher's union sit at the table, then administrators won't join in; and if I let principals, then the union won't participate. It's best just to have the central office and board make these decisions."

- "Our board already knows what they want—why would they listen to a group of stakeholders?"

The resistance to stakeholder involvement is not unlike the subtle resistance to parental involvement in the classroom. "I know that they mean well," the reasoning goes, "but shouldn't we leave the education of our children up to the experts?" The answer, at least in a democracy, is a resounding no. Our history and form of government place extraordinary trust in the common sense of the people. The overwhelming majority of school board members and legislators are citizen volunteers. They exercise enormous power with regard to the resources and policies of school systems, and therefore school leaders exclude citizen leaders from accountability deliberations at some peril. What a school administrator might see as a reasonable division of labor—"leave the details to the experts"—can strike a board member or legislator as contemptuous arrogance. The victims of such misunderstandings are children and schools who are denied the resources they need to be successful.

If, on the other hand, a broadly representative Task Force is both the author of the accountability system and the group that presents accountability information to the board and public, then a different organizational dynamic is present. It is no longer the typical meeting in which the administration presents (and, more often than not, defends) its information in a two-way exchange with the board. Rather, the Accountability Task Force, including teachers, administrators, parents, and other stakeholders, presents information to the school leadership. The board and superintendent are, literally and figuratively, on the same side of the table.

Who are the Stakeholders?

In business, the term "shareholder" refers to the owners of the corporation—the people who own "shares" of common stock. Traditionally, it is the shareholders to whom the organization owes its allegiance. In the past two decades, both corporations and other organizations—school systems, hospitals, and many public and private organizations—have come to understand that their obligations extend far beyond the owners of an enterprise. Employees, clients, customers, community members, students, and others who have a "stake" in the success of an organization can be ignored only at great peril. In the business context, the shareholders may be the owners, but the "stakeholders" in the marketplace and the community must be served for the shareholders to enjoy long-term success. In the context of educational accountability, reports are traditionally given to the board and, in some cases, to voters. I have even seen some accountability reports called the "Report to the Stockholders." My use of the term "stakeholders" does not diminish the importance of the board as an audience for accountability information, but suggests that the job of communicating information about student successes and challenges must not end with the board or even with a report to the voters. All the stakeholders—teachers, administrators, policy makers, parents, students, and community members—have a "stake" in the success of the schools and thus must be considered in the construction of the accountability system.

Who Serves on the Task Force?

The Accountability Task Force is typically appointed by the superintendent, with the advice and approval of the governing body. At the very least, the Task Force should include building-level administrators, teachers, central office administrators (particularly research, assessment, and curriculum leaders), parents, business people, retirees, and other community interest groups. Depending on the dynamics of your community, it may be appropriate to include leaders of the media, as well as political, religious, and community groups, whether or not these groups have a direct affiliation with the school system. The key question to ask is this: Who do we need for support when the going gets tough during the next bond election, legislative dispute, or public controversy? If these people only see school leaders when the latter are asking for money or political support, then no one should be surprised by public cynicism.

Beyond "The Usual Suspects"

Even in those instances where stakeholder involvement appears to be a matter of practice, the depth and breadth of that involvement may be less than ideal. Frequently stakeholder involvement involves little more than committee meetings of the usual suspects—active parents, vocal teachers, veteran principals, community activists, and Chamber of Commerce members whose job description includes serving as a liaison to local governmental and educational institutions. While each of those groups deserves representation, we should not accept as a demonstrated truth that the "usual suspects" are actually representative of the stakeholders in a community.

Active parents are essential for school systems, but many other parents feel disenfranchised and removed from meaningful influence in the schools. This group of parents may remain silent during school committee meetings—after all, they were not invited to the table. But they are not silent during bond issue elections, board elections, and initiatives to support or oppose diversion of public education resources.

Chamber of Commerce members may represent legitimate business interests, but it would serve school systems well to carefully analyze their business community. Where are the numbers? Where is the growth? Where is the employment of students and graduates? Are those enterprises represented only by the members of the Chamber of Commerce, or are those enterprises the thousands of small entrepreneurial businesses that have been the engine of the economic boom at the dawn of the 21st century? If so, then wise school leaders will cast a net throughout the community in order to insure that Accountability Task Force members include traditionally underrepresented—but very important—stakeholder groups.

If a Task Force is to be inclusive, then it is imperative that the leadership of the district cast a wide net, including a diverse mix of stakeholders who hold in common a commitment to public education, but whose differences can be striking. Retired persons, small business owners, single parents, and other unlikely and diverse stakeholders must be at your table. Start by making a list of the "usual suspects" for your Task Force, and then engage in some serious brainstorming to expand the list far beyond that initial list. After you have 30 or 40 names, create the final list of 18 to 24 prospective Task Force members who will be invited to join the group. Only in this way can you achieve the balance, inclusiveness, and ultimate success of the Accountability Task Force.

Asking key members of community groups to serve on the Accountability Task Force sends a clear message: *We need you, but we also will be accountable to you and to the community.* A sample letter of invitation to Task Force members appears in Figure 8.1.

Figure 8.1

Letter of Invitation

Dear _____:

    We would like to ask you to serve on the Accountability Task Force for the Green Valley School District. The purpose of the Task Force is to create an accountability system that will accomplish these objectives:

- ❑ Improve student achievement
- ❑ Communicate with students, parents, and the community
- ❑ Give our board of education reliable information about which educational initiatives are most effective in our community.

    The Task Force will initially meet monthly, starting Friday, October 15th, and on the second Friday of every month through April, from noon to 2:00 p.m., in the district office at 201 Poplar Avenue. Lunch will be served. Please only accept this invitation if you are able to attend these meetings.

    The Task Force will make its recommendations to the Board of Education at its May 21st meeting. After that meeting, the Task Force will continue to meet quarterly to analyze accountability information and to review the accountability reports provided to the board and the community.

    Only 18 people from our community will serve on this vitally important Task Force. We know that your time is valuable and hope that you will give serious consideration to this invitation. If you would like to discuss the duties and role of the Task Force, please call us at any time.

Jane Cohen, Superintendent
Green Valley Schools

Richard Sackett, President
Board of Education

Job Description for Accountability Task Force Members

Even if the letter of invitation is as clear as possible, some future members of the Accountability Task Force may feel as if they have received a cryptic invitation from the superintendent's secretary. They know the meeting is about "education" and perhaps are attracted to the notion of "accountability," but that's as far as it goes. Although there are risks in full disclosure of the challenges involved in membership in the Accountability Task Force, the rewards for the district are far greater. You may consider attaching a version of this description to the letter of invitation.

Job Description:
Accountability Task Force Member

Purpose:
The Task Force will develop a new educational accountability system for our schools and review accountability data for reports to the superintendent and board.

Experience and Education Needed:
Sincere interest in our community and the success of our schools is required. Technical background and educational backgrounds are not necessary. In fact, Task Force members without a technical background in education, testing, and statistics are particularly needed. These members will help the Task Force provide information that is clear to every citizen in the community.

Report to:
Board of Education through the Superintendent of Schools

Duration:
During the first six months, Task Force meetings will be monthly for two-hour meetings (please see the attached schedule). After that, Task Force meetings will be quarterly for two-hour meetings. The term of membership is two years.

Responsibilities:
Prior to each meeting, Task Force members will be expected to read materials distributed by the Task Force coordinator. During each meeting, members will be expected to participate actively in the deliberations of the Task Force. In order to continue membership on the Task Force, attendance at five of the six initial monthly meetings is necessary.

You may choose to use a job description that is somewhat less intimidating, but you must clearly communicate your expectations to the prospective Accountability Task Force members. At the very least, the prospective members must know that you expect them to faithfully attend monthly meetings of 2-3 hours in duration for the better part of a year. In addition, they will be expected to read and think about some complex and difficult documents, ranging from test data to personnel evaluation forms. Finally, they will be expected to deal constructively with conflicting opinions and perspectives. If they find disagreement and strongly held opinions to be unpleasant or distasteful, then this is probably not the right Task Force for them.

Duties of the Accountability Task Force

Although the board of education should give the Accountability Task Force an explicit charter with clear duties, it may be helpful to begin the process with some common responsibilities that this group will undertake:

1. **Identify and describe the existing accountability system.**

   Every school system has an accountability system, whether or not it bears such a label. There are recognition and rewards systems, evaluation forms, achievement reports, and so on. The first duty of the Task Force is to identify the existing accountability systems. Chapter 10 explains how to conduct a study of these systems. All of the work of the Task Force can be undermined if it produces something labeled the "accountability plan" and later find out that the board and community have an alternative agenda—the real accountability system—that was beyond the purview of the Task Force. In the course of their review of the existing accountability system, the Task Force should review the following documents:

   - Strategic Plan

   - Accreditation Plan

   - Building Improvement Plans

   - Board goals and objectives

   - Superintendent goals and objectives

   - Teacher and administrator evaluation forms

   - Bargaining agreements that govern teacher and administrator evaluation forms

   - Research department publications on student achievement

   - State and district "report cards" or other documents that evaluate school performance

   - Independent evaluations, audits, and reports that have been conducted in the past three years.

2. **Define the principles that will govern the accountability system.**

Too frequently groups begin with accountability indicators and argue the merits of one particular test or another. The essential diversity of views of the Task Force will lead inevitably to strong disagreements on such matters. Therefore, the mission of the Task Force is better served if the group focuses first on principles that bring them together. For example, teachers, administrators, parents, and business representatives should all be able to agree that principles such as fairness, equity, and accuracy should govern the system. Chapter 9 offers some additional suggestions for the principles that can govern an accountability system. Values and principles create opportunities for reasonable resolutions to disagreements over the details of an accountability system as well as a means to reassure all stakeholders that the Task Force is not engaging in a "gotcha!" exercise, but rather is committed to an accountability plan that adheres to values held by all stakeholders.

3. **Identify who within and outside the school district is accountable.**

If the only people held accountable are 4th graders and the only accountability mechanism is sending legions of 9-year-olds to summer school, then the deliberations of the Task Force should not be particularly taxing. If, on the other hand, accountability includes not only students, but teachers, administrators, board members, and the community at large, then a completely different set of accountability indicators will follow.

4. **Identify qualitative and quantitative indicators for performance by students, teachers, and leaders.**

Just because something can be measured does not automatically qualify it for inclusion in an accountability system. Accountability is far more than a recitation of test scores. The Task Force will inevitably face two challenges. First, Task Force members will be overwhelmed with data. Despite the apparent abundance of information, they may conclude that some data can be interesting without meeting the requirements for a fair, effective and comprehensive system. Second, the Task Force may find that, despite the overwhelming amount of data (typically test scores) that is available, there are important pieces to the accountability puzzle that are missing. Most school systems fail to measure critical educational practices and results, including classroom-level assessment and teaching practice. These historical omissions should not lead to their exclusion from the accountability system, but rather create a challenge for the Task Force to identify new information that must be gathered at the same time they are identifying some time-honored elements of test reports that may no longer play a meaningful role in the accountability system. Thus the Task Force must consider the data presently available as well as the information that may be important but that has not been traditionally gathered by the school system. Chapter 13 treats this subject more thoroughly.

5. **Determine the architecture of the accountability system.**

Once indicators have been identified, how do they fit into a system? Will every piece of available information be reported on every school? Will schools have some choice with regard to the indicators that they use? A recommended accountability system architecture is provided in Chapter 11. Task Force members can also use the Template for Accountability System Design (Appendix A) as a guide to building the structure of the accountability system and describing the purpose of each part of the system.

6. **Create an accountability communication system.**

Typical accountability systems offer an annual "report card" to the community. Because the amount of information is typically overwhelming, there is inevitable disappointment when the media oversimplifies the process. An effective accountability communication system may well include an annual report, but it will also include information throughout the year. Moreover, because the primary purpose of the accountability system is the improvement of student achievement, reports are not only made in the form of voluminous documents and formal board presentations, but in a series of very brief summaries for a variety of audiences. These audiences include individual students and parents, who can see how their efforts contribute to the accountability system. Other key audiences for accountability reports throughout the year include teachers, principals, and central office administrators, all of whom must be able to use that information to make "mid-course corrections" and improve their own professional practice in pursuit of the goals of the system. In other words, communication about accountability is not merely an exercise in public relations; communication provides essential feedback to the stakeholders in the system so that they can improve. Examples of accountability reports on various levels can be found in Appendix B.

Task Force Coordination and Communication

A senior administrative officer of the school district or an independent facilitator should have primary responsibility for coordinating Task Force affairs and communicating with Task Force members. Effective communication for the Accountability Task Force has the following characteristics:

- **Advance Notice and Time for Reflection**: Agendas and supporting documents are always distributed at least 10 days in advance. It is not reasonable to expect Task Force members to read complex documents during a meeting or to respond to alternative ideas on accountability systems without first taking time to reflect on those ideas. Administrators and Task Force members who attempt to distribute written materials during a meeting should be gently but firmly reminded of the group procedure that all materials must be distributed in advance in order for those items to be considered by the Task

Force. Without such advance distribution, the matter can wait until the next Task Force meeting.

- **Documentation and History**: Every Task Force member should have a large three-ring notebook into which all documents and various drafts of the accountability plan are placed. Subtle changes in wording can have significant implications for the accountability system, and memory of Task Force members is a poor substitute for careful and complete documentation of deliberations and changes.

- **Deliberation Between Meetings**: With the availability of computer email lists, it is easy—indeed necessary—for a constant flow of thought and deliberation to take place between meetings. The problem with most Task Forces and committees is that such between-meeting deliberation is typically limited to a few people who happen to cross paths. It is far more constructive (and less divisive) if these between-meeting deliberations occur openly. Unlike an e-mail exchanged between two people, an e-mail list (ListServe) can allow a single e-mail address to reach every member of the Task Force. Even if a deliberation begins as a conversation between two Task Force members, the use of the ListServe allows every member of the Task Force to follow the thread of the conversation and add their own perspective and contribution to the deliberation. For Task Force members without access to the Internet, the Task Force coordinator should compile paper copies of the electronic memoranda and distribute them to Task Force members at least every two weeks. Task Force members without a computer can then submit their contributions to the discussion through the coordinator who, in turn, will post those comments to the ListServe.

- **Communication Outside of the Task Force**: An imperative for the Task Force is the agreement of members that the deliberations—particularly drafts and trial balloons—are not presented as settled policy or Task Force decisions until they have been approved by the superintendent and board. The Task Force is a deliberative body created for the purpose of making recommendations. It is not a policy-making body, and none of the members should labor under such an illusion. It is particularly inappropriate for Task Force members to talk about their deliberations to the media. That's the job of the superintendent—not Task Force members.

Task Force Procedures

During the first meeting, the Task Force must establish its norms and procedures. Examples of issues to be addressed could include the following:

- Facilitator and/or Chairperson (unless the Superintendent has already identified the person to fill this role)

- Meeting protocols, including length of meetings, timing of breaks, and attentiveness to the person who has the floor.

- Decision-making procedures—will it be consensus, majority, or super-majority?

Decision-making by consensus implies that the entire group will assent. If there is not agreement by the group, the facilitator will seek modification of a proposal that meets the needs of all participants until a consensus is achieved. The process of consensus does not rely upon formal rules of procedure, such as Robert's Rules of Order, with its attendant motions, amendments, and amendments to amendments. Rather, the group as a whole seeks to find a proposal that is acceptable to the entire group. The weakness of the consensus model is that a single person can impede the progress of the entire group. There are times, however valuable consensus may be, that it is necessary to resolve an issue and move on.

In those matters requiring a vote, a majority or a super-majority can decide the matter. A majority—particularly a slender one—can be a perilous course for any decision-making body that is addressing profound community issues. Where widespread public support is imperative, a majority of 51 percent of one committee is hardly the source of community-wide confidence. Moreover, the presence or absence of a single member will influence the existence of a simple majority. An alternative to simple majority is the "super majority," a requirement that a large majority—typically between 66 percent and 80 percent—of members agree on a disputed matter before the issue is regarded as settled.

To the maximum extent possible, consensus is helpful. But at critical points in the Task Force deliberations, some alternative to consensus may be necessary. Without such an alternative, the progress of the Task Force is subject to the veto power of a single member who may be pursuing a personal agenda. On the other hand, a Task Force recommendation from a bare majority of members will have little credibility with the superintendent and board. A reasonable rule of thumb for consensus is 80 percent—it isn't unanimous, but it represents the strong conviction of the vast majority of participants.

Task Force Leadership

Task Force leadership is a delicate issue. It is not unusual for a talented and well-informed person to be selected as the chair of a Task Force. Then, when a contentious issue arises on which the leader's experience, judgment, and information would be essential, the leader is expected to be impartial. This denies to both the Task Force and the leader essential opportunities for contribution and collaboration. A better route to Task Force leadership may be the division of Task Force leadership into two roles: convening and facilitation. A Task Force member can convene the meetings, communicate with members, and serve as a liaison between the Task Force and the district leadership. During the meeting, however, an independent facilitator can allow all Task Force members to have equal voice and vote. Moreover, the independent facilitator can synthesize discussions and decisions so that each meeting ends with a verbal synthesis of the discussion and the next meeting begins with a written record of previous decisions. Finally, an independent facilitator who is experienced in accountability system design can help the Task Force learn from the experiences of other school systems and allow the Task Force to focus on the issues that are most important to that community.

Conclusion

Anyone who has ever served on a dysfunctional committee must wonder, "Isn't there another way? Why must we use a Task Force to do what an effective leader can do?" The very idea of giving the important decisions involved in an accountability system over to a group of people who could be fractious and inefficient is enough to give most school leaders nightmares. This reluctance to trust committees, Task Forces, or other groups may be reasonable and based on wide experience; ultimately, however, this distrust of groups cannot prevail. The alternative, however enlightened and well intentioned, is autocracy. It can be dressed up as vision, dynamism, and many brands of "leadership," but decision-making by a single person or exclusive group remains autocratic and ultimately impotent. The use of the Accountability Task Force will require patience. It will take the members six months to do what the superintendent might be able to do alone in a single day. Nevertheless, the broad representation, thoughtful research, collective insights, and wide-ranging communication that the Task Force structure can provide is vastly superior to the autocratic alternative.

Questions for Discussion

1. What stakeholder groups need to be represented on your Task Force?

2. In addition to the duties outlined in this chapter, what else do you expect of the Accountability Task Force members? Write a draft job description for Task Force members to consider during their first meeting.

3. What personal, interpersonal, and professional strengths should Task Force members possess?

Task Force Membership and Characteristics

Potential Task Force Member	Stakeholder Group(s) Affiliation	Personal and Professional Strengths of This Potential Member

9

CHAPTER

Step 2: Accountability Principles

What are the essential principles of an effective accountability system? The definitive answer rests with the Accountability Task Force for each school system. The following seven principles reflect the input of many diverse board members, community members, teachers, students, and school leaders: (1) congruence, (2) respect for diversity, (3) accuracy, (4) specificity, (5) feedback for continuous improvement, (6) universality, and (7) fairness.

Congruence

First, an effective accountability system must be congruent. That is, the accountability system must be compatible with the rewards and incentives already in place in the school district. The most frequent incongruity in accountability systems is the disparity between personnel evaluation systems (often rather arbitrary and based on administrative efficiency and discipline practices) and educational accountability (often based on test scores). An effective accountability system must provide the same incentives for educational excellence that personnel evaluation systems embody.

Several school districts in Alaska have done a comprehensive job of establishing congruence between academic standards, assessment practices, teacher evaluations, administrator evaluations, and accountability practices. Their efforts stand in stark contrast to the extraordinary number of districts that retain accountability systems that have requirements contradictory to their personnel evaluation systems. For example, an accountability system measures student writing, but student personnel evaluations require teachers to "cover the curriculum," and the performance appraisal system fails to address teacher assessment practices. Such a system rewards what is delivered by the teacher rather than what is learned by the student. Administrative evaluations often emphasize the fiscal performance of an administrator (meaning that the administrator uses funds in traditional ways, consistent with the expectations of business management officials), while the academic accountability system requires principals to use funds in innovative ways. Many "customer service" indicators for teachers and principals penalize courageous teachers and principals for telling parents the truth about sub-standard student performance. Effective accountability systems, on the other hand, require teachers and principals to give parents accurate information about student performance—even when that information is unpleasant or different from what parents have traditionally expected. Personnel evaluation and accountability systems must be consistent in the demands that they place upon teachers, administrators, and others.

Congruence extends beyond personnel evaluations. Many accountability systems have failed simply because they were replaced by new programs or plans. For a season or two, the accountability plan was foremost on everyone's mind. But it was quickly replaced by the accreditation plan, followed by the strategic plan, followed by the school improvement plan, followed by the five-year plan. After each of these plans have come and gone, a new board chair announces that it is time for a "new" accountability plan.

If the principle of congruence is to be implemented effectively, then accountability must be a framework within which all other plans, programs, and documents fit. The accountability plan establishes what is important enough to measure and report. It focuses on excellence and equity. Matters that do not fall within this purview are probably not worth the attention of policy makers and school leaders. Properly implemented, a comprehensive accountability plan can become a source of vital information for all other plans and initiatives in the district. Moreover, it can be a filter through which prospective new programs and ideas must pass. If new initiatives do not support the accountability system, then school officials should seriously question whether or not they should be taken on.

Respect for Diversity

The second principle of effective accountability systems is respect for the diversity of individual schools. "Diversity" must be more than the slogan of the decade. It must be a practical consideration in the reality of complex school systems. Diversity includes not only the apparent differences among students, but also the differences that exist among schools, curricula, programs, cultures, and learning styles. A school system might include magnet and specialty schools such as language immersion schools, schools for the arts, schools of technology, and International Baccalaureate Programs, as well as schools designed to improve the performance of academically disadvantaged students.

As important as diversity is in principle, there is great danger for student learning when the term becomes politicized and thus is little more than a code word for lower expectations among disadvantaged students. Diversity can and must certainly apply to strategies; but there cannot be diversity with regard to the standards of performance expected of students. Uniformity in pursuit of excellence is no vice; diversity as an excuse for poor performance and low expectations is no virtue. In response to the diverse needs of its students, a school district must be committed to maintaining equity and must set high standards and expectations for all students.

At the same time, an accountability system that labels low-achieving schools as "failures," without taking into account incremental progress toward a goal, will fail to motivate faculty, students, and administrators. Moreover, an accountability system that allows some schools to become complacent will ill serve the students and parents of those buildings; they need the same continuous challenge as every other school in the system.

One practical implication of the principle of respect for diversity is that an effective accountability system must include multiple measurements of student achievement and educational practices. Some indicators should apply to all schools, based on what they share in common. Other measurements should apply to individual schools based upon their individual needs.

Accuracy

Third, the accountability system must be accurate. This means more than the typical "reliability and validity" required for educational tests. After all, there are many tests that appear to be valid and reliable, but do not measure adequately the attributes an accountability system seeks to evaluate. The principle of accuracy requires not only that the measurements themselves are correct, but that the measurements are used appropriately.

It is possible, for example, to have district and national test data with completely sound psychometric properties, yet utterly unsound applications, in an accountability system. This occurs, for instance, when norm-referenced tests (those that compare students to national averages) are used to determine the extent to which students have met a consistent and objective standard. The same problem of sound data accompanied by unsound application also occurs when schools are ranked from top to bottom. Such ranking can be done without consideration for whether differences in ranking are accompanied by meaningful differences in academic achievement.

Many accountability systems that are based on test scores alone fail to honor the principle of accuracy because they do not distinguish between the academic achievement of students who have been in a school for one week and those who have been there for an entire year. Moreover, test scores alone fail to reflect the academic achievement of some students who could illustrate proficiency better by using demonstrations, portfolios, or other alternative indications of performance. The use of such alternative evidence is essential for the legal defensibility of tests and accountability systems, particularly when high stakes (graduation, post-secondary educational opportunities, jobs, and money) are associated with the results.

Test scores fail to reflect the educational efforts that are the "antecedents of excellence"—professional development of the staff, involvement by the parents, engagement of the students, excellence in assessment and instructional practices, and a climate of safety and educational achievement in the schools. An effective system must measure all of these indicators if it is to give policy makers the information they need to distinguish among effective and ineffective programs, policies, and practices.

Specificity

Fourth, an accountability system must be specific. The persons responsible for the education of our children must have a clear idea of what they must do to help all students achieve. One survey of principals revealed that more than 80 percent of school administrators in one state did not understand what they were supposed to do in order to succeed in the state accountability system (Ladd, 1996). Given the complex and opaque nature of many accountability systems, this is hardly surprising. Such ambiguity leaves the demoralized staff and school leadership guessing what they should do, and frequently working exceedingly hard at precisely the wrong things.

The practical implication of the principle of specificity is that the accountability system must focus on practices of leaders and teachers, not merely on test scores. In a health care accountability system, it would not be sufficient to give the patient a test score for lung capacity without also adding, "By the way, you'd do much better if you quit smoking and exercised regularly." Such a common-sense system includes causes, not merely effects. An effective accountability system is both descriptive and prescriptive. It is not enough for a system to simply note, "Your math scores are low." An effective system will simultaneously prescribe, "Based on the nature of the state mathematics examination, your students will perform better if you have them write more frequently, emphasize more problem-solving in your math curriculum, and require students to estimate answers and calculate by hand before using electronic calculators." Teachers will embrace accountability only if the system gives them the ability to improve student learning. If the system merely blames them for the effects of the educational system, then resistance, rather than cooperation, will result.

Specificity requires that the accountability system pass the "grocery store" test. That is, any stakeholder should be able to read the requirements of the accountability system on a poster in the local grocery store and have a reasonable understanding of what is required. The newest teacher in the district should be able to understand not merely a general desire for good student achievement, but the specific strategies that the individual teacher can pursue to achieve that goal. Parents whose first child is entering kindergarten and parents whose teenager is studying calculus can understand what they can do to improve student learning and thus how they share in the accountability system of the schools. Specificity is more difficult (and, many would say, more tedious and boring) than rhetoric, mantras, or the usual fluff that masquerades as the latest educational fad. None of the other principles of accountability, however, can be effective if the requirements of the system do not pass the fundamental test of specificity.

Feedback for Continuous Improvement

The fifth principle of effective accountability is feedback for continuous improvement. This means that accountability system data are both summative and formative. Accountability data summarize the results of school improvement and student achievement, but also use the results to inform school improvement decisions and initiatives. Data-Driven Decision-Making Seminars form the basis of such decision making. These seminars can be provided in a variety of formats, but effective data-driven decision-making seminars have several characteristics in common. First, they focus on local student results. My colleagues at the The Leadership and Learning Center have worked with many school systems to provide a "treasure hunt" for school leaders in which they plumb the depths of the data from school, district, and state assessments to learn more about the strengths and weaknesses of their students. Second, effective seminars lead to specific strategies based on school and classroom data. This implies that representatives of different buildings and classrooms can leave the seminar with different strategies. Third, effective seminars give teachers and students the information they need for their current students. This implies that this year's fourth grade teachers, for example, are looking not only at the test scores for the students they taught last year, but also for last year's third-graders—the students now sitting in their fourth grade class. Fourth, effective seminars provide for reflection and intermediate feedback. While annual local, district, and state test scores can be a starting point for data analysis, they cannot be the end of the discussion. Many effective districts supplement their analysis of annual state and district test data with monthly analysis of classroom and building assessments. Thus the annual test information is simply an indication of "where we start" and the classroom and building information are vital pieces of the puzzle to indicate "how we are getting better."

Data-Driven Decision-Making Seminars are designed to set goals based on four key steps. First, school leaders and teachers become more familiar with their accountability data. This requires carefully reviewing and analyzing district and school data from test score reports, demographic analyses, attendance reports, and other information. Second, participants conduct needs analyses. Seminar participants ask themselves and each other two key questions: "Based on thousands of data points, what can we learn about the challenges faced by our students?" and "How can we break away from educational platitudes and determine the needs of our schools?" Third, participants develop specific educational strategies linked to their needs analyses. Fourth, school leaders, parents, teachers, and site council members select goals that are based upon the data of the accountability system. Armed with information, they can resist the facile notion that a "ten percent improvement" is a reasonable goal. Perhaps such an improvement is reasonable, but only with hard data can one determine if it is either impossible or too easy.

The use of Data-Driven Decision-Making Seminars to achieve the principle of feedback for continuous improvement makes another critical point: The audience for accountability extends far beyond the media and policy makers. School leaders and classroom teachers make up the primary audience for accountability information. They must use accountability data in the same way that students must respect and use feedback from teachers. Without feedback, students quickly lose interest and commitment; the same is true of adults in the educational system.

This continuous use of feedback is what Dr. Jeff Howard, president of the Efficacy Institute, calls the "Nintendo Effect." He notes that many children who have been labeled as having Attention Deficit Disorder and are assumed to be unable to concentrate will play Nintendo games for hours at a time. Why? Because they receive immediate and relevant feedback. "How many students," Dr. Howard asks, "would play Nintendo if they didn't receive the score for several months?" Indeed, how many adults would find a process meaningful if the feedback never came to them in either a meaningful or timely fashion? In the context of educational accountability, students, teachers, and leaders need feedback which meet the same criteria.

Universality

Universality is the sixth accountability element. It is unusual indeed to find a school system where there are as many standards for adults as there are for children, and as many accountability indicators for the central office, board, and parents as there are for teachers. Comprehensive accountability systems do not deserve to use the words "comprehensive" or "accountability" if only the performance of children is measured. Teaching and leadership practices, as well as the influences of board policy makers and, to be sure, parents, are critical elements of the system.

I have seen many accountability systems that include parental opinions about the school. I have not seen a single one that asks parents the following questions, recording the percentage who reply "always," "sometimes," and "never":

- I read to my child every day.

- I review homework every day.

- I make sure children have no access to alcohol, tobacco, weapons, or drugs in my home.

- I call the teacher when I have questions about my child's performance.

- I volunteer to serve at least one hour per month (at a time compatible with my work and home obligations) in my child's school.

- I limit television viewing in our home on school nights to two hours.

I have heard irate community members and politicians contend that such a survey, particularly as part of an accountability system, is a gross invasion of parental privacy. The same people will speak eloquently of family values and decry the disintegration of the nuclear family. But the suggestion that their rhetoric should be taken seriously enough to measure the impact of family practices on educational achievement is met with indignation.

Consider the case of school leaders who must choose between effectiveness and popularity when they make tough curricular choices. I recently visited a high school in a relatively small community in the western United States. Both the district and the state had established academic content standards, and administrators spoke eloquently about the need to focus on the academic needs of an astonishingly large number of under-achieving students. I asked, "With the majority of your students failing 9th-grade algebra, would you consider providing additional mathematics instruction in middle school and high school curricula so that these students would have a better chance on the state graduation exam?" "Oh no, we can't do that," came the quick reply. "Our parents, students, and teachers really like all of our electives. In fact, we have more than 400 different courses in this high school, so we just don't have time for the ninth graders to take more math." If one part of the accountability system emphasizes popularity and the other emphasizes achievement, we should not be surprised if administrators find that the feedback they are receiving is inconsistent and valueless.

The principle of universality means that accountability is not simply about threatening 8-year-olds with retention unless they achieve a certain test score; it is not about threatening teachers if their students are ill-prepared for a test; it is not about closing down schools and firing administrators. Accountability, when governed by the principle of universality, applies to all stakeholders—students as well as board members; parents as well as policy makers; teachers as well as administrators. The health of the patient depends not upon the singular efforts of physician, patient, supportive family, or hospital trustee—all of these medical stakeholders can help—or hinder—the successful recovery of the patient. Anything less than a universal effort undermines the health of the system. So it is with educational accountability.

Fairness

The seventh and final element of effective accountability systems is fairness. Children will not long engage in a game where the rules change and are widely regarded as unfair. If their efforts are not reflected in the score of the game, or if they are penalized for events over which they have no control, they wonder whether the game is worth the effort and sometimes quit amidst tears and anger. Listen to the conversations of principals and teachers as they discuss contemporary accountability systems. These conversations will include tales about the frustrations of administering tests to students who cannot read the questions, as well as about the anger and tears of children who are entering their fifth school this year but have yet to be academically engaged. Educator discussions will also include immense pride in the unnoticed accomplishments of students and exceptional work of teachers, and perhaps a bit of cynicism about the public acknowledgment of a teacher or administrator who appears to have a greater gift for self-promotion than education.

Although I understand the efficacy of incentives and consequences, my ultimate faith is placed in fairness. If we begin with the premise that most teachers and administrators want to do a good job, want the tools and information necessary to do a good job, and will be more productive because of fairness and respect than because of intimidation and threats, then we might become more engaged in a process of meaningful accountability.

School leaders should consider, for example, opening a discussion of accountability with this pledge:

> "We agree right now that no teacher in this district will be disciplined or otherwise penalized for low student test scores."

Union and professional association presidents, who have come armed to attack typical accountability systems, will now have to admit that there is some common ground. The school leader continues:

> "We also agree that both students and teachers can only be held accountable for that which they understand and control. That means, for example, that while we will not hold teachers accountable for test scores, we fully expect to hold teachers accountable for their assessment practices. This means that teachers will routinely share examples of the assessments that they use, along with examples of student work that they regard as 'proficient.' We will further hold principals accountable for guiding their staffs to a consensus about what constitutes academic proficiency in student work, and for implementing the consensus of the group in all school instructional and assessment practices. If students, teachers, and school leaders are of one mind in the evaluation of proficiency, and that consensus is based on our state and district standards, then test scores will take care of themselves. But if we only provide or withhold incentives for teachers based on test scores, but never agree on what proficiency means, then we will never really know what helps us improve student achievement."

Every teacher and parent knows that children have an innate sense of fairness. Fairness means that we understand the rules of the game, that the rules of the game are applied consistently, and that everyone has the opportunity to play by the same rules. Unlike adults, who frequently associate games with winning and losing, children know that fairness operates as a universal principle irrespective of notions of victory and defeat. Fairness and accountability are not about "beating" someone else, but they are certainly about winning the battle against inequity, injustice and ignorance. Those victories are beyond our grasp if our students, teachers, and school leaders do not believe that they are governed fairly.

Conclusion

I would argue that a system of accountability governed by the principles in this chapter is far more rigorous and demanding than the typical system of test scores. In a system that evaluates teacher and administrator assessment and instructional techniques, accountability can occur every day, not merely once a year. Moreover, the inevitable legal challenges to the intermediate causes of student test results suddenly evaporate when the elements of the accountability system are under the direct control of individual teachers and administrators. This argument does not suggest excluding test scores from accountability systems. Rather, I propose that test scores be restricted to where they belong—a part of, not the sum of—comprehensive accountability.

Questions for Discussion

1. Analyze your current accountability system based on the seven elements of congruence, respect for diversity, accuracy, specificity, feedback for continuous improvement, universality, and fairness.

2. In which of these areas could your accountability system be improved?

Principles of Accountability

Principle	Our Present Accountability System (Rate on a scale of 1 to 10, with "10" being exemplary)	Possible Improvements in Our System for This Principle
Congruence		
Respect for Diversity		
Accuracy		
Specificity		
Feedback for Continuous Improvement		
Universality		
Fairness		

CHAPTER

10

Step 3: Research Existing Accountability Systems

Researching existing systems is the third step in designing a comprehensive accountability system. This involves two levels of study. First, an internal study must be conducted to identify the factors for which stakeholders are currently being held accountable. Even if a school system lacks a formal accountability system, a great deal of information about programs, plans, and results is available to the Accountability Task Force members willing to conduct the research. These data sources will play an important role in designing the accountability system. Worksheet 10.1 will help to lend structure to this inquiry. Second, an external study should be conducted to learn from the successes and mistakes of other school systems. By studying how other school systems and districts have designed their accountability systems, a school district can learn a great deal and save considerable time and effort. The books, articles, and Internet web sites listed in Appendix G and in the references at the end of this book should be a helpful start to this task.

Internal Study

Many districts may already have accountability systems without even realizing it. Their current efforts may not bear that label, but every superintendent, board member, principal, and teacher has some level of accountability right now. The problem is that these accountability factors, while implied, are often undefined, unclear, and internally inconsistent. To find their "hidden" accountability systems, members of a task force sub-committee should inventory the district's personnel evaluation forms, reward and incentive systems, and current methods for imposing sanctions on schools.

If a local business group or educational foundation provides cash awards and extraordinary recognition for one sort of activity—say, dramatic performances—then we shouldn't be very surprised if people are drawn to such activities. If a high school administrator receives greater recognition for processing paperwork accurately than for helping a student who is in an academic crisis, then it should not surprise us if the administrator responds to that reward system. If the superintendent and central office administrators can only maintain their jobs by responding to daily demands from board members for information, research, and investigations, then we should not be surprised if academic initiatives take a back seat to job security.

In an astonishing number of cases, there are clear contradictions between what school districts purport to reward and what actually garners favor or sanction. A comprehensive accountability system—if it is clearly supported by senior leaders and policy makers—can help school systems move away from espousing one set of expectations while actually rewarding quite another. An effective accountability system can help schools channel their efforts toward clear objectives and realign their reward systems to promote the results they seek. If schools want accountability systems with this kind of congruence, then task force members must explore both the explicit and implicit factors embedded in the district's "hidden" accountability structure.

Explicit Accountability Indicators

Explicit accountability indicators are frequently spelled out in board policies, personnel handbooks, and employee evaluation forms. A sub-committee of the Accountability Task Force must read these documents, however obscure and impenetrable they may be. In the course of this study, sub-committee members should identify the incentives built into the present system and, in particular, any contradictions between espoused and actual expectations. Consider this real example:

> The Superintendent and the Director of Instruction of a school system reviewed recent educational research that suggested high school faculty frequently offer a curriculum that is "a mile wide and an inch deep." The school leaders took the findings of this research to heart and, as a result, developed an outstanding curriculum that focused on "essential questions" in every discipline, narrowed the focus of the curriculum objectives, and used textbooks sparingly as resources rather than as prescriptive elements of a curriculum. They forgot, however, that the personnel evaluation form— approved by the union and the board—included a mandate that teachers "cover the material in the assigned textbook." Moreover, the new curriculum required teachers to create new assessment activities that were beyond the scope of teaching duties outlined in the bargaining agreement. An otherwise excellent program of curriculum and instruction came to a crashing halt because no one had researched how the current requirements might be at odds with the new accountability system.

Other explicit accountability indicators are buried in award and recognition programs, grant funding requirements, contracts, bargaining agreements, work rules, and personnel manuals. If the principle of congruence is to be implemented effectively, then the Task Force must thoroughly investigate the accountability messages currently being sent to teachers and school leaders. It is very unlikely that the indicators in the present accountability system are congruent with other reward and evaluation systems currently in place in the district. This means that an important—and frequently overlooked—responsibility of the Accountability Task Force is to recommend specific policy changes to the board and system leadership so that all rewards and incentives are congruent with the new accountability system.

Implicit Accountability Indicators

Implicit accountability indicators are more difficult to identify. These are the sort of expectations that can have a profound influence on the careers of teachers and principals, but which are rarely spelled out. I have participated in informal review sessions for principals, for example, in which the superintendent spoke eloquently of the need for academic achievement and effective leadership by the principal. But when the conversation turned to specific evaluation of individual principals, the most common theme of the superintendent's review of administrator performance was their prompt attendance at a series of meetings called by the superintendent. Those who failed to attend the meetings and participate enthusiastically were not the "team players" that this superintendent wanted. Academic achievement, the criteria mentioned only moments before, was clearly a lower priority when it came to the implicit expectations of principals. The evaluators never appeared to consider the possibility that some of the missed meetings might have been due to thoughtful and intelligent decisions by principals to spend more time with students and teachers. In my work with teachers and curriculum leaders, I have asked them to "weed the garden" by identifying activities that they will remove or modify in order to make time for more effective instruction and assessment. My invitation to administrators to set the example by weeding their own calendars of excessive and unproductive meetings is, more often than not, met with stony silence or outright resistance.

The Accountability Task Force can only identify implicit accountability indicators by conducting personal and candid interviews with teachers, principals, and senior leaders in the district. A single open-ended question should suffice for these interviews: What do you expect of the teachers and administrators who work for you, and what do you perceive is expected of you? (See Worksheet 10.2)

Other implicit accountability indicators might have to do with the cleanliness of school parking lots, publicity (or perhaps lack of it) in local newspapers, participation in (or perhaps avoidance of) regional and national meetings, the ability to get grants and raise money, and a host of other unstated requirements. An effective Accountability Task Force should ask board members and school leaders what their real expectations are, with a view toward eliciting unspoken, as well as obvious, expectations. While it is unlikely that all of the hidden accountability measures will be identified, there is great value in the "sunlight effect"—the only cure for the destruction of some molds, bacteria, and viruses. Only when implicit—and often obsolete and destructive—accountability measures are brought into the sunlight can they finally be exposed and, if appropriate, discarded.

Implicit accountability indicators can often be a waste of time and the product of miscommunication. I have sat in meetings in which teachers insisted that they were required to do something as a result of expectations from the superintendent, while the superintendent, clearly dumbfounded, insisted that he or she had never issued such a requirement and that the teachers' perceptions were wrong. For each such moment of truth, there are doubtless hundreds of other misunderstandings, some of which continue for years. The efforts of the Accountability Task Force to identify implicit indicators are a first step toward eradicating the most contradictory and insidious of the hidden accountability measures.

External Study

In addition to an internal study for explicit and implicit accountability measures, the Accountability Task Force must conduct an external study of how other states and school systems have designed their educational accountability systems. Conducting external research will accomplish several purposes. First, it will help to ground task force members in the principles and practices of educational accountability and give them a practical frame of reference. Second, it will convince task force members that there is no "single correct answer" to the process of designing an effective accountability system. Third, it will equip the Task Force members to be articulate and well-prepared advocates on behalf of the accountability system that they eventually develop. The inevitable question, "Why don't we do it like THAT district?" can be answered with an understanding of the strengths and weaknesses of the accountability systems of neighboring schools and districts.

A good place to start researching other accountability systems is the internet. Most state departments of education and many independent educational publications have web sites that outline various accountability systems. Appendix G is a listing of some of these websites, along with suggestions for finding others. If Internet access in your district is limited, however, there are other ways to do the research. The Leadership and Learning Center provides assistance to school systems throughout the world on accountability systems. If your task force members do not have Internet access, they can call a toll-free number, (866) 399-6019, and receive reports, research, and assistance free of charge.

Many of the kinds of information that school districts must already gather and report can be converted, without much extra work, to part of the accountability system for that district. These are known as external accountability requirements. Examples of the kinds of accountability indicators used for external reporting are listed below:

- **Federal Level**

  - Student achievement analyzed by eligibility for free and reduced lunch and ethnicity.

  - Student participation in academic and extracurricular activities, analyzed by gender.

  - Student achievement analyzed by specified at-risk categories, such as low reading level, teen parents, drug/alcohol treatment, etc.

  - School safety as demonstrated by environments free of drugs, weapons, and violence.

  - Student achievement as measured by equal access to educational opportunity, regardless of a student's handicap or disability.

  - Student achievement as determined by equal access to educational programming and activities, regardless of students' race, gender, color, creed, national origin, or sexual orientation.

  - Student achievement as assessed by the availability of alternate forms of assessment for those students whose participation in more traditional assessment programs would be inappropriate.

  - School accountability as measured by the implementation and maintenance of accurate, relevant, safe, accessible, yet confidential student record systems.

- **State Level**

  - Student achievement analyzed by specified at-risk categories, such as low reading level, teen parents, drug/alcohol treatment, etc.

  - Student achievement as measured by promotion to the next school grade.

  - Student achievement as measured by percentage of students who successfully complete 8th and 12th grades.

  - Student achievement as assessed by students' average daily attendance rates.

  - School safety as demonstrated by environments free of drugs, weapons, and violence.

  - School performance as documented by continuous improvement in student achievement and the identification and provision of services to schools in need of technical assistance or other interventions.

  - School performance as documented by continuous improvement in student achievement and the identification and provision of services to schools in need of technical assistance or other interventions.

  - Student achievement as measured by equal access to educational opportunity, regardless of a student's handicap or disability.

- Student achievement as assessed by the availability of alternate forms of assessment for those students whose participation in more traditional assessment programs would be inappropriate.

- Student achievement as prescribed by the availability of tobacco, alcohol, and other drug awareness and prevention programs.

- **Private or Regional Level**

    - Regional Accreditation Agencies: System and/or school performance as demonstrated by designated levels of student achievement.

    - Private Foundation Grant Funders: Student achievement sorted by participation in specific instructional intervention programs.

Accountability indicators used for external reporting must be considered because those who gather data for an accountability system will be fierce in their resistance if they see accountability as additional work. If, on the other hand, they see that the new accountability system will honor the work that administrators are already doing and use the data that administrators are already collecting, a bridge of goodwill can replace much of the resistance that plagues the implementation of new accountability systems.

Conclusion

One reason that so many accountability systems are ultimately ineffective is that the developers of these systems have not taken the time to consider the status of their current accountability systems. It is a dangerous myth that a school has "no accountability system." It may be accurate to say that the measures for which teachers and administrators are accountable have not been spelled out, but every school and district has accountability indicators that are implicit, and most have accountability indicators that are explicit. A thorough review of the school district's current accountability system, even if it is "hidden," can help the Task Force reconcile existing expectations with those that will be included in the new system.

An external study of other accountability systems will also help Task Force members ground the new accountability system in fundamental research. Valuable resources can be found in publications and through Internet searches. To complete their research, Task Force members will also want to examine what data the school district must collect in order to meet both state and other external reporting requirements.

Thorough internal and external studies of accountability will provide the Task Force with an expansive view of accountability and provide policy makers with an opportunity for clear communication and genuine reform.

Questions for Discussion

1. Describe your present accountability system. What explicit indicators did you find already exist? What sorts of implicit indicators did you find? How did you go about reconciling your explicit and implicit indicators? Use Worksheet 10.1 to help you complete this task.

2. Describe the accountability systems in at least two other school systems that have opportunities and challenges similar to your school system.

Existing Accountability Mechanisms

Stakeholders	Existing Accountability Mechanisms	Analysis: Integrate Into Comprehensive Accountability Plan, Modify, or Discard?
Students	• Report Cards • Standardized Test Reports • Graduation Requirements • Other Reports on Student Performance	
Teachers	• Personnel Evaluation • Pre-Hiring Evaluation • First Year Teacher Evaluation • Veteran or Tenured Teacher Evaluation	
Teachers	• Professional Education	
Teachers	• Award and Recognition Programs (list below):	

Stakeholders	Existing Accountability Mechanisms	Analysis: Integrate Into Comprehensive Accountability Plan, Modify, or Discard?
Building Administrators	• Personnel Evaluation • Pre-Hiring Evaluation • New Administrator Evaluation • Veteran Administrator Evaluation • Recognition and Reward Programs	
Central Office Administrators	• Personnel Evaluations • Recognition and Reward Programs	
Superintendent	• Personnel Evaluation • Contract Requirements, Incentives, and Rewards	
Other Stakeholders:	Other Elements of Existing Accountability Rewards, Incentives, or Evaluations:	

Interviewer: _____ Date:_____

Interviewee Position:

❑ Teacher

❑ Building Administrator

❑ Central Office Administrator

❑ Board Member

❑ Parent

❑ Student

❑ Community Stakeholder

Introduction: Thanks very much for taking the time to meet with me. This is a confidential interview and your name will not be recorded or reported by me in any way. This won't take more than 20-30 minutes. We need your frank and candid feedback in order to learn about educational accountability in our district and, ultimately, to develop a better accountability system. I am a member of the Accountability Task Force that has been asked by the superintendent and Board of Education to research our current accountability policies and develop some improvements.

Is it ok with you if I take notes while you talk?

1. What do you expect of the teachers in this school system?

2. What do you expect of administrators in this school system?

3.   What do you expect of the Board of Education?

4.   What do you expect from students?

5.   What do you expect from parents?

6. What other expectations do you have of the stakeholders in our educational system—particularly those expectations that you believe should be in our new accountability system?

7. What do you expect of the teachers and administrators who work for you, and what do you perceive is expected of you?

Step 4: Accountability System Architecture

The architecture of an accountability system is similar to the design of a building. An effective design is not a mere recitation of specifications and rough plans, but a purposeful, detailed, and comprehensive description that considers function and form. Although the actual architecture of buildings varies widely, the physics of engineering and principles of design safety remain the same. So it is with the architecture of educational accountability systems. While the details of the system may vary, effective accountability systems have at their core five common design elements: system-wide indicators, school-based indicators, demographic information, qualitative descriptions of the school environment, and clear guidance about the interpretation and use of data.

Most accountability systems have only the first element—system-wide indicators—as measured in test scores, attendance information, dropout rates, and other data related to the entire system. While this information may be interesting, it is as incomplete as a "building" with only a couple of walls, but without a foundation, roof, or any consideration of the environment in which the building must endure. Although the content and design may vary, each of the five elements described in this chapter is essential for an effective and comprehensive accountability system. The Template for Accountability System Design, in Appendix A of this book, provides an example of the elements in a comprehensive system.

System-wide Indicators

System-wide indicators are those measures of educational performance that are used by every building in the system. They represent the core values of stakeholders, those "non-negotiables" that must be measured and considered at every grade in every school. They have broad application from the most elite secondary school to the neighborhood elementary school; from the alternative school for adjudicated delinquents to schools dedicated to meeting the needs of exceptional education students. Examples of common system-wide indicators are measurements of safety, attendance, and student achievement. Your district may have other critical areas that are of interest to the entire system—teacher qualifications, promotion rates, dropout rates, funding ratios, and so on. You can find more examples of system-wide accountability indicators listed in Appendix C.

However they are structured, system-wide indicators must be clear and understandable to all stakeholders in the system. With effective system-wide indicators, everyone knows what the goals, objectives, and achievement targets of the school system are. Providing all stakeholders with clear targets helps them develop confidence that the accountability system is grounded in expectations that will not change. If the accountability system is to have credibility with teachers, administrators, and the public, they must have confidence in the stability of the system, and system-wide indicators help give the accountability system this stability.

Nothing is so demoralizing as a system that claims to represent "accountability," yet changes with the prevailing political winds. Over the past 50 years, tens of thousands of school board members have come and gone in the United States, yet very few, if any of them, have changed a single high school football or basketball rule during that time. On the other hand, the academic game, as defined by accountability systems, appears to change with the seasons. Because it takes time to focus a curriculum, develop a faculty, and gain the attention of students, consistency is a critical element of effective system-wide indicators.

As important as system-wide indicators are, they are only a single element of an effective accountability system. If the goal of accountability is to improve student achievement, then we must do more than merely gather information; we must encourage a diversity of strategies at the building level and systematically analyze the effectiveness of those strategies. That leads us to a consideration of school-based indicators.

School-based Indicators

School-based indicators are the "antecedents to excellence"—the strategies employed by a specific school that lead to academic achievement and the attainment of other system-wide goals. Some school-based goals are explicitly linked to the strategies at a particular school site and with a particular student population. While system-wide indicators focus on results, the school-based indicators focus on the strategies used to achieve those results. The word "strategy" often connotes lofty vision and grand plans; in fact, it is simply a method of achieving a result. Consider this example of a strategy from the school-based indicators of the accountability plan in an urban school system.

> The system-wide indicators included the results of the state mathematics test. Therefore, the school-based indicators should include specific strategies to achieve the result: improved math achievement. The development of an effective strategy at the school level required teachers

and administrators to consider why math scores were low. The typical lecture "math scores are low—so go do some more math" is not particularly helpful. These teachers and school leaders needed to determine the root cause of their poor math performance and develop a school-based indicator that would reflect a strategy that would lead to improved math scores. They discovered that mathematics test scores were low not because students had failed to learn mathematics, but because students in this high-poverty area did not know how to use calculators. In response to this finding, the school developed a "Calculator Proficiency Assessment" and required students to excel on this performance task before they took the state mathematics examination. The school-based indicator was "percent of students proficient or better on the Washington Elementary Calculator Proficiency Assessment." The system-wide indicator was "percent of students proficient or better on the state mathematics examination." The students in this school performed exceptionally well on the next state math test, once they knew how to use the tools required for test success.

Other examples of school-based measures include involvement of parents in school activities, professional development of teachers, student enrollment in rigorous courses, and other measurable indicators that are directly linked to student achievement. While system-wide indicators are consistent, school-based indicators may change with the needs of the students. Research we have conducted at the Center indicates that the strategy of frequent informative writing assessment is linked to higher performance on state test scores (Reeves, 1999). A substantial body of research (*NASSP Bulletin*, April 1998) links participation in the arts with improved academic performance. Other research suggests that increased participation in extracurricular activities at the middle school level is associated with increased student attendance that, in turn, is associated with improved student achievement.

An emphasis on the "process" of school-based indicators alone would be insufficient without the context of the results in the system-wide indicators. The typical emphasis on the "results" of the system-wide indicators is of little use if the stakeholders lack an understanding of the processes that led to the accomplishment of those results through an analysis of school-based indicators. Thus the "process vs. results" debate misses the point: We need both sets of data to understand not only how well students are performing but also what strategies lead (and fail to lead) to successful achievement.

Demographic Information in Accountability Reports

Demographic information is useful when interpreting accountability data, but it is imperative that teachers do not establish expectations for students based on these data. One of the more insidious trends in accountability reporting is the use of sophisticated statistics, usually in the form of mathematical equations designed to predict student test scores. The practical impact of the excessive focus on these equations has been the inflation of the relative importance of demographic data. Crudely put, the color of one's skin or the economic status of one's parents "predicts" the scores on one's test. It might be more elegant to present, as some accountability systems have done (Ladd, 1996), a tidy equation in which a "predicted test score" is equal to the sum of a set of factors such as skin colors, neighborhoods, and money, such as this one:

$$R_{it} = a + bR_{i,t-1} + cM_{i,t-1} + c(R_{i,t-1} M_{it,-1}) + dR^2_{i,t-1} + eM^2_{i,t-1} + u_{it}$$

However persuasive such a mathematical proposition may be, the crudity of the proposition remains. This equation purports to generate, in the form of "R_{it}," the "predicted test score," while the variables on the right-hand side of the equal sign, which supposedly form the test score's components, represent such demographic characteristics as ethnicity, economics, language, and location. The association between certain demographic characteristics and low test scores leads to the "bi-variate fallacy"—one cause leads to one effect. If we accept this fallacy, then low socioeconomic status "causes" low achievement; dark skin color "causes" low test scores; and, for that matter, higher shoe size "causes" increased I.Q. scores. Of course, the real world is not "bi-variate" but "multi-variate." Students with low socioeconomic status and dark skins are disproportionately likely to have less qualified teachers and experience fewer curriculum demands (Haycock, 1999). The "cause" of their poor academic performance lies less in their poverty and skin color than in the challenges and effective teaching that have been withheld from them.

If the bi-variate fallacy is so clear, then why do so many educational accountability systems persist in using demographic information to "explain" student performance? The argument for using these statistics is, on the surface, appealing and goes something like this: "Of course demographic variables influence student achievement. Therefore, it is only fair that accountability results be adjusted to take these variables into consideration. If we fail to make these adjustments, then rich schools will always be favored over poor schools in educational accountability programs."

This argument is pleasing. It has a mix of sophistication and common sense that enthralls some policy makers. Perhaps we should state the same equation with more blunt language and see if the argument remains so attractive:

"You see, you've got your colored students, and everybody knows that they can't add very well. And of course those Mexican kids hardly speak any English, so they can't be expected to read as well as other kids. You've also got kids from the western part of the state, and everybody knows that those kids aren't as good in history as children from the eastern part of the state. And then there are the poor kids, who certainly can't write as well as the rich kids ..."

This statement describes the same "elegant" mathematical equation and patronizing explanation about poverty and poor student achievement. The first explanation is plausible and enticing; the second is offensive and racist. But it is the same equation and the same system.

The Proper Role of Demographic Data

Demographic information is important and should be displayed as part of comprehensive accountability systems, but it must not be used to explain, excuse, or influence the results. Demographic information helps us understand important relationships between demographic variables and student achievement, where those exist. But demographic data do not explain, excuse, or predict student performance. Robert Rosenthal and Lenore Jacobson (Woolfolk, 1995) explained the power of teacher expectations on student achievement more than 30 years ago. Accountability systems that use demographic information to predict the results of student performance explicitly say that we expect less of some students and more of others based on factors they can't control.

Qualitative Information

I have a confession to make. I love statistics. I enjoy statistics. I wish that we used them more. I particularly enjoy the elegant way in which multivariate analysis helps us to understand the complex relationships among many different variables. But in spite of my life-long love affair with statistics, I also know this: Numbers alone cannot describe many important issues—including the effectiveness of schools. Qualitative information provides the lens through which quantitative information can be seen more clearly. Narrative description provides the scene, setting, and characters for quantitative data. Both qualitative and quantitative information is necessary. Alone, neither is sufficient.

Consider the following two schools. Jefferson and Washington Elementary Schools both have mean reading scores in the 58th percentile, with math scores in the 47th percentile. In both schools, 32 percent of the students are eligible for free or reduced lunch, 11 percent are learning disabled, and 6 percent do not speak English in their homes. The average tenure of teachers in both schools is 7.3 years. The teacher-student ratio, funding-per-pupil ratio, and square-feet-per-student allocation are all the same. Statistically speaking, the schools are almost identical.

Now consider the qualitative dimensions of each school as described in annual report narratives:

Jefferson Elementary School

The past year has been a challenging one at Jefferson Elementary. Mrs. Jameson, a popular and talented teacher, was stricken with cancer in the fall, and her gallant, but unsuccessful, fight for survival has taken a toll on the faculty and student body. While there were many opportunities for growth and learning amidst our tears, the impact of her illness and death cannot be overstated. Individual and group counseling, along with a play written and performed by students in memory of Mrs. J., have diverted time and attention away from the academic curriculum. For this decision and the resultant lower test scores, I take full responsibility as principal. Nevertheless, we have followed the course of action that I believed was in the best interest of our school community, and I am fully confident that our failure to completely cover the curricula is more than offset by our attending to the emotional needs of our children.

It is perhaps no coincidence that our third, fourth, and fifth-grade science teams took third, first, and fifth place honors, respectively, in the city science fair. These students demonstrated extraordinary work in Mrs. J.'s favorite subject. This accomplishment represents the best showing of a single school in the 28-year history of the city science fair. Unfortunately, the same level of achievement is not reflected in the district's accountability data for standardized science test scores.

Washington Elementary School

I am proud to report dramatically improved reading achievement by the students of Washington Elementary School. Our "Reading Is Everything" Program has been a smashing success, leading our students to exceed the 60th percentile in reading for the first time. While I know that some parents questioned the wisdom of discontinuing art, music, science, drama, and physical education programs, I determined that the need for higher test scores was far greater than any benefits that might have been derived from these programs. The daily tests, high anxiety, transferred staff members, and a few children's tears were unfortunate but necessary prices to be paid for our improved test scores. I also want you to know that I have donated $25 to the school library from the $2,000 bonus I received for our test score improvements.

Can you imagine the typical quantitative accountability system describing these two schools as "the same"? These narratives may appear exaggerated, but keen observers of school climate know that these descriptions barely scratch the surface of real school complexity. More examples of qualitative descriptions can be found in the Sample Accountability Reports of Appendix B. Qualitative information provides a dimension of reality through which quantitative data can be evaluated more accurately. The use of qualitative information denies us the illusion of precision. We can imagine, absent the lens of qualitative information, that Washington and Jefferson are identical schools. We can pretend, without the truth of these narratives, that the numbers tell the entire story. Our imaginations and pretensions would be wrong. Every sports writer, police investigator, and physician digs deeper than the superficial tale told by the numbers. The wise educational evaluator, policy maker, and leader will be similarly persistent.

Clear Guidance about the Application of Data

Clear guidance about the application of data is the fifth element of accountability system architecture. This element allows all stakeholders to understand how the accountability system tracks and monitors progress. How is accountability information really used? The clarion call for "consequences" in educational accountability would suggest that bad results are punished and good results are rewarded. If reward and punishment are the only applications of accountability data, then we have invested a great deal of time and energy to become rats in the behaviorist maze. While feeding and shocking rats may have some dubious merit in the laboratory, this sequence has little to commend it in the school setting. "Shocked" teachers and administrators are not removed, but merely demoralized and convinced that they are failures despite their efforts to help students in need. "Fed" teachers and administrators are similarly bewildered, particularly if their rewards are unrelated to the efforts that they have expended in pursuit of student achievement.

There is a better way. An accountability system that has clear direction with respect to the use of information is absolutely transparent. Schools receive unequivocal guidance about the number and kind of system-wide and school-based indicators for which they will be held accountable. Stakeholders are provided with information about the systems that have been established to determine the degree to which schools are meeting expectations and which schools are in need of improvement and/or intervention. Details about how users should interpret accountability data and apply it to the improvement of student achievement are also provided. In particular, qualitative information provides a lens through which quantitative information is better understood. Essentially, this element of accountability system architecture provides users with guidance about how accountability results should be used to distinguish effective from ineffective activities and thereby improve classroom teaching and learning.

If we use accountability information only to "keep score," then guidance about the use of data is unnecessary. After all, it's not how you play the game, but whether you win or lose. But if accountability information transcends superficial record-keeping and achieves its ultimate objective of improving student achievement, then stakeholders can look at Washington and Jefferson schools and understand the differences that the numbers fail to explain. Washington's draconian strategies are no success; Jefferson's compassionate and heroic accomplishments are no failure. Statistical equivalence notwithstanding, the two schools are not the same.

Conclusion

The architecture of accountability systems will vary depending upon the needs of schools and stakeholders. Every sound accountability system design shares some characteristics in common. A foundation of accountability principles supports the walls of accurate and consistent information, and accommodates the inhabitants of the building. Of course, to complete the metaphor, we should acknowledge that while the building is a school and children are the inhabitants, the adult policy makers are both landlords and custodians. Their financial support and leadership as well as their frequent maintenance of the system are required in order for the dream of the architect to survive.

An accountability structure without all five elements discussed in this chapter has an unstable foundation. Without comprehensive quantitative and qualitative information, it lacks windows that admit light and show us the world. Without demographic information, we have no understanding of our context and location. Without a commitment to the same standards for safe and sound structural engineering, we tacitly admit that some buildings in some neighborhoods are destined to offer better appearance, safety, and protection from the elements than other buildings. Without clear guidance about how accountability data should be applied, the building will be nothing more than a hollow facade—nice to look at, but not functional at all. The design of the accountability system may be creative or traditional, but without the elements discussed in this chapter, it will be incomplete.

Questions for Discussion

1. What system-wide indicators should your district include in its accountability system? Review the menu in Appendix C. What kind of information would these indicators provide? How could various members of your school community use this information to improve student achievement? (Worksheet 11.1)

2. What school-based data should be included in your district's accountability plan? Review the menu in Appendix D. What strategies with measurable impact are in use in your school system? List additional school-based strategies that can be analyzed and measured. Remember that school-based indicators are strategies that directly support the achievement of the results in the system-wide strategies. (Worksheet 11.2)

3. What demographic information should be included in your district's accountability plan?

4. Create a sample qualitative description of two schools in your district that have similar achievement data. Consider the Sample Accountability Reports in Appendix B. How does the qualitative information help you to better understand the quantitative data?

System-wide Accountability Indicators

System-wide Indicators	Information Provided	Use of This Information to Improve Student Achievement

System-wide Indicators	School-based Strategy to Support the System-wide Indicator

Demographic Information

Demographic Criteria	Data to be Recorded in Accountability Report

Qualitative Information—Interpretation of Quantitative Data

School A		School B	
Quantitative Data	Qualitative Information	Quantitative Data	Qualitative Information

Describe the *Qualitative* Differences Between These Two Schools:

School A: School B:

Step 5: Critical Review of Accountability Plan Design

As the Scottish poet Robert Burns once wrote, "The best-laid plans of mice an' men gang aft agley." The phrase applies well to accountability systems, for no matter how careful the architecture, system design, and community support are planned, things can go wrong. This chapter discusses five pitfalls that endanger even the best accountability endeavors.

Pitfall #1. Statistical Quicksand

"We don't have time for all that stuff; just give us the numbers!" the school board president thundered at the superintendent. This apparently reasonable demand was issued amid murmurs of agreement from the other board members. "All these charts, graphs, and other information just cloud the issue. Can our kids read well or can't they? Just get to the point!"

The frustration from the perspective of board members is clear. Decision-makers want clarity, and we respond with complexity. The board wants test scores, and we insist on placing information in context and giving it meaning. They want numbers and we provide narrative. They insist on summaries, and we find detail imperative. Since one of the unspoken laws of school administration is, "One rarely wins arguments with board members," what is the school leader who wishes to support comprehensive accountability supposed to do when the board demands "accountability lite?"

First, we must focus the argument not on the details of the accountability system, but on the principles of effective accountability (Chapter 9) on which the board agreed before the first element in the accountability system was created. One of these principles is "accuracy." The board has agreed that a fundamental tenet of any discussion of student achievement is that the information at hand must be accurate. Accuracy demands context, including comprehensive data and multiple data sources. Does this mean that school boards are doomed to another three-hour presentation from the assessment department, full of incomprehensible slides and laborious handouts? Certainly not. There is room for balance, and this balance can be found in the focus provided by an effective accountability system. In fact, a complete presentation of accountability data can require far less time, even as it provides more meaningful information, than the typical recitation of test results.

Much of the information provided by testing companies is the stuff of recreational statistics. ("Thanks ever so much for the standard error and measurement and normal curve equivalents; now please pass another serving of the standard deviations!") Board members want to cut to the chase and be done with it. In less time than they typically spend on the minutia of test data, they could consider accountability information in which test data has already been screened for statistical distinctions without differences and place this information in a meaningful context. Rather than suffer through line after line of reading scores from a document the size of a Los Angeles telephone book, the board can consider the broad conclusions of the Accountability Task Force, whose members have already separated the statistically meaningful wheat from the chaff.

Effective accountability systems focus on few indicators—typically five or six system-wide indicators and another five or six school-based indicators. Board members get to the "bottom line" they seek because they can focus on the key indicators that are of most importance. Only with this degree of focus can policy makers and leaders avoid descending into the quicksand of meaningless data distinguished by their quantity and complexity more than by relevance and meaning.

Pitfall #2. The Testing Trap

Closely related to statistical quicksand is the pitfall that involves excessive focus on test results. Test results are, to be sure, an important indicator of student achievement. Test data are necessary but insufficient sources of information for analyzing educational accountability. By far the most common error in accountability systems in education today is the exclusive focus on test data without an accompanying focus on the causes of student performance (FairTest, 1998; Bracey, 1999; Reeves, 2000). The impact of the Testing Trap goes well beyond errors in board policy, as the board chases every program, promise, and silver bullet in order to increase last year's test scores. The classroom impact is even more insidious, as teachers frantically attempt to follow the board's demands for improved test scores and drill children on the test questions from the previous year. Even when board members have access to fair and accurate test data for one year, it is too easy to leap to the conclusion that those test results are the consequence of the current year's curriculum and instruction. Of course, learning is cumulative, and test scores are the result of several years of curriculum, instruction, and assessment strategies.

Those who avoid the pitfall of the Testing Trap know what appears to be a well-guarded secret in educational accountability circles: This year's third-graders are very likely to be next year's fourth-graders. An even more elusive corollary to this insight: The performance of fourth-grade students in reading, writing, and mathematics is the sum of at least five years, perhaps eight or nine years, of education, and is not the exclusive consequence of the techniques of the fourth-grade teacher and district curriculum director. These insights, however obvious they may appear, have serious implications for members of the Accountability Task Force and researchers who analyze accountability data. The "effect variables" for one year must be analyzed in the context of "cause variables" for several preceding years. Without such a systematic analysis of causes, we are left with little more than associations between program implementation and test scores, and the serious work of determining what specific instructional interventions were most effective remains incomplete.

This pitfall poses particular challenges for the analysis of students in school systems with high mobility. If a substantial number of students taking a state test in the spring were not present in the fall—and certainly not present in the previous years that we must analyze—then the search for the "causes" of isolated test scores may be fruitless. One answer to this dilemma is the "two-column" technique. The first column of the accountability report includes the scores of all students for a particular assessment; the second column includes only those students who were continuously enrolled in that school for a full year or more. This sort of analysis can be laborious—it requires unique student identification codes and a database that is capable of analyzing student records rather than classroom records. Such an effort pays dividends not only in analytical insights but also in staff morale. While average test scores may offer a host of misinterpretations, the key question for every educator and leader is this: Did the students for whom I am responsible improve during the time they were in my school or classroom? If so, what were the other instructional variables that were associated with the success of those students?

Too frequently the discussion of test information leads to a false dichotomy of warring factions. "Tests are unfair, discriminatory, and of no value!" cry the critics. "Tests are the only independent and reliable information we have to measure student achievement!" say the defenders. Consider a more reasoned middle ground. In order to avoid the testing trap, we must be willing to critically analyze the relevance of average scores and typical presentations of test data. We must be prepared to acknowledge that not every test score has merit for evaluation. In brief, we must insist that the test information is accurate, complete, and in context.

Pitfall #3. Revenge of the Nerds

Not long ago, a large consulting firm placed full-page advertisements in the *Wall Street Journal* and other publications with the following taunt: "Remember that nerdy kid with the thick glasses, leaking pen, slide rule, and pocket protector? Well, now he works for us, and you really need him to solve your business problems." "Cute," we thought, as we half-wondered, half-worried about whether the implied threat of the advertisement was true. Of course, not all of the nerds went to work for international business consulting firms; many work in universities, and not a few found their way into district assessment and research departments and educational consulting firms.

Complexity rules when the nerds have their revenge. They relish the role of data wizard from whom mere mortals must seek information. Accountability thus becomes not a means to improve student achievement, but the exclusive province of the quantitatively able cognoscenti.

Of course, there is nothing wrong with being a nerd—I count myself among their number, equipped with slide rule, pocket protector, and black plastic glasses. The serious issue facing the Accountability Task Force is the analysis of complex data in a manner that is accessible to the community and educational stakeholders. Because public credibility is a precious and rapidly evaporating asset for many school systems, it is imperative that the sources of data and the processes by which data are analyzed are transparent. One of the most important elements of an effective accountability system, therefore, is a technical appendix that explains in clear and unambiguous terms how each element of the system was calculated along with the source of the information used.

Pitfall #4. Just the Facts—As Long as They're My Facts

The most consistent pitfall in accountability systems is the selective use of data. While bias may be inherent in human nature, it need not be a fixture of accountability systems. Some bias is intentional, such as the common practice of comparing a school's test data to national norms and excluding school-based indicators and achievements. Other biases are inadvertent, such as the labeling of academic areas like "mathematics" or "science" based on the description of test items, thus failing to recognize that math and science questions reflect several areas of student proficiency, including reading and writing. Most biases are, to be charitable, the result of careless analysis. The misuse of international test data, such as the Third International Math and Science Study (TIMSS) have been frequently documented (Bracey, 1998, 1999), yet the purveyors of misinformation about the performance of American students persists (Gerstner, 2000).

The most disturbing elements of bias are the use of inflammatory, exaggerated, and inaccurate descriptions that accompany test data. I have witnessed instances of significant growth in student achievement being either ignored or suppressed, apparently because evidence of quality in public education did not conform to the election-year convictions of those whose political success depended upon evidence of public education failure. Few political challengers, after all, can succeed in unseating the incumbent with the slogan, "Student achievement is improving!" The need for change—a new occupant of a seat in the legislature or on the school board—implies a rationale for change—the status quo is an abject failure. Data to the contrary are most inconvenient for purveyors of doom.

Of course, bias is not the exclusive province of political challengers. Incumbents can, purposefully or not, distort educational data to imply a higher level of student performance than is warranted. I have witnessed school officials carefully nurture the illusion of success based on mean test scores in the 65th percentile. The same leaders exhibited genuine surprise when they learned that 40 percent of their students in third through fifth grades were, according to the district's own records, below grade level in reading. Selective consideration of data is not the exclusive province of one political persuasion or another, but is a frequent fixture in the debate surrounding educational accountability systems.

One solution to our national predilection for bias in educational analysis is the careful scrutiny of published reports by those who are willing to expose the data and accompanying analysis to the harsh light of logic and reason. One of the best examples of such analysis is the "Bracey Report," published annually by the *Phi Delta Kappan* journal (Bracey, 1998, 1999). Researcher Gerald Bracey systematically analyzes published educational reports and awards both Golden Apples and Rotten Apples to deserving recipients.

Pitfall #5. A Distinction without a Difference

Even the best accountability systems flounder on the issue of categories and ranking. We want to know not merely whether or not schools are succeeding. We must know, "Who is best?" We desire not merely some effective intervention strategies for schools in need, but demand to know "Who is worst?" This impulse—what I shall call the "comparative imperative"—leads to some of the more silly errors in educational analysis. In general, these errors are what every beginning statistics student would call a "distinction without a difference."

Consider the task before paleontologists, biologists, botanists, and other natural scientists as they try to answer the question, "In order to label a species as new, how different does it have to be from other species?" Medical diagnosticians face similar challenges. Many people have different white blood cell counts, but how significant must the difference be in order to signal a medical alarm? Does any variation constitute a "trend," or must the data be considered in the context of other symptoms and medical data? Before medical intervention—particularly when it is painful, expensive, and inconvenient—takes place, we demand to know that the diagnosis being made is one that is not a minor statistical distinction from our previous state of health, but that it is a genuinely meaningful difference. The difference must be so profound that intervention is clearly justified. On the other hand, we do not want to be complacent based upon an analysis of a couple of reassuring diagnostic numbers. Our entire state of health must be considered in order for us to placidly accept our present condition. Whether the question is one of the taxonomy of fossils or the diagnosis of a loved one, the same question presents itself: Is the information I have sufficiently significant, important, and meaningful that I can make an informed decision?

The question before educational analysts is similarly complex: Given myriad data about different schools, how do we determine whether the differences between them are sufficiently meaningful to say that one school is a "success" and another one is in need of immediate and decisive intervention? The traditional responses to this question are distinctly unsatisfying, as they merely rank or label schools without offering insights about how to improve performance. Ranking assumes that the "bottom third" of schools is different from the middle and upper third, as schools are ranked based on test scores and other data.

How do errors of ranking and labeling invade school accountability systems? The statistical practice that routinely leads to the "distinction without a difference" error is the use of categories. A school where less than 70 percent of the students meet the reading standard is regarded as failing, while a school where more than 70 percent of the students meet standards is adequate. While newspapers covet such simplicity, few editors would tolerate such facile diagnoses of their personal health. They would hardly settle for a diagnosis of adequate health with a statistic of 70 and then face radical surgery with a statistic of 69. They would insist that the diagnostician carefully analyze what test results really made the difference between health and illness. The sports editors offer perhaps the best standard of complete reporting. They do not merely rank baseball teams, but meticulously report the number of "games back" each team is from the leader. This allows the most casual observer to understand that the difference between the teams in 3rd and 4th place is not at all the same as the distance between the teams in 4th and 5th place. We should expect the same degree of care and precision from the reporters on the education beat.

If we are to avoid ranking and categories, what do we do? How do we help the public understand the data on school performance? One way of synthesizing complex accountability data is the use of a point system in which schools receive points for their performance on system-wide and school-based indicators. Consider this example: A school system has five system-wide indicators that show academic achievement (for example, state and district test scores) and five school-based indicators that reflect improvement in building-level strategies (for example, classroom assessment practices, parent involvement, instructional intervention). Each school can earn from zero to ten points on each of these ten indicators.

> Roosevelt School scored an eight on each of the ten measures—good achievement on the system-wide indicators and good improvement on the school-based indicators—and thus earned a score of "80" in the accountability system. Wilson School began the year with a history of very low test scores, but it's getting better. On its five system-wide achievement indicators, Wilson scored only a five on each indicator, but the school's improvement was significant, earning it a "10" on each of the school-based improvement indicators. That means that Wilson's total point value was "75" for the

accountability system—25 points on the achievement indicators and 50 points on the improvement indicators. Taft School has always been fortunate, with a history of high test scores. In fact, in the old system that measured only test scores, Taft was always the top of the heap—"the best school in the city," their principal said with complacent satisfaction. In the new system, Taft received the maximum of ten points for each of the system-wide achievement indicators. But Taft is not improving very much and, hence, received only four points for each school-based improvement indicator. Thus, Taft received a total of 70 points in the accountability system—50 points on the achievement indicators and 20 points on the improvement indicators.

In all three of these cases, the policy makers and leaders needed to know detailed information about student and school performance, but also needed to get to the bottom line: are these schools in crisis? In all three cases, the point system allowed the board, leadership, and public to conclude that, despite their differences, these schools were satisfactory because of their achievement, their progress, or both. Despite their similar ratings in the accountability system, leaders and stakeholders had valuable insights into the specific areas of progress worth of celebration and specific areas of challenge worthy of concern.

In the comprehensive accountability model advocated in this book, school leaders and policy makers would also have the benefit of extensive qualitative information. This qualitative information would create a lens through which they could better analyze the quantitative data in the accountability system. Readers of the accountability report would not only have summary point totals, but would also have detailed information about the performance of each school on all ten of the accountability indicators.

Conclusion

The accountability process can be contentious and difficult, even when the Accountability Task Force agrees on principles and procedures. At least some of the difficulties faced by the Task Force can be minimized if the group is aware of the pitfalls outlined in this chapter.

Questions for Discussion

1. Review the data package provided to your district assessment office. How can the information in that package be synthesized and communicated to policy makers in a coherent manner? What information is essential? What information is unnecessary for policy makers to review?

2. What indicators other than test scores will be included in your accountability system?

3. Discuss your reaction to the "comparative imperative." To what extent, if any, does the "comparative imperative" pose an obstacle to standards-based accountability for your district? What concrete steps can you take to overcome this obstacle?

4. What information will you need to include in your technical appendix to explain how data were calculated and from what sources data were obtained?

Data Analysis and Synthesis

Review the data package for a state, district, or national test that has been provided to your school system. Analyze the usefulness of the data using this worksheet.

Data Element	Utility for Policymakers	Necessary for Accountability Report?

Accountability Indicators Other Than Test Scores

Accountability Area	Indicators (NOT Test Scores)
Language Arts	
Mathematics	
Science	
Social Studies	
Other Areas:	

CHAPTER

Step 6: Select System-Wide Accountability Indicators

The next step in the development of a comprehensive accountability system is the selection of system-wide indicators. These indicators represent the most broadly shared values and goals of a school system. Every school, regardless of the focus of its curriculum, the economic status of its students, or any other unique characteristics, must share a common commitment to a core set of objectives. Often, this set of core objectives is identified through a district's strategic planning process. Once a comprehensive accountability system has been put into place, accountability information can be used to drive a district's planning process toward those core objectives. Planning offers a district the opportunity to reflect upon its current successes and failures in order to determine the direction it wants to take. Out of this reflection and planning process, school systems are able to assess which of their current efforts have resulted in higher achievement for students, and which initiatives have failed to benefit students and other district stakeholders. A district's goals and objectives represent those steps that the system believes will help it close the gap between its vision of where it would like to be and the current reality of where the district is. While strategies and leadership techniques may vary widely from one school to another, every school within a system shares—or should share—some common values and objectives. System-wide accountability indicators put these common values and objectives into measurable terms that the district can then use to assess its progress toward meeting its goals.

Although it is the responsibility of the Accountability Task Force, in collaboration with school leaders and others, to identify system-wide indicators, it may be useful to begin the process with a look at some examples (see Table 13.1). Additional examples of system-wide indicators are included in Appendix C.

Table 13.1

Examples of System-wide Accountability Indicators

Indicator Type	Sample Data Source	Sample Wording of System-Wide Indicators	Remarks
Academic Performance	Standardized Tests	Percentage of students who achieve a score of "proficient or higher" on the state 8th grade mathematics test.	Note that this is not a "percentile." It will be necessary for the Accountability Task Force to determine the number of correct responses that constitute "proficient" performance. This will require test vendors to provide item analysis data, not simply the scale scores or the percentile ranks achieved by students.
	Locally Created Tests	Percentage of students who achieve a score of "proficient or higher" on four out of five school-based writing assessments.	The comparison of this information with state and national test data allows policy makers to determine the relative rigor of locally created tests.
	Teacher Observations	Percentage of students who teachers score as "proficient or higher" on state (or district) academic content standards.	The use of this information, in conjunction with other assessment data, allows teachers and school leaders to reflect on the consistency and accuracy of teacher feedback to students. If teachers tell students that their performance is "proficient" or "exemplary" when other tests suggest that the performance is inadequate, then some professional development on student evaluation may be appropriate.
Safety Indicators	School Records	Percentage of days without safety violations (or student injury, etc.).	Note that it is best to express accountability indicators in a consistent direction—that is, "high" numbers are good.
Student Engagement Indicators	School Records	Attendance	Some systems exclude students who are not legally required to attend school, such as those under 6 or over 16.

How Many Indicators?

How many system-wide indicators is enough for the average accountability system? While those people assigned to implement an accountability system can be tempted to bury their readers with data, my recommendation is that system-wide indicators be limited to only five or six indicators for each level of school. That is, five or six indicators for elementary, perhaps a separate five or six indicators for middle schools, and another five or six indicators for high school. The reason for such a limitation is the requirement for focus. School improvement plans with 20 or 30 goals lack focus. School leaders have often found it easier to set many goals than to analyze the achievement of those goals. Deliberate focus on fewer goals enables districts to monitor and get feedback on goal achievement more frequently. This makes the accountability process more meaningful.

System-wide indicators may, of necessity, vary depending upon the type of school and the data available. It is reasonable, however, that all elementary schools will have the same five or six system-wide indicators, because all elementary schools share common values, such as reading, mathematics, and safety. Similarly, all middle schools and all high schools should share a common set of indicators.

Demographic Data

The demographic data about schools—student population, percentage of students eligible for free and reduced lunch, number of students receiving special education instruction, and so on—should be included as part of an accountability report because they can provide important contextual information for the reader. These data are *not accountability indicators*, however, but are only included in the report to provide an analytical frame of reference. As a matter of equity for schools and high expectations for students, it is imperative that all schools—regardless of the demographic characteristics of their student populations—choose system-wide indicators that are challenging and rigorous. This does not occur when a district establishes different student performance expectations based on the demographic characteristics of a school.

One of the more dangerous national trends in educational accountability is the notion that expectations for academic performance should be adjusted based on the ethnicity and economic status of students. Once a school district descends the slippery slope of changing expectations based on demographic characteristics, it has institutionalized a system of low expectations for some students based on their economic or ethnic status. However elegant the statistical rationale for such a procedure may be, decades of research are unequivocal: low expectations have powerfully adverse results for students. As I write this paragraph, I am returning from a school district in which well-intended, decent teachers and administrators have accepted a system of accountability in which goals for student achievement are a function of demographic characteristics. The administrators in this system mean well, but their system screams this epithet: "That school didn't do very well, but they did all right for a bunch of poor minority kids." These are not people of malicious intent; they have simply fallen victim to the national trend to allow demographic data to overwhelm rational expectations.

School districts that define expectations based on demographic data invariably have lower performance expectations for poor students and for students from ethnic minority groups. The defense of these systems typically includes statements such as "This is the best that 'they' can do" and "Students and teachers will get discouraged if we demand the same standards of 'those students' than we require of other kids." Although these words come from people who regard themselves as education advocates, it is difficult to reconcile a policy of low expectations for minority and poor children with educational progress or justice. Fortunately, a growing number of school systems with high percentages of students from low-income minority families are creating a counter-revolution in accountability, with consistent expectations of all students regardless of their demographic characteristics. Examples of these include Pueblo School District, Colorado; Milwaukee Public Schools, Wisconsin; Riverview Gardens School District in St. Louis, Missouri; Metropolitan School District of Wayne Township in Indianapolis, Indiana; and Princeton City Schools in Cincinnati, Ohio.

Selecting Accountability Indicators

Where is the best place to start when selecting system-wide indicators for the district's accountability plan? An important first step is to conduct a "data inventory." This inventory should include every measurement that is routinely taken by a school system, including assessment and test data, attendance, tardiness, suspensions, expulsions, surveys, course enrollment, and so on. Such an inventory will likely leave Accountability Task Force members surprised by the sheer volume of data collected by its school district. Some of this data may be useful for the accountability system; a great deal of it will not. The best way to discern the meaningful useful data from the irrelevant information is this question: Will this piece of data help a classroom teacher change curriculum, assessment, and instruction and thus improve student performance? The Task Force may determine that some critically important pieces of information are missing, and that some additional data gathering or additional analyses of existing data may be necessary. For example, data from classroom assessments and building analyses of teacher assessment practices can be vital pieces of information, but these are frequently omitted from traditional accountability systems.

Specifications for Analysis and Collection of Data

The Accountability Task Force must not only identify system-wide indicators, but must also specify the manner in which data will be analyzed and collected. For example, all schools maintain attendance data and grade data, but not all schools collect data on the grades of students who have attendance rates of 90 percent or higher. All schools maintain test scores and routinely disaggregate this data based on income, gender, and ethnicity; not all schools go the extra step of also collecting the test scores of students who actually attended the school for the majority of the school term. The common assumption that test scores reflect the curriculum and teaching of a particular school year is appropriate *only if the students were in class for that year*. While this statement may be obvious to most readers, researchers and school boards frequently use test data without any analysis of whether the students being tested actually attended school and received the curriculum and instruction that are purportedly under evaluation.

Whenever the suggestion is raised that specifications for analysis and collection of data should consider student attendance and other characteristics, some allege that such analysis reduces school accountability. The argument goes something like this: "If you're only going to include those students who attend school all year, aren't you saying that you have no accountability for those students who enrolled in your school in February?" Similar arguments are made about students in special education or programs for English language learners. The specifications for analysis and collection of data are not intended to exclude students from accountability but, rather, to insure that accountability information is as accurate as possible.

Consider the case in which the Accountability Task Force decides to evaluate student attendance. To get the most accurate information possible, the Task Force decides to include only the scores of those students who have attended school for 90 percent of the school days in the six months before a test is administered. This in no way implies that teachers and administrators can forget about the other students. In fact, my recommendation is to report two sets of data: the "all student" data and the data for the specified group. For example, if we want to measure the performance of students who participated in the curriculum and instruction of a specific fourth-grade class, and we also wish to have universal accountability, it makes sense to include two sets of test information in the accountability system. The first set of test data includes the scores of only those regular education students who attended the class 90 percent of the time. The second set of test data includes the scores of all students, including special education students, transfer students, and students who were absent frequently.

Inappropriate Incentives

The importance of including these technical specifications for how data should be collected cannot be overstated. Indeed, it is imperative that this information be included if teachers and staff members are ultimately to have confidence in the accountability system. In addition, the technical specifications are the key to avoiding inappropriate incentives for teachers and principals. The most perverse incentive in educational accountability systems occurs when some students are subtly encouraged to be absent from school on testing day and unavailable for make-up testing. This is particularly true when districts mandate that all students be included in testing on one hand but, on the other hand, calculate average test scores as if the average scores were representative of educational quality. Parents can be gently encouraged to assert their right to withdraw their children from testing (some districts even provide convenient copies of test exemption forms for parents to sign), or students can receive the unmistakable signal that they need not attend school on test day. While it may be popular sport to blame teachers and administrators for the high numbers of students who fail to participate in school testing, it is actually the inappropriate incentives of the accountability systems that are to blame.

Conclusion

System-wide accountability indicators should focus on the commonly held values and objectives shared by all schools in a system. They should be few in number—not more than five or six—and should therefore permit school leaders to focus on a clear set of important educational indicators. In addition to identifying the system-wide indicators, the Accountability Task Force must also specify how the data for these indicators will be collected and analyzed. When proper specifications are given for how data should be collected and analyzed, all system stakeholders can have confidence that the accountability data shared with the public are accurate reflections of the performance of students, teachers, and the school system.

Questions for Discussion

1. What are the common goals and objectives of your school system or district? Consult district documents about your mission, vision, goals, and strategic plans.

2. What would be indicators for each common goal and objective?

Indicators for Achievement of System Goals

Common School System Goals	Accountability Indicators
All schools:	
Elementary Schools:	
Middle Schools:	
High Schools:	
Pre-School Programs:	
Central Office:	
Other Programs and Goals:	

CHAPTER

Step 7: Select School-based Accountability Indicators

School-based accountability indicators are specific and measurable actions at the classroom and building level. These indicators reflect specific strategies that are linked to the achievement of system-wide goals. The best school-based indicators reflect the unique needs and challenges of that building environment. They are selected based on a careful analysis of assessment and diagnostic information, as well as the professional judgment of teachers and leaders within each individual school. When properly used, school-based indicators provide continuous feedback to leaders, teachers, and students. While the system-wide goals are typically district and state assessments that are tracked only once a year, the school-based indicators represent classroom and building-level data that can be tracked every month or more frequently.

Synergy Between System-wide and School-based Indicators

School-based indicators are more than the typical list of goals from school improvement plans, strategic plans, or other documents. The essence of effective school-based indicators is *synergy*. This term has been so overused in the context of business and organizational development models that many people have forgotten the primary meaning of the word. Synergism was originally a medical term referring to the "interaction of elements that when combined produce a total effect that is greater than the sum of the individual elements" (Flexner, 1987). In the context of educational accountability, the synergy between system-wide indicators and school-based indicators occurs when their combined use creates a greater effect than the use of those two indicators in isolation.

How does synergy work? Typically, accountability systems report isolated variables—test scores—and teachers are implored to improve those results in the future. The implication is that the path to improvement is some change in effort or practice by students and teachers, but little is known about improvement until the next year's test scores are provided. By producing information on the strategies and practices teachers use to achieve student results, school-indicators have a direct impact not only on instructional practices, but on the student achievement measured in system-wide indicators.

Consider this example: Burroughs Middle School in Milwaukee, Wisconsin had student attendance as a system-wide indicator. Every school in the district tracked and reported attendance, and the numbers for Burroughs were not pretty. Truancy, tardiness, and other absences were out of control. One of the school-based indicators used by Burroughs was "Percent of students involved in two or more extracurricular activities." The principal, Mr. Victor Brazil, and his teacher-leader team reasoned that in the middle school environment, peer pressure for success in extracurricular activities would lead to high attendance rates. Every teacher was involved in coaching or advising at least one activity. With the help of students, scores of new clubs and activities were invented to meet a wide variety of needs and interests. During the first year of this initiative, significantly more students were involved in a large number of extracurricular activities and student attendance improved by 22 percent. Of course, as attendance improved (the system-wide indicator), the participation in extracurricular activities (the school-based indicator) grew even more. That, in turn, led to continued improvement in attendance. That's synergy.

Another example of synergy is the cross-disciplinary impact of writing. In a number of districts we have studied, the consistent pattern that emerges is this: when students and teachers increase the frequency of their informative writing assessments, student scores increase not only on state and district writing assessments, but also in mathematics, science, social studies, and reading (Chapter 20 describes this relationship in fuller detail, as does Linda Darling Hammond's 1997 book, *The Right to Learn*). In this way, the improvement on a single school-based indicator, "percentage of students who are proficient or better in informative writing" or "number of interdisciplinary writing assessments" can have a positive impact on several system-wide variables.

Can You Really Trust Schools to Pick Their Own Indicators?

The board president was shocked and upset to learn that the Accountability Task Force had recommended that the school-based indicators in the new accountability system would be chosen by local school committees. "They'll just give themselves softballs!" the president lamented. While this concern is understandable, my experience suggests that trusting local educators and leaders to select school-based accountability indicators is a wise policy. Rather than easy-to-accomplish "softball" goals, school-based indicators tend to be creative, relevant, and challenging. Moreover, the architecture of a comprehensive accountability system offers an automatic check to discourage easy goals and encourage challenging indicators at the school level. If the published accountability report shows that on system-wide indicators a substantial number of students are not meeting state and district standards, but the school-based indicators suggest that everything is rosy because superficial and easy goals have been attained, then the school leadership clearly lacks credibility. If, on the other hand, the school goals are aggressive, challenging, and substantive, then it will be clear to the stakeholders and policy makers reading the accountability report that the school leadership is aggressively pursuing improved student achievement. For a menu of sample school-based indicators, please see Appendix D.

Focusing School-based Indicators

Anyone who has participated in a school planning process knows that this process of dreams, visions, and plans can lead to dozens of goals and reams of paper. When goal setting becomes politicized, then every interest group, every discipline, every activity must have its own goal in order to have an aura of significance. At the end of the day, however, these exercises seldom provide a clear focus and the resulting goals are futile. Fewer goals, with everyone pulling in the same direction, will lead to better focus and improved achievement.

How many goals and school-based indicators are too many? It is impossible to be precise and prescriptive, but it is fair to say that when the number of goals exceeds ten, the faculty and leadership risk losing their focus. My colleagues at The Leadership and Learning Center work with outstanding school systems that have four to six system-wide goals and a similar number of school-based indicators for each building. If, for example, the goals focus on reading, writing, math, and safety, the implication is not that science, social studies, music, art, and physical education are unimportant. Rather, there is a clarion call for all of the latter activities to avoid the typical curriculum isolation that prevails in so many schools and pull together in a concerted effort to achieve those four goals. In these schools, the physical education teachers help students in measurement, the social studies teachers encourage student writing skills, and the science teachers improve problem-solving abilities. The music teachers do not lose their aesthetic value and artistic commitment because they help students with fractions, vocabulary, and critical thinking skills. In other words, the focus on a few school-based indicators does not diminish the importance of curriculum and activities, but it elevates every activity, unit, and class into a critically important academic activity.

Conclusion

The selection of effective school-based accountability indicators is the very heart of educational improvement. Decades of effort in the creation of detailed planning documents have produced thousands of goals that frequently are distinguished more by their complexity and abundance than by their impact on student achievement. But in the careful selection of a handful of school-based indicators, an Accountability Task Force will be rewarded with the synergy of progress toward system-wide indicators and improved student achievement.

School-Based Indicators

System-Wide Indicator	School-Based Strategies to Support This System-Wide Indicator	Possible School-Based Indicators to Measure Achievement Related to This Strategy

15

CHAPTER

Step 8: Accountability Reports

Accountability is of little value without communication. While the media may focus on test scores and mislabel them as "educational accountability," the communication of accountability data entails far more than test data. This chapter identifies the key reports that must accompany an effective accountability system. Ideally communication about accountability is not a mammoth tome delivered on an annual basis, but rather a reporting *system* that provides a steady stream of information to school leaders, teachers, and the community.

District Accountability Reports

The annual accountability report begins with a district summary and includes individual information on each school in the system. The district summary includes the system-wide indicators as well as an analysis of trends in school-based accountability reports. The district summary should focus on five key questions:

- What were our goals?

- What was our performance compared to our goals?

- What was our performance compared to previous years?

- What strategies worked well to improve student achievement?

- What does the information in the accountability report tell us about how to improve student achievement?

Recently a superintendent asked, "Why don't we just report the test scores? After all, that's what people really want to see." There is an understandable impatience with long reports and unnecessary detail. These five questions, however, lie at the heart of effective accountability. The omission of important information in the district summary is an invitation to superficiality and over-simplification. We should be guided by Einstein's maxim that "things should be as simple as possible, but not more so." The appropriate balance between complexity and simplicity might be, as I suggested in Chapter 2, the sports page of your local newspaper. This information about men and women playing games is neither limited to box scores nor the subject of encyclopedic examination. In the reporting of every game, there is

Accountability in Action

a blend of scores, analysis, and inferences. Surely we can aspire to a balance at least as careful in the reporting of educational information.

School Accountability Reports

Some school systems recoil at the idea of including information about individual schools in a district accountability report. I heard one senior administrator say, with a straight face, "If people in the community want information about individual schools, then they can just go to the schools and get it." The reluctance to share individual school data as part, the district report is based on the fear that the public would compare schools to one another and develop rankings that would hurt the morale of the faculty and students. The strategy of the administrators appeared to be that failure to disclose school data would lead journalists and other curious members of the public to give up and presume that all is well with the state of education. In fact, in the minds of education critics, the line between reluctance to share data, however benign the motives, and "hiding" information with sinister intentions is a thin one. When the information does come out, as it inevitably must, those prone to compare and sort and rank schools will do so with gusto, their methodology unencumbered by logic or analysis. As a consequence, school leaders are invariably better served by providing complete information—not simply the test scores to which the indolent journalist may resort, but all of the system-wide and school-based indicators, along with brief narratives on each school.

Intermediate Accountability Reports

The extraordinary effort involved in the creation and maintenance of a comprehensive accountability system should yield more than annual district and school reports. Accountability is, above all, a tool for improving student achievement. With the help of the research department, the Accountability Task Force should review data throughout the year, perhaps at quarterly meetings, that helps to address the question, "What can we learn from the accountability data about strategies to improve student achievement?"

Intermediate accountability reports include a search for associations between school-based indicators and system-wide indicators. In addition, analysis of accountability data can focus on schools with particular characteristics. Here are some examples of research questions that have been addressed with accountability data from school systems around the nation:

> *Do schools with high poverty and high achievement have leadership and teaching practices that are different from schools with high poverty and low achievement?*

A review of system-wide indicators reveals 14 schools that have more than 90 percent of the student population eligible for free or reduced-price lunches and more than 90 percent of the student population who met or exceeded the state academic standards. A review of the school-based indicators in these 14 schools indicates that 12 of the 14 schools shared the following school-based goals in common:

- Increase the percentage of students who are proficient or better in a school-based informative writing assessment.

- Increase the percentage of art, music, and physical education classes that include a focus on writing, measurement, or problem solving.

- Increase the percentage of science, social studies, and math assessments that include requirements for student writing.

We did not find frequent use of or success in these school-based indicators in high poverty schools that did not experience high levels of student success. From this information, we believe that there is an association between more writing by students (and more assessment of writing by teachers) and improved performance by students in high-poverty schools. In addition, successful high-poverty schools in our district appear to have a consistent emphasis on academic performance in every subject, including art, music, and physical education. Of course, these are successful practices in *any* school, not only schools with many students eligible for free and reduced lunches. The experience of these schools indicates that high levels of poverty in a student population are not necessarily a reason that students are unable to meet our academic standards and perform well on state assessments.

> *Do schools with high mobility and high achievement have leadership and teaching practices that are different from schools with high mobility and low achievement?*

A review of system-wide indicators reveals that we have 12 schools with mobility rates (defined as the percentage of students enrolled in the school in April who were not enrolled in October, compared to the total number of students enrolled) in excess of 60 percent. Of those 12 schools, 4 of them showed exceptional academic performance, with 80 percent or more of the students meeting or exceeding state standards. By contrast, the other eight high-mobility schools showed significantly lower performance, with less than 50 percent of the students meeting or exceeding state standards. A review of the school-based indicators in the four high-mobility, high-achievement schools reveals the use of strikingly different practices than prevailed in the eight high-mobility, low-achievement schools. These practices included:

- Significant increases in parental involvement, including parent contribution to assessment design and student coaching.

- Significant increases in school-wide focus on discipline, including frequent communication, assemblies, and conferences with students and parents on behavioral expectations.

- Significant increases in student writing in language arts and other academic and non-academic subjects.

An analysis of data from the four high-mobility, high-achievement schools indicates that the student populations with higher levels of poverty had better achievement than schools with the high-mobility, low achievement profile. As a result, one cannot conclude that the higher achievement by those four schools was due to greater wealth of their student populations. Instead, it appears that some instructional and assessment strategies are particularly effective, and that these strategies can have a positive impact on student achievement even in high mobility and high poverty schools.

Conclusion

Accountability reporting can be greatly improved if it is clear, comprehensive, and useful. These objectives cannot be met with a recitation of test scores or a litany of excuses that hide critical information from the public. When they have a clear link to the mission and values of the school system, accountability reports can help the reader understand not only what the numbers are, but what the numbers mean relative to the important objectives of the school system. When annual reports are supplemented with analytical insights throughout the year, then accountability is no longer a *"Gotcha!"* used to embarrass, humiliate, and demoralize teachers and students, but is a constructive force for improved student learning and enhanced leadership and teaching practice.

Questions for Discussion

1. Create a mock annual accountability report. Consider the examples in Appendix B. It may be helpful to select an actual school so that you can determine how difficult it is to gather and report data for the system-wide and school-based indicators in the accountability system you have developed.

2. Develop some research questions that are important for your school system. Consider the questions raised in this chapter on the impact of teaching and leadership practices in high poverty and high mobility schools. What are the most challenging questions that data from your accountability system can begin to address?

Research Questions

Research Question	System-wide Indicators Related to This Question	School-based Indicators Related to This Question

16

CHAPTER

Step 9: Build the Central Office into the Accountability System

The central office, where the work of senior administrators and staff is carried out, must be included in a comprehensive accountability system. Most superintendents have heard this pointed question: "What do all those people in the central office do anyway?" When a board of education member poses this question during a budget discussion, the ax can fall quickly on central office functions that may be important, but have been invisible to the public and policy makers. The use of a comprehensive accountability system gives central office functions visibility, responsibility, and accountability. Such a system can serve not only as an effective advocate for central office functions, but it can also send the clear message to teachers and community members that the senior administrators in the district are held accountable in the same way that teachers and principals are held accountable.

The central office has traditionally experienced both extremes of accountability: When things go wrong, the board of education issues the clarion cry that "heads will roll," and the heads most likely to roll are those with minimal job protection—senior administrators. The other extreme is represented by the notion that only teachers should be accountable for student performance, and that the role of the central office is to implement the accountability system, not to be subject to it. This chapter is devoted to the proposition that senior leaders and members of a district central office are important participants in an effective, comprehensive accountability system. Their roles exert direct influences on system-wide goals, school-based goals, and student achievement.

Format of the Central Office Accountability System

The architecture of the central office accountability system is parallel to that of the school accountability system. The central office accountability system contains three levels: common goals, departmental goals, and narrative descriptions of the performance of the department. Central office common goals are established by the Accountability Task Force and approved by the school board. Central office departmental goals are established by the accountability team of each department of the central office, and reviewed by the Accountability Task Force. For the sake of clarification, common goals for the central office accountability system should not be confused with system-wide goals for the school accountability system. Though each has an effect on the other, they are two different sets of objectives.

Measurement of central office goals includes a focus on both absolute achievement and yearly improvement. In the suggestions below, the common goals focus on consistent measurements of absolute achievement, while the departmental goals focus on yearly improvement.

Central Office Common Goals

The common goals represent those shared by every department in central services. Every department, from the office of the superintendent to the human resources and food service departments, can identify contributions that they make to common goals as they serve students, the community, and internal clients. Central office staff serve two sets of clientele: external clients—school stakeholders not employed by the school system or district—and internal clients—school stakeholders employed by the school system or district. For example, the principals who must find qualified teachers to fill particular positions in buildings are the internal clients of the personnel department. Department heads and teachers are internal clients of the curriculum department. Senior administrators, teachers, and principals are all internal clients of the assessment department. Examples of external clients include students, who are clients of the food service, transportation, curriculum, and assessment departments. Parents and community members are external clients of the assessment departments.

Some examples of common goals for central services are listed in the table below:

Table 16.1

Examples of Central Office Common Accountability Goals

Category	Examples of Central Office Common Goals
Safety	• Percentage of employee days without work-related illness. • Percentage of work areas modified for ergonomic design. • Percentage of safety inspections completed with zero violations. • Percentage of cost savings resulting from fewer job-related injuries.

Category	Examples of Central Office Common Goals
Human Resources Practices	• Percentage of employees meeting professional development goals. • Percentage of months in which equal opportunity hiring goals have been achieved. • Percentage increase in the pool of qualified applicants for critical skills. • Percentage of employees who have participated in comprehensive performance appraisals within the previous 12 months. • Percentage of cost savings resulting from the procurement of a less costly medical benefits provider.
Technology	• Percentage of employees certified to use current computer network software. • Percentage of employees who have completed Internet training. • Percentage of cost savings resulting from automation of manual procedures.
Service to Schools	• Percentage of employees who participate in direct contact with students or in teacher support roles. • Percentage of employees who participate in school-to-work activities. • Percentage of employees who bring business/community partners into classrooms. • Percentage of employees who sponsor community/ workplace outings for students. • Percentage of employees who develop ways to engage students in solving real-world problems.
Communication	• Percentage of public presentations made by department employees to a community or service organization. • Percentage of cost savings resulting from the use of the district website, electronic mail, and other communication technologies.

Category	Examples of Central Office Common Goals
Risk Reduction	• Percentage of employees who have completed risk management training. • Percentage of workdays without an employee complaint or union grievance. • Percentage of cost savings resulting from fewer on-the-job injuries.
Cost Control	• Percentage of budget used for employee benefit costs. • Percentage of budget used for office supplies. • Percentage of budget used for long-distance telephone and facsimile (fax) costs.

Departmental Goals

In the same way that schools have unique needs that can be reflected in school-based indicators, each department in the central office of a school system can identify departmental goals. Just as school-based indicators reflect improvement in a particular school and contribute to the achievement of system-wide goals, central office departmental goals should also be designed to reflect improvement in a specific department and contribute to the achievement of central office common goals. Although every department should be free to establish its own rigorous and relevant goals, the following examples may serve to stimulate some thought by the Accountability Task Force and departmental team members as they develop and review departmental goals.

Examples of departmental goals are listed in the following table.

Table 16.2

Examples of Departmental Goals

Department	Examples of Central Office Departmental Goals
Food Service	• Increase the percentage of patrons who rate food "excellent" or better on customer satisfaction surveys.
	• Reduce the percentage of processed food costs due to negotiated agreements with selected suppliers.
	• Increase the percentage of patrons who choose Food Service options rather than vending machine selections or home lunches.
	• Increase the percentage of special menu items available for patrons.
	• Increase the percentage of employees who participate in "reading buddies" or other programs in schools in need of reading improvement.
Finance	• Increase the percentage of employees who work directly with students as "math mentors" at least once per week.
	• Reduce the percentage of paper costs due to the use of electronically produced reports.
	• Increase the amount of school funding allocated to schools identified as having large populations of "at-risk" students.
	• Reduce the percentage of time required for cost accounting information to be delivered to department heads, principals, and other "internal clients."
	• Increase the number of principals and department managers who complete a seminar offered by the Finance Department in "Cost Management and Budgeting."

Department	Examples of Central Office Departmental Goals
Technology	• Increase the number of technology applications that replace paper forms and transactions, improve customer service, or demonstrably save departmental time.
	• Increase the percentage of district employees who complete training in the "Technology Core Curriculum" to improve core skills in the use of e-mail, word processing, and presentation software.
	• Increase the percentage of department employees working directly with a student or teacher as a "technology tutor" at least once each week.
	• Increase the number of visitors to the district website.
	• Increase the number of teachers who use computerized progress and grade reports.
	• Increase the number of staff who use the district's electronic mail system.
Human Resources	• Increase the size of the qualified applicant pool for middle school and secondary science teachers.
	• Increase the size of the qualified applicant pool for middle school and secondary mathematics teachers.
	• Increase the size of the qualified applicant pool for all administrative, teaching, and non-certified personnel affirmative action employment goals.
	• Increase the number of days without a union grievance or employee complaint.
	• Reduce the number of days that elapse from the time an employee files a grievance or complaint to the time the matter is resolved.
	• Increase the number of staff members who complete training in how to conduct an effective performance appraisal.
Facilities	• Increase the number of school buildings that have the electrical wiring necessary to support the use of computers and other forms of technology.
	• Increase the number of school buildings rated as having excellent or good appearance and maintenance on customer satisfaction surveys.

Department	Examples of Central Office Departmental Goals
Risk Management	• Increase the use of safety checklists in order to reduce potential liability for job-related accidents. • Increase the number of department directors who report either reduced or avoided costs based on a review of data from previous years. • Increase the percentage of accurate payroll records. • Increase the percentage of government reports submitted on time. • Reduce the number of employee and student injuries. • Increase the fairness and legality of employee interviewing, selection, promotion, and discipline. • Decrease the incidents of illegal uses of technology. • Eliminate any instances of workplace substance abuse and/or violence.
Student Services	• Increase the percentage of parents and students who rate the efficiency of the enrollment process as "excellent" or "good" on customer satisfaction surveys. • Increase the percentage of parents and students who rate student records operations as "excellent" or "good" on customer satisfaction surveys.
Staff Development	• Increase the percentage of staff development programs that receive a thorough "after-action" audit of results. • Increase the percentage of teachers who use what they learn in staff development in their own classrooms. • Increase the percentage of staff development programs that are tailored directly to the needs of individual schools based on their school-based goals. • Increase the percentage of faculty who attend staff development workshops that target either system-wide or school-based goals.

Department	Examples of Central Office Departmental Goals
Instruction	• Increase the percentage of teachers who use at least one standards-based performance assessment every month.
	• Increase the number of department directors who identify a specific student achievement indicator from the school accountability system and focus resources on the improvement of that student achievement indicator.
	• Increase the number of department directors who identify specific school-based goals and provide direct assistance to principals and schools to achieve these goals.
	• Increase the percentage of teachers using supplementary reports of student achievement beyond the "report card." These supplementary reports make specific reference to the standards of the state and district and can include other issues that the teachers regard as important, such as the time management, organization, and behavior of students.
	• Increase the number of contact hours spent between departmental and divisional leadership and principals, teachers, and students.
	• Increase the number of teachers who give students and parents feedback at least once per week about student achievement and improvement.

Departmental Narrative

The third level of the central office accountability system is the departmental narrative. This gives the superintendent, board, and public the "story behind the numbers." Issues of morale, community volunteerism, direct work with schools and students, and a host of other activities that may not be evident in the sterile numbers of other reports can be highlighted in the departmental narrative. In the example in table 16.3, the recreation department of the central office is able to tell a compelling story and show readers the relationship between this central office function and student achievement.

Table 16.3

Sample Narrative Report

WAKEFIELD PUBLIC SCHOOLS

Recreation Department

The Recreation Department completed the year with programs involving 3,802 youth in 34 summer programs and another 18 programs during the school year. As the numerical data in our report indicate, we completed the year 1.5% under our budget, experienced no serious accidents, and incurred only four minor student injuries. The activities of the Recreation Department have had a more significant impact on this community than the raw numbers may reflect.

Student Attendance

Improved student attendance has been an important goal of the district. While the average attendance rate for the district is 89%, the average attendance rate of students participating in recreation programs during the school year exceeds 95%. The average attendance rate of summer school students was 78%; for those students participating in the summer recreation program, the average attendance rate was over 90%. While few people would associate the Recreation Department with academic achievement, it is fair to say that the students we serve are exposed to excellent adult role models and a consistent emphasis on attendance and good citizenship. While our recreation specialists may not be certified teachers, they certainly have an impact on attendance and, as a result, on achievement.

Community Service

Eagle Crest High School has implemented a community service program as part of their school accountability program. Our five professional staff members in the Recreation Department were supported by student and staff volunteers from Eagle Crest. These volunteers collectively contributed more than 700 hours to serving students in recreation programs. In addition, our services expanded this year to include services to physically challenged students. Twenty-two students with physical and developmental disabilities participated in our regular recreational activities; the Department provided logistical and training support for Special Olympics in which another 56 students participated.

Professional Development

Two of our staff members completed their college degrees with majors in education. While they continue to be employed by recreation services, they hope to find positions in the district physical education program. Whichever schools are lucky enough to get these outstanding professionals will each gain a "first year" teacher with more than ten years of experience in the Recreation Department. We have also provided professional development opportunities to district employees through our "Healthy Lunch" series. Our staff provides important information while the food service staff provides a carefully prepared healthy lunch for participants. Our classes for employees include stress reduction, stretching, weight training, fitness, and personal health.

Every department has a story to tell, and neither budget numbers nor employee counts tell that story completely and accurately. A one-page narrative allows every department to proactively respond to the question, "What do those people in the central office do, anyway?"

Conclusion

Most of this nation's efforts toward school accountability have focused almost exclusively on teachers and principals. However, the central office profoundly influences the activities of and resources available to teachers and principals. It is essential that this influence becomes visible and accountable in a systematic way, and this is only provided by a comprehensive accountability system.

Questions for Discussion

1. What common goals are appropriate for the various functions of the central office of your system or district?

2. What departmental goals are appropriate for the central office of your system or district?

Category	Central Office Common Goals
Safety	
Human Resources Practices	
Technology	
Other Categories	

Central Office Department Goals

Department _____

Common Goal	Department Strategies to Support This Common Goal	Possible Department Goals to Measure Achievement Related to This Strategy

Step 10: Use Accountability Data to Improve Teaching, Learning, and Leadership

The theme of this book is simple: *The purpose of educational accountability is to improve student achievement.* That goal remains elusive if we stop at the ninth step and simply report the results of student achievement. The most well-designed accountability system in the world is an irrelevant waste of time if the information provided by the system is not used to improve teaching, learning, and leadership. Because accountability information is so frequently associated with blame, excuses, and political agendas, it is easy to let the discussion shift away from the only appropriate focus: improving student achievement. This chapter will consider how accountability information can be used by teachers and school leaders to analyze and improve their strategies and student results.

Better Teaching: The Key to Improved Achievement

The impact of teaching on student performance may seem so obvious that it needs little documentation. There is, however, a pervasive feeling of powerlessness among many educators who see the impact of family and social factors as overwhelming the classroom environment. The importance of teaching, therefore, is an issue that requires exploration. The question is not simply, "Is teaching important?" but rather, "Is teaching *more* important than all the other factors that influence student achievement, including poverty, language, and other external factors that are beyond the reach of the educational system?" Although conventional wisdom, political platitudes and some serious scholars (Murray and Herrnstein, 1994) may hold the position that family and demographic characteristics are determinative, the preponderance of the evidence (Darling-Hammond, 1997; Haycock et al, 1999; Wong, 2000; Reeves, 1998, 1999) is on the other side. Teaching not only is important, but it is more important than all demographic characteristics combined. This is not the Pollyanna view that poverty and linguistic factors are irrelevant; that extreme view is as unhelpful (and as unsupported by the evidence) as the other extreme view that contends that demographic factors overwhelm the efforts of excellent teachers and school leaders. The middle ground, where both reason and research are found, is that while demographic factors such as poverty and second languages are clearly associated with lower student performance, the impact of these factors is less than the impact of great teaching and school leadership. The success of a growing number of schools in high poverty areas is not the stuff of inspirational anecdotes; it is a mountain of evidence that demonstrates that successful teaching progress substantially mitigates the impact of the demographic factors that, in many educational circles, continue to be regarded as the unchangeable road to failure.

If teaching practice is such a critical variable, how can accountability information be used to improve teaching practice? There is a substantial body of opinion that holds that teaching is far more art than science and that the heart and commitment of great teaching is not subject to analysis and replication (Ohanian, 1999). The same argument could be made with respect to medicine: Great physicians have some qualities of caring and insight that are not easily defined in scientific terms. Nevertheless, no amount of medical artistry relieves a physician from rigorous and systematic inquiry, analysis of patient information, and use of that information to treat the patient using the best practices medical science can offer. Similarly, one can acknowledge the existence of such a thing as the "art" of teaching, while not sacrificing the need to apply rigorous analysis to the field. Without such analysis, accountability is little more than an expensive and time-consuming nuisance. With reflection and analytical rigor, however, accountability information can offer teachers and school leaders insights into effective practices to improve student achievement.

Accountability in Action: Using Data to Improve Practice

In the previous chapter, we explored examples of how an analysis of accountability data led to the discovery of leadership and teaching practices that were predominantly associated with excellent achievement in schools with high poverty and high mobility. At the school level, detailed analysis of accountability data can yield insights into effective (and ineffective) strategies employed by teachers and principals. The following vignettes have been created based on my observations of many different schools that have systematically used assessment and accountability information to improve teaching and leadership practices. The stories are not designed to be elegant or profound research studies, and the analyses and conclusions are certainly not presented here as definitive research findings. Rather, they are a synthesis of real world cases in which teachers and school leaders used accountability data *from their district* to improve instruction and student achievement *in their schools*. The intention is not that the reader copy these findings, but rather that teachers and leaders replicate this process:

1. Use system-wide accountability and assessment data to identify the challenge;

2. Use school-based accountability information in your own and other schools to identify potential solutions; and

3. Create meaningful and realistic goals for student achievement and improved teaching and leadership practices.

Math, Measurement, and Multiple Learning Strategies
Adams Elementary School

The system-wide accountability data were puzzling. Although student achievement had improved in many other areas, mathematics scores remained stubbornly low. As they reviewed the accountability information in detail, the faculty and leadership of the school discovered something that was more revealing than general information about low math scores. Lurking behind the system-wide indicator that read, "percentage of students meeting or exceeding the state mathematics standard—34 percent" was a confusing set of sub-scales. While the total math score was mediocre, the sub-scales told a different story. In geometry, more than 80 percent of the students met the standard, while in measurement and problem solving, less than 20 percent of the students met the standard.

The faculty and leadership of the school asked two critical questions. First, "What do these sub-scales tell us about our students and our curriculum in math?" Second, "What are other schools that are similar to ours doing in math that we are not doing?" The discussion of the first question led to a consideration of the school math curriculum. Why was something relatively easy, such as measurement, so low?

"Easy," said Sheila Rabinowitz, the 4th grade teacher. "That's the next to the last chapter in the book—we never get to it until well after the state test has been administered." And why do the same students do so well in geometry? "Beats me," said Ms. Rabinowitz—"I didn't think I was doing anything special in that area at all."

"But I was," said James Brooks, the art teacher. He hadn't been invited to this meeting to analyze math test scores, but was grabbing his usual lunch of a donut and a coke in the faculty lounge.

"You've got our attention," said Sheila, surprised.

James continued, "All year long we've done polygons and patterns. We used triangles and rectangles as the building blocks for many of our art projects—kids know how they fit together. They even figured out why the area of the triangle is half the base times the height—you know, two triangles make a rectangle ..."

Ms. Rabinowitz interrupted, "But I don't even teach that in 4th grade."

After an awkward pause, the principal, Dimitri Stoyanov, said, "Perhaps we're on to something here. The big difference between geometry and measurement tells us that there is nothing wrong with the math ability of these kids. It also tells us that both Ms. Rabinowitz and Mr. Brooks are terrific teachers—but we aren't teaching students everything that they need at the time they need it." The district accountability report was sitting on the table, thus far unopened. Mr. Stoyanov continued, "Let's see what's happening in the schools that are similar to us but have much better math scores. Look, here's High Plains Elementary: same demographics as we have, but 92 percent of their students were proficient or better in math. What are their school-based accountability indicators?" The report said it all:

Indicator #3

Increase in the number of instructional units in art, music, physical education, and social studies that assess student proficiency in measurement and problem solving—300%.

"They *tripled* the number of opportunities kids had to learn measurement outside of math class—pretty impressive," said Ms. Rabinowitz. "Why not do the same thing that Mr. Brooks has done with geometry in other areas—problem-solving, measurement and graphs?"

"I'm game," said Mr. Brooks. "Let's get the whole faculty involved in this next time—it looks like it's a lot more than just a math issue ..."

Competence and Computers
French Middle School

"I don't understand it," said Stanley Stalter, the principal of French Middle School. "We received a grant for $1.5 million for new computers. Every class is connected to the Internet. I've even tracked our usage—the ratio of connection time per student is more than double this year compared to last year—but our reading and writing scores went down on every system-wide indicator in the accountability report! Don't tell me that this technology initiative has all been a waste of time."

"Wait a minute, Stan," offered Ms. Campbell. "Computers aren't the cause of improved achievement and they aren't the cause of lower achievement—it's how they are used. Let's see the records of what was actually happening in the classrooms: look at 7th grade English. We have five different classes, and all of them followed your requirements, more than doubling their per-student computer use. But only one of them met our school-based goal of increasing the frequency of writing performance assessment, and that's the one class that had higher scores in writing and reading."

Ms. Moore broke the uncomfortable silence that followed Ms. Campbell's statement. "Look, we don't have a 36-hour day. You wanted more computer time, we gave you more computer time. But something had to give, and that was writing assessments. We didn't have time to do both. If you want us to do writing next year, then we'll have to cut back on technology."

"How did *you* do it?" said Ms. Campbell, directing her inquiry to Ms. Cleland. Her class was the one that had doubled student time on computers and also increased the frequency of writing performance assessment. Her class was also the only one that showed increased scores on the reading and writing tests.

"I don't think I did anything different than my colleagues," said Ms. Cleland tentatively. "You know that I don't have students with better learning backgrounds or higher economic status—I've got the same challenges facing every classroom in the school. I guess the only thing that I did differently was that I never used computer time as a special allocation time because I didn't want it to compete with the other areas of curriculum. For my kids, computer time was always part of another unit. Sometimes it was geography, sometimes music or art, sometimes literature. Of course, I know that the kids mess around sometimes, but I just didn't have time in class to spend on any computer games or unstructured Internet searches. I certainly couldn't give up my writing assessments—that's been one of the best sources of improved reading and writing performance for my kids."

"I've got to own this one," said Mr. Stalter. "The problem isn't the computers and it certainly isn't any of you—it's the way that I crammed the technology goal down the faculty's throat. I was so focused on justifying the grant and showing that we were using the computers that I didn't keep the focus on the essentials. Computers are just tools. Measuring their use without thinking about how they are used doesn't make sense. How can we express our school-based goals for next year in a way that focuses on teaching practices that really improve student learning?"

Science and Sequence
Davis High School

"The firings will continue until the scores improve," said Frank Morales, the thirty-year teaching veteran who was the chairperson of the science department at Davis High School. No one laughed. All of the teachers in the department meeting knew two things—they were working harder than ever before, and yet their scores on the state science exam had declined once again. "That's no joke," said Bianca Angel without a smile. "We *are* under the gun, and we all know the problems. We've got a 9th grade biology textbook that some kids can't read, and we've got a state science test that kids don't take until the spring of their 10th grade year. Some of the information they're tested on was taught almost two years before they took the test!"

"I don't know," said Mr. Morales. "What does the information in the accountability report really say—are our kids in that much trouble?" The group looked at the system-wide indicators and saw that the percentage of students who scored at the "proficient" level or higher in science had declined for two consecutive years. "Let's dig deeper. What do we know about kids who did well on the test?" asked Mr. Morales. "Are they just smarter than the other kids, or are there some things different in their curriculum and instruction that we can discover?"

It didn't take long for some trends to emerge as the science faculty reviewed the accountability data for each student. "Look at this," offered Tina Anderson, a substitute teacher who was on a long-term assignment in the science department. "I don't know a lot about this, but it looks like only 38 percent of our students overall were proficient or better, but 64 percent of Mr. Vasquez's students were proficient."

"That can't be right," countered Mr. Morales. "Mr. V. has the students in the intervention program—they're the ones who couldn't take science in 9th grade because they needed an extra year of literacy. They were the so-called "at risk" kids. After the extra literacy class in 9th grade, they wind up in Mr. V's two-period science class as 10th graders. We were just trying to save those kids and get them ready for high school—and you're telling me that they are doing better than our regular kids on the state science test?" Tina offered the department chair the written reports. "See for yourself," she said.

"We've had it backwards," offered Bianca. "We thought that the number of students who needed remedial assistance was a bad thing—that a higher number might count against us. It's pretty clear that a school-based goal ought to be increasing the number of students who participate in the intervention program. Those are the kids who are doing best on the science test—perhaps because they are better able to read the books. Who cares if they do it in 10th grade rather than 9th grade?"

Mr. Vasquez quietly added, "For whatever it's worth, they really seem to like science."

Conclusion

The effective use of accountability data requires the commonplace use of research, assessment, and communication by teachers and school leaders. This means that we must move beyond the "priesthood of statistics"—the prevailing philosophy that leaves assessment and accountability data in the hands of the statistical cognoscenti. Although the vignettes in this chapter indicate the value of detailed analysis of accountability by teachers who are willing to ask common-sense questions, those scenarios are only possible when teachers and school leaders are entrusted with the information they need. This means that teachers and leaders at the classroom, department, and school level need all of the accountability data—not just superficial score reports on their students or their school. They need the system-wide, school-based, and narrative information for every school in the district. There are no secrets and no danger of the data being used to rank, embarrass or humiliate colleagues. Indeed, there is a systematic search for effective practices in which colleagues can say to one another, "It looks as if you were successful in circumstances similar to ours. Let's talk about how you did it and what we can learn."

Agenda for Faculty/Department Meeting to
Review Accountability Data

Agenda Item	Facilitator	Next Steps
1. **Strengths**—What does the accountability report tell us are the strongest areas for our students? (Review system-wide indicators, including sub-scales of state and district assessments)		
2. **Challenges**—What does the accountability report tell us are the most challenging areas for our students?		
3. **Strategies in Our School**—What do the school-based indicators tell us about the instructional strategies we used that were associated with our achievement results? What inferences can we draw from this? Which strategies were effective? Which strategies were not effective?		
4. **Strategies in Other Schools**—Identify some schools that had success in areas where we had challenges. What were the school-based indicators employed by those schools? What can we learn about the strategies that those schools used?		
5. **Unnoticed Strategies**—What was happening in our school (perhaps revealed in the narrative part of the accountability report) that might have influenced our student achievement? What does this suggest for our school-based goals for next year?		

PART

The Role of Standards in Educational Accountability

PART III

CHAPTER

Why Standards?

The case for rigorous academic standards has been made by a number of researchers (Tucker & Coddings, 1998; Mitchell, 1992; Reeves, 1996). This chapter will briefly review the inextricable link between effective accountability systems and a standards-based approach to educational evaluation. The unfortunate truth is that while 49 of the 50 states and many private and international school systems have articulated a commitment to standards, educational accountability systems remain overwhelmingly based on norms and averages rather than on consistent standards. The national tendency toward a norm-based system is unwise and dangerous for three reasons. First, such a system is inaccurate, giving neither students nor parents a clear idea of what students really know and whether or not they demonstrate proficiency in either subject or skill areas. Second, norms encourage complacency, allowing students who are incompetent on certain critical skills but "above average" on test performance to enjoy—at least temporarily—the bliss of ignorance. Third, norm-based assessments rarely measure comprehensive student achievement, but indicate the speed and agility with which students take a particular test instead.

Standards Are More Accurate Than Norms as Measurements of Student Achievement

Nowhere is the folly of norm-based accountability systems more apparent than in the growing number of states and districts that presume that "80 percent of our students should be above the 50th percentile, or average test score." It apparently does not occur to the developers of such goals that, in any distribution of data, about 49.9 percent of those who take the test will *always* be below average, and about 49.9 percent will *always* be above average. Even if student scores improve drastically, the notion that, by definition, half of any data set is in the "lower half" of a distribution apparently eludes many educational policy makers.

The central issue with testing and standards has nothing to do with either sympathy for poor test takers or envy of good test takers; the central issue is accuracy in the measurement of student performance and progress. Policy makers of every political stripe should agree on the simple principle that accountability and test information should be accurate. Our assessment of professionals and other people who must be licensed to perform a task depends on objective measures of proficiency. This demand for standards-based measurement applies to airline pilots and teenage drivers, physicians and x-ray technicians, trial attorneys and automobile mechanics. In every instance, the challenge is to meet an objective standard, not merely to beat the other people taking the test. No advocates of norm-referenced testing would fly with a pilot who merely scored "above average" on the examination administered by the Federal Aviation Administration. Rather, they would insist that the pilot have demonstrated his or her ability to make a specific number of take-offs and landings safely. The defenders of the norm would never allow their teenage drivers to make the excuse, "Sure, I wrecked the car and got four speeding tickets, but I'm still a better driver than Harry!" They would insist that the teenager meet standards of safe and competent driving, regardless of favorable comparisons with other teenage drivers.

Academic standards provide accuracy in a way that comparisons to the average can never offer. Educational leaders, teachers, students, and parents must know whether a student is proficient. They take no false pride in the fact that one child is relatively more capable than other kids, nor do they undergo humiliation because the reverse is true. The central focus of a standards-based system is the achievement of standards by as many students as possible.

Standards Fail to "Sort and Select"

For all that standards-based systems can accomplish, there is one thing that they fail to do very well: sort and select students. If a test is designed to select only the "top one percent" of students, who will be admitted to an elite school, then an educational system that produces large numbers of students who perform at high levels will fail to select students for this purpose. The degree to which this is a valid criticism of standards rests upon two premises, both questionable. The first premise is that traditional norm-referenced tests accurately identify the "top 1 percent." It is certainly true that some statistical techniques including, among others, item response theory, can be used to make any distribution of test-takers fit a normal curve. Once this has been done, those students who have test scores higher than 99 percent of the other test-takers can be identified. But following this procedure does not necessarily allow us to identify the 1 percent of students who are most deserving of enrollment in an elite school, the students best able to benefit from additional educational opportunities, or even the most intelligent test-takers (Perkins, 1995; Neill, 1998).

The second questionable premise is that the function of public schools is to sort and select students. This premise rests on the notion that the valedictorian of a high school class is remarkably different from those who are not the "top" graduates. School administrators (and legions of those who were close to being valedictorians) can share stories of how the difference between the presence or absence of this signal honor was measured in either hundredths of decimal points, the decision of a ninth-grader to take a class for pass/fail credit rather than for a letter grade, or the growing use of "quality points" to change the method of calculating grade point averages. Not only is there a mathematically meaningless distinction among these top students (grade point differences notwithstanding), but the gamesmanship prompted by the sorting and selecting premise can lead to poorer performance and lowered academic pursuits for students seeking comparative rankings. Perhaps the reader has heard a student shy away from a challenging and rigorous class because "It might mess up my grade point average."

More importantly, the premise of sorting and selecting should be challenged because this is not the appropriate function of a school. To the extent that a method is needed for the allocation of scarce resources among similarly qualified candidates (such as college admissions), then external tests and the growing use of holistic reviews of student profiles are appropriate. These processes can all take place while allowing schools to evaluate students based on their proficiency—not based upon comparisons of which student was "better" than other students. In sum, standards-based assessment practices are indeed an abject failure if their goal is to sort and select students. If, however, the goal is to provide the best learning opportunities for the greatest number of students, then standards-based assessment is the superior alternative.

Standards Provide Necessary Challenges to "Above Average" Students

Whenever I ask an audience if they have students who have scored in the 60th percentile on the "English" portion of a nationally normed test, audience members raise their hands in large numbers. When I ask the same group if a good number of these "above average" students are unable to write a coherent essay, an equally large number of hands are raised. The plain fact is that we have a large number of students and parents who are inappropriately complacent because students have been labeled as "above average" on a nationally normed test when, in fact, their performance, as measured against academic standards, is inadequate.

The "above average" English student may not be able to write an essay. The "above average" math student may not be able to apply an algebra concept in a real-world situation. The student who receives an "above average" score in reading may not be able to compare one piece of literature to another. In brief, a comparison to the "average" not only hurts the most disadvantaged students, but it also hurts those children whose test-taking abilities have allowed them to achieve false notions of mastery. Their inappropriate complacency is based on the ability to "beat" other children rather than their ability to meet rigorous and demanding standards.

Standards are Fair

Any parent—certainly any teacher who has pulled playground duty—has heard the plaintive cry, "That's not FAIR!" Children have a concrete notion of fairness, and they are unequivocal about voicing their opinions about fairness on the playground whenever anyone attempts to change the rules in the midst of the game. Their behavior in the face of clear incidences of unfairness in the academic game is only slightly subtler. We say that teachers convey the rules of the academic game to students in the expectations that they set forth at the beginning of the school year. But when a standardized test—frequently amplified in importance by letters to parents and dire warnings from principals—includes content and format that a student has never seen, it is once again clear that the rules of the game have changed. The kids are right: THAT'S NOT FAIR!

Standards communicate what students are expected to know and be able to do. Benchmarks identify specific expectations for certain grade levels or groups of grade levels. Scoring guides (sometimes called "rubrics") provide the most specific expectations for students by identifying what they are expected to accomplish on individual assignments and assessments. When a student achieves the expectations identified in a scoring guide, this provides evidence that a benchmark has been met. When a student achieves the expectation of a benchmark, then we have evidence that a standard has been met. Students can only be counted upon to meet these expectations when the standards are clear and unchanging.

Of course, the integrity of academic standards depends upon the link between standards and assessments. When (as is the case in many states today) the standards say that the writing process is important, but the state-sanctioned test renders writing irrelevant or requires students to write without using the writing process, then the lack of connection between standards and assessment is clear. Students may not rise up in a testing session and yell, "THAT'S NOT FAIR!" but they certainly may act out their feelings about being treated unfairly in other ways. Random response patterns, the absence of responses, or the deliberate selection of wrong answers are all ways that students attempt to send messages to the test authors. "After all," they reason, "if I mark 'A' as the response to every question, I should get at least 25 percent of the answers right. Surely if I get 0 percent right, then someone will notice that I'm doing this on purpose." (As the parent of adolescents and a veteran teacher of bright children, who defy standardized test logic, I can certify that this is the way they think.)

Neither children nor adults will play a game for very long if the rules of the game keep changing. Standards are the rules of the game, and we should not be surprised if children refuse to play the testing game once they realize that the rules will change constantly.

Accountability in Action

Conclusion

Life, along with school boards and state-mandated tests, the reader may argue, is unfair, and thus our students should be able to cope with this unfairness. What is the practical way to address the common situation in which students are exhorted to meet academic standards in writing, but tested only in multiple-choice frameworks? It is the answer to this question that brings us to the heart of the connection between accountability and school effectiveness. If we have a comprehensive accountability system, then we can begin to address which teaching practices are associated with the best results in student learning and academic performance in a systematic way. The next chapter will be devoted to research findings that help to establish this connection.

Questions for Discussion

1. To what extent are the students in your district held to standards-based rather than norm-referenced standards? What steps would need to be taken to make a standards-based approach more pervasive?

2. Based on your school's performance data, what curricular areas should be emphasized? What support would teachers and others need to make changes in curricular focus?

CHAPTER

The 90/90/90 Schools: A Case Study

Research conducted at The Leadership and Learning Center on the "90/90/90 Schools" has been particularly instructive in the evaluation of the use of standards and assessment. The research includes four years of test data (1995 through 1998) with students in a variety of school settings, from elementary through high school. Our analysis considered data from more than 130,000 students in 228 buildings. The school locations included inner-city urban schools, suburban schools, and rural schools. The student populations ranged from schools whose populations were overwhelmingly poor and/or minority to schools that were largely Anglo and/or economically advantaged.

One reason that the research in these schools was so productive is that the districts maintained careful records on actual instructional practices and strategies. This allows researchers to investigate associations between instructional strategies and academic achievement results. It is important to acknowledge, however, that these results are only associative in nature. We make no claim that a single instructional intervention can be said to "cause" a particular achievement result. What we can say with a high degree of confidence, however, is that there are some consistent associations between some classroom strategies (for example, performance assessments that require writing) and student achievement in a wide variety of tests and subjects. One final note: We make absolutely no claim that the schools in the study were the beneficiaries of any proprietary "program" or "model" of instruction.

The research literature in every field from pharmaceuticals to education contains too many "studies" that purport to show the effectiveness of treatments that the authors of the research have used. Our role in this investigation is that of journalist and researcher, not of architect of any program or intervention. Hence, we do not claim any credit for improved academic achievement that is rightfully due to the students, teachers, and administrators in the study.

Accountability in Action

Characteristics of 90/90/90 Schools

The 90/90/90 Schools have the following characteristics:

- More than 90 percent of the students are eligible for free and reduced lunch, a commonly used surrogate for low-income families.

- More than 90 percent of the students are from ethnic minorities.

- More than 90 percent of the students met or achieved high academic standards, according to independently conducted tests of academic achievement.

The educational practices in these schools are worthy of notice for several reasons. First, many people assume that there is an inextricable relationship between poverty, ethnicity, and academic achievement. The graph in Figure 19.1 expresses the commonly held belief that poverty and ethnic minority enrollment are inextricably linked to lower levels of student achievement.

Figure 19.1

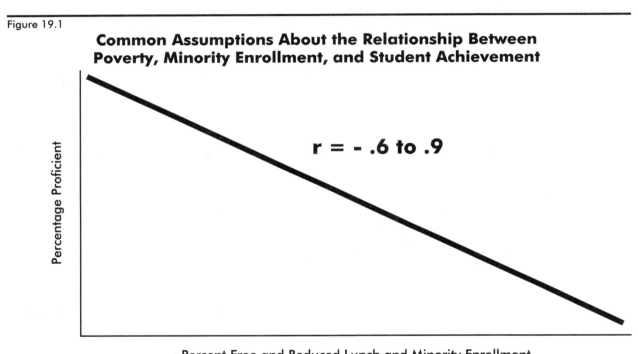

Common Assumptions About the Relationship Between Poverty, Minority Enrollment, and Student Achievement

Percentage Proficient

r = - .6 to .9

Percent Free and Reduced Lunch and Minority Enrollment

In this chart, the prevailing hypothesis leaves no room for students in the upper right-hand corner of the graph—that is, schools that have high academic achievement coincident with high poverty and high minority enrollments. This is consistent with national observations dating back to the 1960s in which demographic characteristics were regarded as the dominant variables influencing student achievement. In fact, the actual data from the December 1998 Comprehensive Accountability Report of the Milwaukee Public Schools shows a different story. In individual schools, there are striking numbers of students who are poor and who are members of ethnic minorities who are also academically proficient. Throughout the entire system of more than 100,000 students, the relationship between poverty and student achievement is not the postulated -.6 to -.9, but rather a -.2. While the impact of poverty clearly has not been eliminated, the prevailing hypothesis that poverty and ethnic minority status are invariably linked to low student achievement does not conform to the data.

Common Characteristics of High Achievement Schools

Our research on the 90/90/90 Schools included both site visits and analyses of accountability data. The site visits allowed us to conduct a categorical analysis of instructional practices. In the same manner that the authors of *In Search Of Excellence* (Peters and Waterman, 1982) identified the common practices of excellent organizations, we sought to identify the extent to which there was a common set of behaviors exhibited by the leaders and teachers in schools with high achievement, high minority enrollment, and high poverty levels. As a result, we found five characteristics that were common to all 90/90/90 Schools. These characteristics were:

- A focus on academic achievement

- Clear curriculum choices

- Frequent assessment of student progress and multiple opportunities for improvement

- An emphasis on nonfiction writing

- Collaborative scoring of student work

Focus on Academic Achievement

After visiting all of the 90/90/90 Schools, we noticed profound differences between the assessment and instructional practices of these schools and those of low-achieving schools. First and most importantly, the 90/90/90 Schools had a laser-like focus on student achievement. The most casual observer could not walk down a hallway without seeing charts, graphs, and tables that displayed student achievement information, as well as data about the continuous improvement students had made. The data were on display not only in principals' offices, but also throughout the schools. In addition, we saw school trophy cases full of exemplary academic work, including clear, concise essays, wonderful science projects, terrific social studies papers, and outstanding mathematics papers. In short, the 90/90/90 Schools made it clear to the most casual observer that academic performance was highly prized.

The focus on achievement in these schools included a particular emphasis on improvement. The comprehensive accountability system in use by these schools forced every school to identify five areas in which they measured improvement. Although the school could choose the goal from a menu, the common requirement was to focus on a few indicators of improvement in contrast to the typical school improvement plan that contains a large number of unfocused efforts to improve. The focus on improvement is especially important in an environment where many students come to school with academic skills that are substantially below grade level. The consistent message of charts showing weekly improvement from the fall through the spring was, "It's not how you start here that matters, but how you finish." Improvements of more than one grade level in a single year were common, and teachers and administrators paid particular attention to students whose deficiencies in reading and writing would have a profound impact on their success in other subjects. Some students spent as many as three hours per day in literacy interventions designed to get students to desired achievement levels. There did not appear to be any consistency with regard to the intervention programs in use by these schools. Some used Success for All, others used Reading Recovery, while others used the Efficacy Model. Others had no specified program at all, but consistently applied focused intervention for students in need using their own teaching staff.

Curriculum Choices

Such a focus on achievement inevitably leads to curriculum choices, spending more time on the core subjects of reading, writing, and mathematics and less time on other subjects. It is possible, for example, that many of the teachers in these schools did not "cover the curriculum" in the strict sense of checking off objectives from a wide variety of curricular areas. They chose—wisely, we believe—to emphasize the core skills of reading, writing, and mathematics in order to improve student opportunities for success in a wide variety of other academic endeavors later. It is interesting to note parenthetically that, despite their disproportionate emphasis on language arts and mathematics, these schools also significantly out-performed their peer schools on science tests as well. This makes an important point that eludes those who remain committed to a "coverage" model: tests of science, social studies, study skills, and virtually every other subject area are, in fact, tests of reading and writing.

Frequent Assessment of Student Progress with Multiple Opportunities for Improvement

Many of the high-poverty schools included students whose skills were significantly below grade level in academic achievement as they entered the school. The consistent message of the 90/90/90 Schools is that the penalty for poor performance is not a low grade, followed by a forced march to the next unit. Rather, student performance that is less than proficient is followed by multiple opportunities to improve performance. Most of these schools conducted weekly assessments of student progress. It is important to note that these assessments were not district or state tests, but were assessments constructed and administered by classroom teachers. The consequence of students performing badly was not an admonishment to "Wait until next year" but rather the promise that "You can do better next week."

A frequent challenge to this practice is that students should learn to "get it right the first time." The flaw in such a statement is the implied assumption that the traditional "one-shot" assessment is successful in leading students to "get it right the first time." In fact, when students know that there are no additional opportunities to succeed, they frequently take teacher feedback on their performance and stuff it into desks, back packs, and wastebaskets. Students in this scenario are happy with a "D" and unmotivated by an "F." After all, there is nothing that they can do about deficient performance anyway. In a classroom assessment scenario in which there are multiple opportunities to improve, however, the consequence for poor performance is not a bad grade and discouragement, but more work, improved performance, and respect for teacher feedback. In this respect, the use of teacher evaluation based on assessment scoring guides looked much more like active coaching after which improvement was required, and much less like final evaluation from which there was no reprieve.

Written Responses in Performance Assessments

By far the most common characteristic of the 90/90/90 Schools was their emphasis on requiring written responses in performance assessments. While many schools with similar demographic characteristics employed frequent assessment techniques, many of the less successful schools chose to emphasize oral student responses rather than written responses. The use of written responses appears to help teachers obtain better diagnostic information about students, and certainly helps students demonstrate the thinking process that they employed to find a correct (or even an incorrect) response to an academic challenge. Only with a written response from students can teachers create the strategies necessary to improve performance for both teacher and learner.

In virtually every school we have evaluated, student scores on creative writing are significantly higher than informative and narrative writing scores. As a result, teachers in the successful 90/90/90 Schools placed a very high emphasis on informative writing. They typically used a single scoring rubric to evaluate student writing and applied this scoring guide to every piece of written work. Whether the student was writing a book report, lab report, social studies report, analysis of a sporting event, description of a piece of music, or a comparison of artists, the message was the same: this is the standard for good writing, and there are no compromises on these expectations for quality.

The benefits of such an emphasis on writing appear to be two-fold. First, students process information in a much clearer way when they are required to write an answer. They "write to think" and, thus, gain the opportunity to clarify their own thought processes. Second, teachers have the opportunity to gain rich and complex diagnostic information about why students respond to an academic challenge the way that they do. In contrast to the binary feedback (right/wrong) provided by most assessments and worksheets, the use of performance assessments that require written responses allows the teacher to diagnose obstacles to student learning. By assessing student writing, teachers can discern whether the challenges faced by a student are the result of vocabulary issues, misunderstood directions, reasoning errors, or a host of other causes that are rarely revealed by typical tests.

The association between writing and performance in other academic disciplines was striking, and this gets to the heart of the curriculum choices that teachers must make. At the elementary level, for example, teachers were faced with a formidable set of curriculum standards in both science and writing. Many of the most successful schools reported that they had to sacrifice time allocated to every other curriculum area except reading, writing, and mathematics. Nevertheless, more than 80 percent of the 135 elementary schools in the study improved in science scores in 1998, compared to 1997. The Pearson correlation between writing improvement and science improvement is striking: .74—a large correlation in virtually any area of social science research. This correlation took place without any changes in the science curriculum and few apparent modifications in teaching methods. I would offer the same caution as provided earlier in the chapter that correlation is not causation. Nevertheless, when two variables appear to behave in such a similar way, it is difficult to escape the conclusion that an emphasis on writing improvement has a significant impact on student test scores in other disciplines, including science.

External Scoring

Another striking characteristic of the 90/90/90 Schools was frequent external scoring of assessments. While many schools continue to rely upon the idiosyncratic judgment of individual teachers for a definition of "proficiency," the high-achieving schools made it clear that no accident of geography or classroom assignment would determine expectations for students. Rather, these schools developed common assessment practices and reinforced those common practices through regular exchanges of student papers. One teacher would exchange papers with another teacher; principals would exchange papers with another school; and in one of the most powerful research findings, principals would take personal responsibility for evaluating student work.

When teachers exchange papers, it is imperative that they have a uniform basis on which to evaluate student work. The degree of agreement among teachers in their use of performance assessment scoring can be measured by "inter-rater reliability." Reliability, when the term is applied to traditional tests, is a measure of consistency. In the case of measuring consistency in scoring, it is simply the percentage of teachers who score an identical piece of student work the same way. If, for example, ten teachers evaluate a piece of student work, and eight believe that the work is "proficient" and two believe that it is only "progressing," then there is an 80 percent reliability rating for that test. This degree of reliability—80 percent—is the target at which teachers should aim as they jointly evaluate student work. It is very unusual (but not unheard of) for that level of agreement to be achieved the first time that teachers jointly score student work. More frequently, there are disagreements among teachers on the evaluation of student work. These disagreements usually stem from one of two causes. First, teachers frequently use implicit scoring criteria that are not part of the official scoring guide. Examples of implicit criteria include such statements as "He should have written in cursive," or "She knew that she should have included that character in her essay." While these expectations may have been reasonable to these teachers, those criteria did not appear in the scoring guide. It is therefore little wonder that other teachers, who did not share those implicit expectations, failed to mark students down for these failings.

The second cause of teacher disagreement is the lack of clear specifications in the scoring guide itself. Too frequently a disagreement among evaluators leads to an argument rather than to an exploration of how agreement can be achieved through a revision of the scoring guide. "If we change the definition of proficient from this to that, perhaps we could agree on how to mark this paper." Words such as these are the basis of a far more meaningful discussion than, "Of course it's proficient! Don't you see?"

Long-Term Sustainable Results without Proprietary Programs

One of the most powerful findings of the 90/90/90 study is the continuous nature of the success of these schools, even as the poverty of students attending these schools remains intractable. Several of the schools listed below have consistently appeared on the 90/90/90 list, even as students change from year to year, as the effects of poverty grow more onerous, and as parents participating in welfare reform programs are less likely to be at home before and after school. Moreover, these schools are achieving their success without proprietary programs. Let there be no doubt: Our role in this research is as researcher and reporter. None of the 90/90/90 Schools used a specific "program" or any other proprietary model in order to achieve their success. On the contrary, we observed effective teachers and administrators using strikingly similar techniques without the assistance of externally imposed methods of instruction. The techniques used by these schools are replicable, but there is certainly not a need for schools to purchase special textbooks, curriculum materials, or secret information to achieve the level of success enjoyed by these schools.

Non-Proprietary Instructional Practices

In an era in which school leaders appear to engage in a perpetual quest for the magic bullet of educational success, it is noteworthy that none of the 90/90/90 Schools relied exclusively upon a proprietary program to achieve their success. Instead, these schools used consistent practices in instruction and assessment, with support from local teachers. For those who believe that education remains an interactive process that cannot and should not be "teacher-proofed," these research findings are encouraging. The other edge of this particular razor is that we cannot depend upon proprietary systems to save us. It is the collective work of teachers, students, parents, and leaders that will ultimately lead us out of the present malaise. Every one of the 90/90/90 Schools had academic content standards, but so do many ineffective schools. The distinguishing characteristic of the 90/90/90 Schools was not merely that they had standards, but rather, how the standards were implemented, monitored, and assessed.

Data from the "90/90/90" Studies

A current list of some of the 90/90/90 Schools from Milwaukee, Wisconsin, is provided by the school system in their comprehensive accountability report. Since the publication of the first list in 1998, the number of schools qualifying for the designation has more than tripled. The data were independently verified by Schmoker (2001) in direct interviews with Milwaukee administrators. These schools have graciously hosted hundreds of visitors in the past few years as their successes have become more widely recognized. Researchers and educators should always be willing to share their sources of information and welcome the reviews of colleagues in the field. However, I cannot help but note how profoundly disturbing it is to me that I am frequently requested—demanded is not too strong a term—to produce the names and locations of these schools. In fact, these schools have received significant public attention through the Video Journal of Education, Volumes 802 and 803 (Linton Professional Development Corporation, 1998). Research should, of course, be subject to verification and scrutiny. Nevertheless, I cannot avoid noticing that in my many years of conducting, writing, and reviewing educational research, I have never seen such a demand for "names, dates, and places" accompany the allegation that children who are poor and children of ethnic minority groups perform badly on tests. When *The Bell Curve* (Herrnstein and Murray, 1994) was published with the widely accepted assertion that children who are black and poor perform badly on academic achievement tests, I cannot recall a single instance of demands for the names of students who were subjects of the studies cited. When we have demonstrated that poor and black children perform well, we are inundated with demands for verification. These demands speak volumes about the expectations of children based on their appearance and economic status.

After the original accountability report documenting the 90/90/90 Schools, Milwaukee Public Schools has issued subsequent accountability reports. The findings from these reports are striking. In brief, these findings include the following:

1. Techniques used by the 90/90/90 Schools are persistent. The students are still poor and their economic opportunities have not improved. Nevertheless, more

than 90 percent of the students in these schools continue to meet or exceed state standards.

2. Techniques used by the 90/90/90 Schools are replicable. The first time the district tracked these schools, only seven 90/90/90 Schools were identified. In the most recent report, 13 schools meet the criteria for this distinguished label.

3. Techniques used by the 90/90/90 Schools are consistent. These schools are not lurching from one fad to another. While they differ in some respects with regard to implementation, they are consistent with regard to the following areas of emphasis:

   - Writing—students write frequently in a variety of subjects.

   - Performance Assessment—the predominant method of assessment is performance assessment. This does not mean that these schools never use multiple-choice items. However, it is performance assessment in several different disciplines that local observers have associated with student progress.

   - Collaboration—teachers routinely collaborate, using real student work as the focus of their discussion.

   - Focus—teachers in these schools do not try to "do it all" but are highly focused on learning.

Additional Information on Success in Challenging School Environments

Over the years, I have continued to hear doubts and challenges that poor students can perform well. Indeed, the charge is frequently leveled that comprehensive accountability systems are disadvantageous for poor schools. In fact, systematic research from comprehensive accountability systems allows us to document and celebrate the success of students in these schools. Two additional sources of research on this subject come from strikingly different sources. Casey Carter, author of the "No Excuses" case studies from the Heritage Foundation (1999), provides a conservative viewpoint. The details of these cases are available at www.heritage.org. A politically liberal viewpoint is often associated with Kati Haycock and the Education Trust (1998, 2001). Their landmark research on student success in high poverty schools makes a striking case that these schools are not isolated anecdotes. Indeed, the fundamental finding from the Education Trust studies is that however important demographic variables may appear in their association with student achievement, teaching quality is the most dominant factor in determining student success. It turns out, of course, that teaching quality and subject matter certification are much more likely to occur in economically advantaged schools.

The case made by Haycock and others at the Education Trust is clear: the key variable is not poverty, but teaching quality. While poverty and other demographic variables may be important, they are not determinative in predicting student success. The detailed research from the Education Trust, including an interactive program allowing the user to specify the characteristics of a school and find specific data on comparable high-performing schools throughout the nation, is available at www.edtrust.org.

The consensus of the evidence from very different perspectives is clear: effective teaching and leadership make a difference. The lessons of the 90/90/90 Schools as well as the lessons of other studies provide convincing evidence that accountability systems, properly designed, can provide a wealth of information for those desiring to find the keys to improved achievement for all students.

Using the 90/90/90 Practices to Improve Achievement and Close the Equity Gap

Researchers and practitioners must always confront the gap between theory and reality, between anecdote and evidence. "Sure it worked there," the skeptics say, "but our kids are different." The ultimate test of the 90/90/90 research is whether it is sustainable and replicable. Simpson (2003) provides compelling evidence that the practices of the 90/90/90 Schools can be applied in a diverse urban environment with similar results:

> Like the city, Norfolk Public Schools, the first public school system in Virginia, has seen its fortunes go up and down. It's an urban district that serves a diverse population: 67 percent of students are black and 28 percent are white. More than 65 percent of students qualify for free and reduced-price lunches.
>
> - 100 percent of our schools met the state benchmarks in writing in all grades tested.
>
> - 100 percent of our high schools met the state benchmarks in chemistry.
>
> - 100 percent of our middle schools are fully accredited in earth science.
>
> - 100 percent of our middle and high schools showed positive trends in reading, literature, and research.
>
> Also, our schools reduced the achievement gap between white and black students in third, fifth, and eighth grades, with both groups continuing to improve. They decreased disciplinary actions by 15 percent, the number of long-term suspensions by 14 percent, and the number of expulsions by 66 percent. In addition, we have two "90/90/90 schools." These are schools with more than 90 percent of students eligible for free and reduced-price lunch, more than 90 percent are minority students, and more than 90 percent of

students met high academic standards on the state's Standards of Learning tests. (Simpson, 2003, pp. 43-44).

At the beginning of the 2002-2003 school year, I examined the accountability reports of each of the schools in Norfolk, Virginia, and conducted numerous site visits and interviews. In particular, I wondered if the buildings that experienced gains of 20 percent or more in their academic achievement in language arts, mathematics, science, and social studies were significantly different than their counterparts in other schools. The schools with the greatest gains were not similar demographically, as they included high-poverty and low-poverty student populations. The financial support, staffing patterns, union agreements, and central office support were similar for all schools. Therefore, neither the demographic variables of students nor the external variables of funding and labor agreements could explain the extraordinary differences between the schools. The keys to improved academic achievement are professional practices of teachers and leaders, not the economic, ethnic, or linguistic characteristics of the students. The Norfolk accountability system revealed striking similarities to other research on the characteristics of successful schools. Although surely there are many other traits shared by effective organizations of all types, the Norfolk Accountability System provided an insight into measurable indicators that were linked to the largest gains in student achievement. These characteristics also make clear that successful accountability is not the exclusive domain of the "Department of Accountability" in the central office, but rather is a responsibility shared throughout the system on many levels. The observations made on the basis of this inquiry are strikingly similar to observations I have made in other school systems over the course of several years. The following paragraphs highlight the nine characteristics that distinguished the schools with the greatest academic gains.

The Impact of Collaboration

First, the schools devoted time for teacher collaboration. This was not merely an exercise in idle discussion nor at attempt to get along in a friendly and collegial fashion. Rather, collaboration meetings were focused on an examination of student work and a collective determination of what the word "proficiency" really means. At first, teachers identified wide variations in their opinions and were alarmed to see how differently they evaluated the same piece of student work. In the course of many sessions, the most effective schools made time for collaboration very frequently and in some cases did this every day. Where does the time come from for effective collaboration? None of these schools had extra money in the budget or more hours in the day. Rather, they used the time that they already had with an intentional focus on collaborative scoring of student work. For example, the principals made their faculty meetings "announcement-free zones." Rather than drone through a laundry list of announcements (with inevitable comments and controversies), their rule was that the transmission of information would always be in writing. This allowed time formerly devoted to faculty meeting announcements to be dedicated to collaboration. The principals were literally on the same side of the table as their faculty members, with faculty members who were experienced in collaborative scoring taking turns facilitating faculty meetings. The other source of time for collaboration was professional development meetings. Rather than presentations by outside staff developers, a significant degree of the professional development time was allocated to collaborative scoring. These educators knew that collaboration is hard work. Moreover, they understood that it is a skill acquired over time. Hence these remarkably effective schools did not have a "collaboration day" or a "collaboration workshop" but rather made the collaborative scoring of student work a part of their regular routine.

The Value of Feedback

Second, the schools with significant improvements provided significantly more frequent feedback to students than is typically the case with a report card. Emulating their most successful colleagues in music and physical education, teachers provided feedback in real time. They knew that a basketball coach does not provide hints on an effective jump shot nine weeks after an error, nor does a great music teacher note the improper position of the violinist's left hand weeks after noticing the mistake, but rather coaches and musicians provide precise and immediate feedback. In some cases, teachers took a triage approach, providing traditional report cards to successful and self-directed students, while providing weekly reports on their progress to students who were struggling. Their approach to feedback was consistent with Robert Marzano and his colleagues whose meta-analysis of research on student achievement revealed that feedback had a profound impact on student achievement, provided that the feedback was timely, accurate, and specific (Marzano, Pollock, and Pickering, 2001). The emphasis that these teachers placed on accuracy in feedback was remarkable. Unlike the "positive distortion" that clouds so much classroom feedback (Foersterling and Morgenstern, 2002), teachers with large gains were committed to feedback that was consistently accurate, with student performance compared to unambiguous expectations.

The Impact of Time

Third, the schools with large gains made dramatic changes in their schedule. Although they had the same budget, state requirements, teacher's union contract, and other restrictions as other schools in the system, the schools with large gains made remarkable schedule changes. At the elementary level, they routinely devoted three hours each day to literacy, with two hours of reading and one hour of writing. At the secondary level, they routinely provided double periods of English and mathematics. This was not a shell game in which they used the block schedule to double up some times but cut back on English and math in other times, but rather represented a genuine increase in instructional hours of math and English. The essential nature of instructional time is hardly a new idea, yet in an astonishing number of schools, the schedule is revered more than the Pledge of Allegiance, Constitution, and Magna Carta combined. To break the mold in student achievement, these schools discovered, they had to break the schedule. It is interesting that this commitment to time for literacy instruction occurred in a state in which social studies and science content examinations were required. These teachers and principals did not change the schedule to over-emphasize literacy because they disregarded science and social studies, but rather because they knew that literacy was essential for success in every content area.

Action Research and Mid-Course Corrections

Fourth, teachers engaged in successful action research and mid-course corrections. In many of the schools with the greatest gains, their school accountability plans were not static documents set in concrete before the beginning of the school year, but dynamic and flexible guides. They asked the central office for permission to change goals and strategies that were not effective and start new ones that held promise, even during the school year. Moreover, these faculties and leaders learned from one another. An illustration of their commitment to the application of action research is the use of word walls at the secondary level. Because both the school improvement data and the instructional techniques associated with those improvements are transparent in a system of holistic accountability, the teachers who had achieved great things with students were subject to being questioned by colleagues throughout the system about their success. When in earlier years, elementary educators reported that significant improvements in vocabulary and reading comprehension results were associated with the implementation of word walls, the secondary science and social studies educators decided to adopt the idea. They created walls with words containing essential science and social studies vocabulary, sometimes associated with vivid visual images, and used those vocabulary words throughout the year. In other examples of effective action research, teachers replicated one another's writing rubrics, interdisciplinary assessments, and student motivation practices.

Aligning Teacher Assignments with Teacher Preparation

Fifth, principals made decisive moves in teacher assignments. Some writers have argued that when test scores are down, the entire school should be reconstituted and the entire faculty dismissed. In my observations, however, principals have made impressive gains by reassigning teachers to different grades within the same school. Consider what has happened to the curriculum—particularly in the fourth, fifth, and sixth grades—over the past decade. There has been an enormous growth in the complexity of the curriculum, particularly in math and science, with an accompanying set of assumptions about the undergraduate curriculum of the teachers responsible for those grades. Those assumptions have sometimes been wildly inappropriate. When the fourth grade curriculum requires an understanding of algebra and scientific inquiry and the teacher's undergraduate preparation does not include those subjects, there is a challenge that will not be solved with a one-day staff development course in academic standards. The teachers whose undergraduate backgrounds fail to match the standards are not bad people nor are they unprofessional educators. Rather, their preparation is better suited to a different grade level. Effective leaders know that they should seek not to "fix" the person, but rather find a job (and accompanying set of standards) that best meets the teacher's abilities and backgrounds. By making decisive moves in teacher assignments, these principals saved the careers of some teachers and dramatically improved the achievement of their students.

Constructive Data Analysis

Sixth, successful schools included an intensive focus on student data from multiple sources, and specifically focused on cohort data. They were less interested in comparing last year's fourth grade class to this year's fourth grade class (which are, in most instances, different children) and more interested in comparing the same student to the same student. Their most important questions were not, "Is this year's class different from last year's class?" but rather:

- "What percentage of a group of students is proficient now compared to a year ago?"

- "What percentage of our students have gained one or more grade levels in reading when we compare their scores today to their scores a year ago?"

- "Of those students who were not proficient a year ago, what percentage are now proficient?"

- "Of those students who were proficient a year ago, what percentage are now advanced?"

In brief, these teachers compared the students to themselves rather than to other groups of students. This analysis allowed them to focus their teacher strategies on the needs of their students and not on generic improvement methods.

Common Assessments

Seventh, the schools with the greatest improvements in student achievement consistently used common assessment. This is a dangerous recommendation to consider in an era in which the most frequently heard complaint across the educational landscape is that students are over-tested. To be sure, many students are over-tested; but they are under-assessed. The distinction between testing and assessment must be clear. Testing implies an end-of-year, summative, evaluative, process in which students submit to a test and the results—typically many months later—are used by newspapers and policy makers to render a judgment about education. By the time the results are published, they are ancient history in the eyes of the student and teacher. Contrast this to the best practice in assessment, in which students are required to complete a task and then very soon—within minutes, hours, or days—they receive feedback that is designed to improve their performance. Effective assessment is what great music educators and coaches routinely provide to their students. Moreover, great educators use assessment data to make real-time decisions and restructure their teaching accordingly. The track coach, for example, does not use the previous year's data to make decisions about assembling relay teams or selecting students to compete for the state finals. Rather, the most recent data available is far more important than the final results from the previous year. Similarly, the data from last quarter on a school-based assessment is far more helpful than the data from last year's test. Common assessments also provide a degree of consistency in teacher expectations that is essential if fairness is our fundamental value. Although individual teachers must have discretion on a day to day and hour to hour basis to teach, re-teach, and otherwise meet the needs of individual students, they do not have the discretion to presume that their students "just can't do it." The use of a common assessment for each major discipline allows for a combination of daily discretion and independence by teachers, while preserving a school-wide commitment to equity and consistency of expectations.

The Value of Every Adult in the System

Eighth, these remarkably successful schools employed the resources of every adult in the system. In holistic accountability systems, we can explore the extent to which professional development is distributed among all adults in the system. In a few remarkable cases, for example, there is profound respect for every employee, including bus drivers and cafeteria workers. The respect for these employees is evidenced by their inclusion in professional development opportunities in classroom management and student behavior. Leaders recognized that the student's day does not really begin in the classroom, but on the bus or perhaps during free breakfast. By committing their systems to consistency in the education and behavior of adults, these leaders ensure that every adult leader, from the bus driver to the food service employee to the classroom teacher, is regarded as a significant adult leader in the eyes of students. The language concerning student behavior, sanctions, and rewards is consistent and the results are impressive. Concomitant with gains in student achievement, these schools witnessed dramatic improvements in student behavior, including a reduction of bus misbehavior and disciplinary incidents outside the classroom.

Holistic accountability (Reeves, 2001) reviews allow a consideration of other extraordinary performances, including those by school nurses, library/media center specialists, school secretaries, custodians, counselors, psychologists, security guards, and many other unsung heroes whose exceptional efforts are disregarded in the typical accountability report. While holistic accountability does not provide a cookie-cutter approach to school success, it does reveal the remarkable impact of every adult in the system on student achievement.

Cross-Disciplinary Integration

Ninth, there is explicit involvement of the subjects that are frequently and systematically disregarded in traditional accountability systems—music, art, physical education, world languages, technology, career education, consumer and family education, and many other variations on these themes. Analysis of holistic accountability data reveals that the involvement of these seemingly peripheral subjects in academic achievement is neither serendipitous nor insignificant. Rather, there is a deliberate strategy of involvement in these subjects in the improvement of academic results for all students. A few examples will serve to illustrate the point. Teachers meet to review student achievement data at a deep level, including the sub-scale scores. The discussion is not that "math scores are low" but rather that "the sub-scales reveal that we need to work in particular in fractions, ratio, and measurement." This leads the music teachers to develop activities in which musical rhythms reveal the relationship of whole notes, half notes, and quarter notes. Art teachers work on perspective and other representational art that makes explicit use of scale. Physical education teachers allow students to choose to run either a millimeter or a kilometer, and when they make the wrong choice, it is a lesson most students remember well.

In a striking example of collaboration in Norfolk, the teachers in music, art, and physical education collaborated to teach a social studies unit about African studies and the nation of Mali, the home of many of the students' ancestors. Using dance, literature, vocabulary, geography, history, song, and other engaging activities that crossed disciplinary boundaries, the teachers took the Mali unit out of the shadows of the final week of school and infused it throughout the school year. It is hardly an accident that these students also displayed astonishing improvements in their performance on state social studies tests.

Other Urban Success Stories

Norfolk is hardly an isolated example of success in urban school systems. In Indianapolis, Indiana, the Wayne Township Metropolitan School Corporation is among many that has demonstrated that academic improvement is compatible with high percentages of minority and poor students in the student body. In St. Louis,

Missouri, Dr. Chris Wright and her colleagues have led successful initiatives in both Riverview Gardens and Hazelwood school districts. Now, under the leadership of Dr. John Oldani and Dr. Dennis Dorsey of the Cooperating School Districts of St. Louis County, these techniques are having an impact throughout the St. Louis area. In Los Angeles County and Orange County, California, urban, suburban, and rural school systems are collaborating to create significant gains in student achievement.

The Wayne Township results are particularly interesting, as they represent not only an example of successful accountability, but also the ability of a complex urban school system to replicate the success of other systems. The Wayne Township experience demonstrates that holistic accountability is not merely the result of idiosyncratic case studies, but rather the result of systematic replication of best practices from within and outside a school system. The demographic characteristics of Wayne Township might be those of any urban system, with 26 different languages spoken by the students, free and reduced lunch enrollment as high as 80 percent in some schools, and minority enrollment increasing in a number of schools to the point that a majority of students are from minority ethnic backgrounds in some buildings. What is unusual, however, is the relentless focus of this school system on collaboration, academic standards, and nonfiction writing at every level. In particular, the years from 1999 through 2003 represent an extraordinary effort to augment the state's accountability system with a district-based holistic accountability system. In addition to the state tests, the district administers pre- and post- tests for every student in the fall and spring of each academic year. For the year ending in June of 2002, every single school made significant gains in mathematics and language arts. In addition, the schools with the highest poverty levels made the greatest gains, perhaps because those schools displayed the most intensive focus on changing schedules, instructional practices, building-level assessment, and leadership. It was therefore no surprise that when the state tests were administered in the fall of 2002, every building displayed significant growth, but those buildings with the highest poverty levels displayed the greatest growth in academic achievement. These gains exceeded 20 percent in the case of several schools within the district.

Without a constructive accountability system, these results might be passed off as the temporary reaction to test preparation resulting from pressure from state authorities. The facts contradict such a presumption. Every school in Wayne Township tracked specific practices in leadership and teaching. In the case of those schools with the greatest gains, there were common assessments on a monthly or quarterly basis. In addition, faculty meetings and staff development sessions were routinely devoted to collaborative scoring of student work. Each of the schools had common scoring rubrics so that there were consistent descriptions of what the word "proficient" means in practice. Following the lead of the district, each school embraced the use of "power standards" so that teachers were able to focus on a few of the most important standards rather than every single standard established by the state. This is among the most important observations of this holistic accountability study: higher test scores resulted not from mindless test prep and frantic coverage of every standard, but rather from the thoughtful application of the most important standards to creative and engaging teaching strategies.

It was noteworthy that the schools that had the greatest gains did not eliminate special area courses, such as music, art, physical education, and technology. Rather, these courses were explicitly a part of the academic preparation of every student. In schools with the highest gains, each teacher in the special areas was given the standards in mathematics and language arts in which students needed the greatest amount of help. Each of these teachers incorporated some of those language arts and math standards into their daily lessons.

Finally, the principal was personally involved in the evaluation of student work. The building leader regularly met with students and parents to discuss student achievement in specific terms. Moreover, the principals personally administered common assessments every month in language arts and math. By giving up faculty meetings, the principal helped to provide additional time for collaborative scoring of student work. The principal also encouraged every teacher to display proficient and exemplary student work in a highly visible manner. The result of these displays was that every student, parent, and teacher had a clear and consistent understanding of what the school-wide scoring rubrics meant in practice.

The Impact of Holistic Accountability on Equity

As impressive as the improvements in academic achievement were in Wayne Township, the gains in equity were nothing short of extraordinary. Figure 19.1 showed the typical negative relationship between poverty and student achievement. The more likely a school is to have high percentages of poor and minority students, the less likely the school is to have a high proportion of the students achieve academic proficiency.

The line extending from the upper left to the lower right shows that as the percentage of students in poverty (as defined by those eligible for free or reduced lunch) increases, the achievement (as measured by test scores) decreases. This relationship is not perfectly negative (-1.0) but it is substantial in most national research, ranging from -.6 to -.9. The prevailing assertion in more than four decades of research on the topic is that variables such as student poverty account for 90 percent or more of the variation in student test scores (Marzano, 2003). If we stop with a consideration of Figure 19.1, then these prevailing assertions will carry the day. The accountability evidence, however, suggests that there are specific teaching, leadership, and curriculum strategies that will mitigate the impact of poverty.

Figures 19.2 through 19.5 indicate that the negative relationship between student poverty and student achievement is not a certainty. Although the grade 6 language arts scores are disappointingly negative (- .35), in both grades 3 and 6, the relationships between poverty and achievement are far lower than is the case nationally, and in three out of four examples, the relationships are almost flat. In other words, this school system has demonstrated that the relationship between poverty and student achievement can be negligible.

Figure 19.2

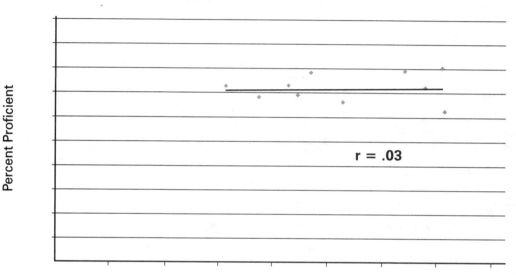

Relationship Between Poverty and 3rd Grade Language Arts Achievement

r = .03

Percent Proficient

Percent Free and Reduced Lunch

Figure 19.3

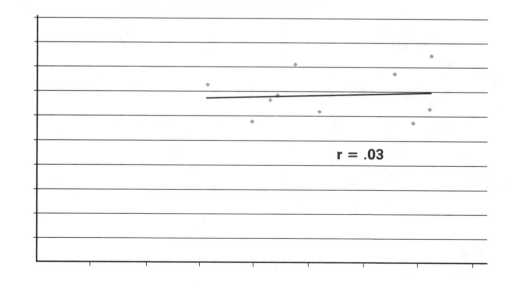

Relationship Between Poverty and 3rd Grade Mathematics Achievement

r = .03

Percent Proficient

Percent Free and Reduced Lunch

Equity Need Not Be A Dream

The Wayne Township experience demonstrates that equity need not be a dream. Every single building in the district—elementary through high school—achieved one of the following two equity indicators: The difference between students eligible for free and reduced lunch and the average was less than 10 percent, or the difference between the largest minority group of students and the average was less than 10 percent. These data points are totally consistent with the improvements in equity in Milwaukee, Freeport, Riverview Gardens (St. Louis metropolitan area), and others.

While no one disputes that poverty, linguistic differences, and culture can be important variables influencing student achievement, the research is clear that variables in teaching, curriculum, and leadership are profoundly important. In fact, these variables, that teachers and leaders can control, are more influential over student achievement than the intractable variables of poverty, culture, and language.

Figure 19.4

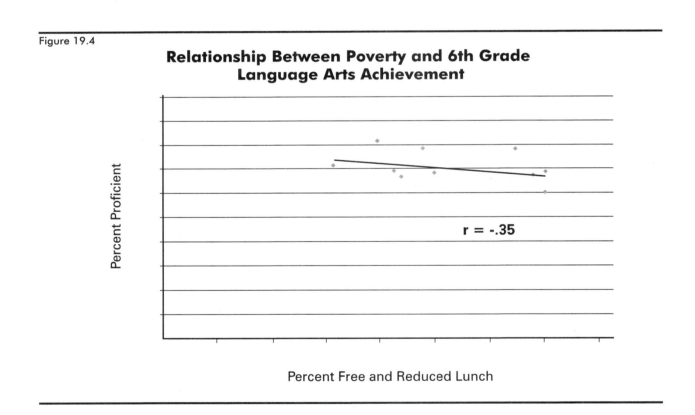

Relationship Between Poverty and 6th Grade Language Arts Achievement

Percent Proficient

r = -.35

Percent Free and Reduced Lunch

Figure 19.5

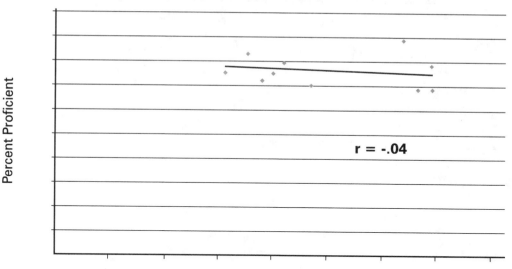

Relationship Between Poverty and 6th Grade Mathematics Achievement

Percent Proficient

r = -.04

Percent Free and Reduced Lunch

Critics, Cynics, and Urban Education Success

We must take a few minutes to address the inevitable critics who appear to be constitutionally unable to believe that a success story in urban education exists. Whenever I share results such as those in Norfolk, Wayne Township, Milwaukee, Riverview Gardens, Freeport, or other successful urban schools, critics inevitably roll their eyes and allege that this surely must be a flash in the pan, the product of a frenzy of test preparation rather than sustainable reform. Others have claimed that the results must be due to the exclusion of under-performing children on test day. Still other critics claim that the students and teachers must be engaged in a massive cheating conspiracy. Others take issue with the methodology of the research, particularly if careful research controls (such as mobility and attendance) are used. The presence of those controls inflates achievement, the critics charge. After all, the studies reflect students who actually attend school. Of course, the absence of those controls would lead to charges of sloppy research. Either way, the critics find a way to ignore the continuing pile of research, of which my studies represent only a few pebbles. Marzano (2003) has assembled the most impressive evidence, using meta-analytic techniques that indicate the importance of teaching, curriculum, and leadership relative to poverty and ethnic identity. Demographic characteristics are relevant, but the preponderance of the evidence indicates that these characteristics are not destiny when it comes to academic achievement. The following is a brief consideration of challenges that I have heard made to the 90/90/90 research:

The only measure of success in this study is test scores, and there are better ways to assess student achievement. Test scores are a way, but by no means the only way, to assess student achievement. It is interesting that one of hallmarks of the 90/90/90 Schools was an unwillingness to tolerate annual state or district tests as the sole measurements of achievement. These schools consistently elevate the importance of classroom-based, teacher-made tests that are collaboratively scored and used to provide immediate feedback to both students and teachers. From a research and policy perspective, however, it is necessary to have some consistent data in order to understand student achievement. While accountability should indeed be a holistic endeavor with multiple assessments of achievement, common tests of literacy and mathematics are useful to evaluate student achievement over time. Finally, the best accountability systems, including the one used in the original 90/90/90 research, included a balance of state, district, and school-based measures. Moreover, it included a narrative report from each school, providing a balance of qualitative observation and quantitative data.

The excessive time devoted to reading means less time for science and social studies. This is true. Schools in the study were required by state law to take science and social studies tests, yet they made a deliberate trade-off to devote more time to reading comprehension and nonfiction writing, even if it meant that they had fewer hours of social studies instruction. This trade-off was wise for two reasons. First, their scores in social studies and science did not decline, but increased. One can speculate that it might have had something to do with the improved ability of students to read and understand the questions on the social studies and science tests. Second, our interviews of social studies and science teachers at the secondary level revealed their nearly unanimous conviction that the key to greater success in those disciplines at the secondary level was not more social studies and science instruction in elementary school, but students who could enter secondary school able to read on grade level. A substantial body of research (Foersterling and Morgenstern, 2002; Klentschy, Garrison, and Amaral, 2000) supports the teachers in this conviction.

The controls for attendance and mobility provide a positive bias for 90/90/90 Schools. This is not true. The accountability system provided "two-column" reporting for students in order to display the impact of mobility and attendance. In one column, the report shows the results for all students, and in the next column it shows the results for those students who were continuously enrolled during the school year. For attendance, the "all student" number was separated from the results for those students who attended school at least 90 percent of the time. These controls were made for all schools, not just the 90/90/90 Schools. Therefore, a parallel comparison was made to high poverty, high minority schools for students with good attendance and continuous enrollment, but who did not have the success of students in the 90/90/90 Schools. This is just good research design. In pharmaceutical research, we compare patients who receive the medicine (the experimental group) to those who receive a placebo (the control group). The research is only useful if those in the experimental group really take their medicine. If we are studying the impact of certain strategies in curriculum, teaching, and educational leadership, our research is of questionable value if we analyze the effects on students who were not present for the curriculum, teaching, and leadership strategies. Finally, it was noteworthy that the schools that had high mobility (as defined by more than 80 percent of students taking the spring test not enrolled in September) and also high achievement, had strikingly similar characteristics to the 90/90/90 Schools, with an emphasis on writing and collaboration.

The 90/90/90 Schools used expensive programs, such as Success for All. This is not true. Some schools used Success for All, and others did not. This makes emphatically clear that the brand name alone of a literacy program is not the predictor of success, but rather the professional practices employed by teachers and leaders in the building. In fact, some Success for All schools had high results, while others had poor results. It was the replicable professional practices, not particular programs, that were associated with student success.

The effects are transient and dependent upon a particularly effective principal and faculty. This is not true. The effects are sustainable, with some schools maintaining this designation through different principals and high faculty turnover. The effects are replicable, with schools in other places (where there is also high turnover and teacher inexperience, particularly in high poverty schools). In the words of one teacher in the original study, "nobody volunteered to come to this school." Nevertheless, their collaboration, focus, and professional practices delivered results.

Conclusion

Perhaps the most compelling argument against any research about success in high poverty schools is the observation that there are cases where teachers are doing all of the right things, and yet student achievement remains low. There are no magic potions to deliver improved student achievement. The best that researchers and policymakers can do is to examine the preponderance of the evidence and draw appropriate conclusions. When a jury is presented with the evidence in a court case, it rarely has a perfect data set with unquestionable research. Rather, the jury confronts conflicting information, including information with errors, uncertainties, and differing interpretations. From this mix, we ask twelve people of good will and common sense to draw an appropriate conclusion based on the preponderance of the evidence.

The 90/90/90 research and the other evidence offered in this article fall far short of perfection. It does, however, contribute to the larger body of evidence that, in its totality, suggests useful strategies for high poverty schools. Moreover, in any research project, we must recognize that perfection is not an option. Rather, we can only choose among the errors that we commit, and attempt to minimize the risk of our errors. From a research perspective, we must choose between the risk of confirming a hypothesis that is not true and the risk of failing to confirm a hypothesis that is true. In the case of the professional practices recommended in this article, we also have two potential errors. One error is the replication of these practices, including an increase in our commitment to literacy, nonfiction writing, and collaboration, and the subsequent discovery that the students really did not need all of that extra work after all. What is the risk of this strategy? Excessively literate students? Teachers who collaborate too much? The other error is the failure to act while we search for perfection or persist in a state of disbelief. Risks attendant with such delay will be debilitating for another generation of students. I do not claim that the 90/90/90 research and its many counterparts in the literature are perfect. I only suggest that the risks of this research being wrong are minimal. The risks if the research is correct and ignored are grave.

Questions for Discussion

1. What implications do the research findings on "90/90/90 Schools" have for your school or district? How would you implement these in your school or district?

CHAPTER

Standards and Accountability

Standards are fair and effective. Standards-based school systems focus on the extent to which their students meet or exceed standards; and not on whether they have exceeded the national average. Rather than searching for a comfortable spot on the bell curve, standards-based school systems continue to climb the mountain of student achievement. It is essential that teachers and leaders understand the relationship between standards and accountability. Typically, every initiative in a school system is viewed as idiosyncratic and additive—"one more thing, one more report, one more program, one more diversion from my work with students." In fact, accountability and standards are not separate initiatives, but are integrally linked; the success of each depends on the other and progress in one area builds progress in the other.

Standards Give Focus to the Accountability System

In the process of facilitating numerous accountability meetings, there is inevitably a moment when, with exasperation, an administrator says, "Just give it to me straight—is this going to be more work for me or less work for me?" The clear implication is that the accountability report is a burden on top of the building improvement plan, the accreditation report, the program evaluation reports, the strategic plan report, and the periodic board demands for school responses to other board goals. If a school system has embraced a standards-based approach to education, however, this diffusion of effort, attention, and reporting can be thwarted before it begins.

Every report, every initiative, every investment of time and energy must respond to this acid test: does it further our efforts to achieve our standards? If not, then one of two things is true. Either our standards omitted something quite important or, more likely, the new demand for time, attention, and resources is outside the scope of those things that our standards indicate are most important. Note that the question does not address popularity, enthusiasm at a recent meeting, or the latest program or fad. The question that separates instruction and achievement from wasteful diversion is how the enterprise relates to standards.

Standards for Students and Adults

Every state has embraced some version of academic content standards, with 49 states establishing these expectations of what students should know at the state level and one (Iowa) requiring school districts to establish standards. Only a few states (Alaska is a notable example) have been as diligent in establishing standards for the adults in the system as they have in the establishment of standards for students. If standards and accountability are to reach their potential of mutual reinforcement and synergy, then the standards-setting effort cannot conclude with academic expectations for the children in the system. Standards for teachers, leaders, policy makers, and (dare I say it?) parents and communities are all integral elements of student success. Just as an effective accountability system includes measurement of academic success (system-wide indicators) and the strategies that lead to that success (school-based indicators), so do effective standards include both the expectations of students and the requirements for teaching and leadership that help students reach those expectations.

Examples of standards for teachers and administrators are in Figure 20.1 and 20.2, respectively. These examples are taken from standards established by the Alaska Department of Education (1997).

Figure 20.1

Standards for Alaska's Teachers

1. A teacher can describe the teacher's philosophy of education and demonstrate its relationship to the teacher's practice.

2. A teacher understands how students learn and develop, and applies that knowledge in the teacher's practice.

3. A teacher teaches students with respect for their individual and cultural characteristics.

4. A teacher knows the teacher's content area and how to teach it.

5. A teacher facilitates, monitors, and assesses student learning.

6. A teacher creates and maintains a learning environment in which all students are actively engaged and contributing members.

7. A teacher works as a partner with parents, families, and with the community.

8. A teacher participates in and contributes to the teaching profession.

Figure 20.2

Standards for Alaska's Administrators

1. An administrator provides leadership for an educational organization.

2. An administrator guides instruction and supports an effective learning environment.

3. An administrator oversees the implementation of curriculum.

4. An administrator coordinates services that support student growth and development.

5. An administrator provides for staffing and professional development to meet student learning needs.

6. An administrator uses assessment and evaluation information about students, staff, and the community in making decisions.

7. An administrator communicates with diverse groups and individuals with clarity and sensitivity.

8. An administrator acts in accordance with established laws, policies, procedures, and good business practices.

9. An administrator understands the influence of social, cultural, political, and economic forces on the educational environment and uses this knowledge to serve the needs of children, families, and communities.

10. An administrator facilitates the participation of parents and families as partners in the education of children.

Academic Standards Are Improved Through Comprehensive Accountability Systems

Fueled by articulate advocates on all sides of the question (Ohanian, 1999; Bracey, 1999; Finn et al, 1998; Kohn, 1999), the debate over the proper form and source of standards rages at the beginning of the 21st century. One side of the debate contends that good standards are specific and voluminous, stemming from the wisdom of the state. The other side maintains that standards must be the exclusive province of the classroom teacher, with any guidance outside of the classroom walls an uninvited intrusion on academic freedom and the art of pedagogy. Neither extreme advances the cause of reason. A search for the middle ground in this argument might consider these premises:

- Students and teachers deserve fairness in evaluation.

- Fairness requires knowledge and understanding of what is expected not only during the current year, but also in future years; not only in the current hour, but also in the next hour.

- Standards that are too voluminous lead inevitably to superficiality, while standards that are vague or absent lack descriptive rigor (Popham, 1997) and leave excessive power in the mysterious domain of test writers.

- Accountability systems require policy makers, leaders, and educators to make wise choices—neither embracing every line of every standard, nor abandoning all hope of a common understanding of what is important for student achievement.

In other words, the information we get through the process of creating a comprehensive accountability system can inform the standards debate by identifying a small sub-set of state or district standards that will be measured. The articulation of accountability indicators requires a process of discernment that rarely occurs in the articulation of standards. The question governing most discussions surrounding standards is, "Did we leave anything out?" The question governing effective discussions of accountability systems is, "What is most important?"

Conclusion

Standards are neither panacea nor plague. Properly implemented, standards provide a framework for effective teaching and learning. When linked to a comprehensive accountability system, standards become not a pipe dream for student achievement, but a focused set of objectives and a clear set of strategies to meet those objectives. When academic content standards are accompanied by clear expectations for the adults in the educational system, then the standards movement can begin to claim that it offers fairness and effectiveness for schools and the students they serve.

Questions for Discussion

1. What standards govern your school system? Find a copy of them and review them.

2. How do your academic content standards compare to the expectations of your accountability system? What is included in the accountability system that is omitted from the standards? What is omitted from the accountability system that is included in the standards?

3. Does your system articulate standards for teachers, administrators, board members, and parents to the same extent as for students? If not, what are the expectations of the adults in the system? What documents express those expectations? To what extent are the standards for the adults in the system supported by the requirements of your accountability system? See Worksheet 20.1.

Standards for Adults

Adult	**Existing Standards** *Documented, Explicit Expectations*	**Potential Standards** *General, Undocumented Expectations*
TEACHER: Preparedness		
Subject Matter Knowledge		
Certification		
Others:		
ADMINISTRATOR: Effective Leadership Practices		
Certification		
Others:		

Adult	Existing Standards *Documented, Explicit Expectations*	Potential Standards *General, Undocumented Expectations*
PARENT:		
BOARD MEMBER:		
OTHER ADULTS:		

PART

Leadership and Policy in Educational Accountability

PART

IV

CHAPTER

The Role of the Board of Education in Accountability Systems

Policy Leadership or Administrative Leadership?

The role of the board of education is to set policy. Such a statement may seem so pedestrian that it is superfluous. Nevertheless, the number of times in which a board of education engages in the day-to-day administration of schools makes it clear that the difference between policy and administration is neither obvious nor overstated. This difference lies at the heart of effective board membership and progressive policy leadership. Boards that become immersed in administration cannot lead policy.

One of the most frequent frustrations that I hear from superintendents and other senior leaders of schools throughout the nation is the failure of school boards to confine their work to committed policy development. "I've got four out of seven board members who are former teachers and administrators," one superintendent lamented, "and all of them believe that their service on the school board is their chance to finally become the superintendent."

Board members see things differently. "I want to be supportive and stick to policy issues," a frustrated board member reports, "but the superintendent treats us like children. Every time we ask a legitimate question, the superintendent huffs and insists that we really don't need to know such things. It's infuriating." Board members have a legitimate need to create policy based upon accurate and contemporary information. Superintendents have an equally legitimate responsibility to exercise administrative leadership in the implementation of policy. Both roles involve leadership; both roles require accurate information. Neither role can operate in isolation. The issue is not, "Who is really in charge?" but rather, "What is the scope of our individual functions, and how do they complement each other?" Both the board and superintendent exercise leadership, but policy leadership must be clearly distinguished from administrative leadership.

Accountability in Action

Resolving the Paradox: Policy and Leadership

How can these two roles be reconciled? A comprehensive accountability system can provide board members with a blend of very specific school-level information, along with qualitative and narrative data that puts this information in proper context. The same accountability system can also give superintendents, senior leaders, and other members of a school community important information on which they can base initiatives that improve student achievement. This chapter identifies some methods that school board members can use to help districts design and implement a comprehensive accountability system. These methods include building the system architecture with clear accountability indicators and deciding when and how often data should be reported, and how it should be used. The school board also plays a critical role in using accountability as a permanent framework for all other district programs and keeping the focus by prioritizing issues within the framework of the accountability system.

System Architecture

The board of education has ultimate approval authority for accountability system design. By selecting specific accountability indicators for the system itself, the board speaks with a clear voice. In effect, the board is saying, "This piece of information is important, and we intend to look at it closely." Setting clear policy about what indicators will be examined most closely avoids the "gotcha's" that can later contaminate reviews of schools and educational systems by policy makers. Unless board members provide school leaders with clear guidance, a single piece of information, gathered haphazardly and reported out of context, can suddenly become ammunition used to make a political point. School leaders, unclear about board expectations, have no way of knowing that this particular piece of information will be the focus of a board member's wrath.

When the architecture of a comprehensive accountability system is clear, however, then the rules of the game are made clear for both policy makers and school leaders alike. All parties know which data are important and subject to critical and public scrutiny.

The board can also influence accountability system architecture in another fundamental way by deciding on an appropriate combination of indicators. Some indicators should report data about absolute achievement. Other indicators should be used to track levels of improvement. In general, the more heterogeneous the schools in a district, the more balanced the indicators should be. That is, if a system includes both high-achieving schools and those with significant hurdles to climb, then an even mix of improvement and achievement indicators allows both kinds of schools to demonstrate accomplishment in the accountability system and permits no school to become complacent.

Complacency can be engendered in accountability systems that focus on the easy wins. For example, upper socioeconomic school districts with a history of good test scores might focus on achievement variables alone and become self-satisfied with mean scores that appear to be well above the national average. If these same districts fail to report the percentage of students who are not meeting reading and math standards, however, they are not including critical areas about which school boards will be concerned. The average can mask important trouble spots. Reporting mere test score averages fails to reflect the performance of students who have not yet achieved proficiency.

Conversely, an accountability system that places too much emphasis on improvement indicators allows similar degrees of complacency to occur. Such systems, while they reflect improvement, fail to come to grips with the plain fact that student achievement remains inadequate. Many of the "value-added" accountability approaches that are now in vogue use this misleading kind of analysis. The faulty reasoning of such systems appears to be, "We're doing a good deal better than we expected to based on our history, so congratulate us for our success and please ignore the fact that many of our kids still can't read."

In a more homogeneous district (that is, a district in which the levels of achievement are more consistent), a case can be made that indicators should be weighted in one direction or the other—either toward achievement indicators or improvement indicators. Some poor states have chosen to emphasize improvement indicators, while wealthy suburbs might pursue absolute indicators of achievement. In general, however, board members are better served with a combination of indicators that show policy makers both the strengths and challenges in their districts. Consult Appendices C and D for more detailed examples of accountability system indicators.

Data Reporting

Board members can exert an extraordinary influence on the timeliness and relevance of accountability systems if school boards pay close attention to how frequently accountability data are reported. Traditional accountability results are typically reported to school boards in much the same way that annual reports are presented to shareholders of major corporations. The executives who are responsible for shareholder reports know, however, that quarterly earnings reports are monitored closely, and that companies also have an obligation to communicate information regularly to analysts and the general public. School boards would be wise to adopt a like commitment to periodic reporting of educational data. Rather than an "annual report," every meeting of the board should include a review of at least one or two elements of data from the accountability system.

Periodic data review sends a clear message to the public, the administration, and to new board members that the school system or district adheres to the principles of data-driven decision-making. Moreover, a continuous focus on accountability system data can reduce the number of impromptu information requests made by board members. This, in turn, can eliminate hundreds of person-hours of administrative time devoted to doing last-minute research in response to these requests. By defining well in advance what data will be required, when the reports will be made, and how they will be analyzed, the board can reverse the tradition of haphazard data reporting that occurs in so many school systems.

Accountability as a Framework

Perhaps the most important role of the school board in the implementation of a comprehensive accountability system is the establishment of accountability as a framework. An accountability system provides the framework within which all other initiatives, programs, evaluations, plans, and other educational policy matters must be placed. Does this really mean "all"? Indeed. The failure of the best accountability systems—in fact, the failure of most educational reforms—is not found in a lack of school system energy or insight, but in the lack of sustained effort and follow-through. Old ideas (that is, anything older than one school board election cycle) are regarded as stale and inadequate. Thus, an accountability system is replaced by standards, which are replaced by strategic plans, which are replaced by comprehensive improvement models, which are replaced by total-quality initiatives, which are replaced by yet another idea. Unfortunately, many of these so-called innovations are distinguished more by their novelty than by their effectiveness. Only accountability can survive, because even as political agendas change and policy makers come and go, accountability remains an inevitable part of every initiative. This is why accountability cannot be viewed as a "program," but, rather, as the framework within which other programs and initiatives must fit.

Board members continually ask such critical questions as, "How do we measure success? How do we know if we've achieved our objectives?" Whether the answers are expressed in dollars, test scores, achievement of academic standards, numbers of students, parental involvement, or any other indicator, a comprehensive accountability system can provide the answers. With a data gathering and analysis system in place, board members need not ask for new data on an idiosyncratic basis. They can have the assurance that key indicators in the accountability system openly disclose district and school weaknesses, appropriately proclaim strengths, and systematically identify what is working and what is not. With the consistent use of accountability as a framework for all other programs, the board says clearly, "What is worth doing is worth measuring. If we're not going to measure something within the framework of this accountability system, then it may not be worth doing."

Focus

The use of accountability as a framework inevitably sounds too exclusionary. What about a program that doesn't appear to fit within the accountability framework? When school board members encounter these kinds of programs, then they must ask the following tough question: "When we adopted our accountability system, we said that these things (achievement, safety, fiscal responsibility, for example) were important. Are we really ready to say that these issues are now less important because we want to focus our attention elsewhere?" Such a thoughtful and provocative question is too rarely posed as exciting new programs are brought before a school board.

In the end, policy makers never control schools, even though the instances of school boards voting on grading policies and football coaches are reaching alarming proportions. What policy makers really control is focus. Where will the attention of leadership, indeed of the community, be in this school system? Sometimes the clerk who prepares the board meeting agenda establishes this focus. If this is the case, then the school board is reduced to a group of figureheads, fulfilling vague duties, but rarely addressing the critical issues facing the school district or system. When this happens, substantive discussions of educational policy get sandwiched between "new business" items. These rarely receive attention before ten o'clock in the evening, and by that time, most school board members are only too happy to defer these items to the administration.

The first characteristic of a focused board is that they are able to filter out peripheral issues. Issues brought before the board that do not fit within the accountability framework are not considered bad or even irrelevant. These issues simply don't merit board time and attention. A focused school board understands that time is a zero-sum game. Every hour spent on one project or discussion is an hour forever lost from another project or discussion.

The second characteristic of a focused board is that it is data-driven. Accountability data are not merely published for the consumption of the news media. The board uses accountability data to make informed decisions. Before they fund, extend, or cancel a program, the focused board asks, "What do the data tell us about this issue?" At every meeting, board members have the most recent accountability information in front of them. Since they have conducted reviews of accountability data at each meeting, they are accustomed to requesting presentations about and analyses of accountability data. They then use this information to make better data-driven decisions.

Third, focused boards create alternative venues for policy exploration and analysis. They liberally use task forces, hearings, and community forums to provide the outlets for analysis and expression that sometimes dominate traditional board meetings. These school boards recognize that the focus on accountability advocated in these pages cannot be used to deny citizens the right to express themselves on vital public matters. They also recognize that the regular board meeting may not be the best forum for this kind of public discussion. The traditional process of giving 50 angry people two minutes each to make their points often sheds more heat than light on the educational topic under discussion. Hearings, task forces, and community forums can provide extended opportunities for citizens to have input in the policy process without destroying the effectiveness and focus of board meetings.

With the widespread prevalence of open-meeting laws, it is very difficult for board members to meet together in informal sessions to address policy issues. Under these circumstances, it is even more important for school boards to maximize the limited time that they have in their meetings.

A focused board can maximize its meeting time. First, the board sets the agenda. The priorities are clear because they have been embedded in the design of the accountability system. What is important gets measured, and school board members monitor and discuss accountability data at every board meeting. Board members do not make accountability reporting an annual endeavor that invites superficiality, but maintain focus throughout the year on the areas of greatest importance. A focused school board makes its priorities clear, does not waste its time or energy on peripheral issues, and uses data-driven decision-making to establish policies that will ultimately improve student and system achievement.

Conclusion

A comprehensive accountability system offers several benefits, including clarification of the role of the school board. With the system in place, little time is wasted determining jurisdiction, but is instead used to make informed decisions about district policy using current data. By carefully defining indicators which will keep the school board on task and also give the superintendent and public an idea of what is expected of them, the school board can review accountability data and use the system as a framework for existing programs, as well as a method to weed out any unnecessary tasks. By clearly defining the direction in which a school board's attention should be focused, a comprehensive accountability system can help these policy makers make the most of their positions.

Questions for Discussion

1. Review the minutes of board meetings for the past two years. Identify the initiatives, policies, and requirements that board actions have created that directly involve teaching and learning and that require administrative reporting.

2. To what extent are the board actions of the past two years consistent with the accountability system that has been developed by the Task Force?

Board Policy and Accountability

Board Policy Initiative (Description and Date)	Relationship to Accountability System (Identify System-wide Indicator or Indicate "none")	Reporting Requirement for Board Policy	Reconciliation of Board Policy (Integrate into accountability system, rescind the policy, or continue as a policy outside of the accountability system)

CHAPTER

The Role of the Superintendent in Educational Accountability: The S.T.A.R. Leader

As demands on the superintendent grow, the number of people with an appetite for the job is steadily declining (Henry, 2000). While the pay and recognition are appealing to outsiders, the real demands of 18-hour days, no job security, perpetual second-guessing, and personal attacks on top school leaders take their inevitable toll. Nothing in this chapter can make the job of school superintendent easy. Effective implementation of a comprehensive accountability plan can, however, allow the leader's vision to transcend politics and achieve results.

While a comprehensive accountability system (or anything else, for that matter) will never provide job security for a superintendent, it will certainly help the leader's vision for student success endure even as the political winds are shifting. Consider the case of Milwaukee Public Schools. Since the implementation of the Milwaukee Public Schools Accountability Plan in 1995 by Superintendent Robert Jasna, the superintendency changed hands four times in four years. The board changed dramatically. All deputy superintendents and many directors were replaced at the central office. Only the accountability system endured. Despite the chaos and uncertainty at the leadership and policy level, the accountability system continued to provide clear expectations for the system and for individual schools. School achievement rose dramatically and the district has an impressive catalog of practices that have a demonstrable impact on student achievement in the local environment (Milwaukee Public Schools, January 2000). While no one would claim that this or any urban system is perfect, the evidence is clear: Many students in the nation's 16th largest district are out-performing their suburban counterparts on many indices of achievement despite continuing social challenges and poverty. While the accountability system surely is not the cause for these successes, it is fair to say that the presence of a consistent and comprehensive accountability system provided school leaders with vital information and clear focus. In the end, school superintendents are far more motivated by the success of the students they serve than by the transient appreciation (or condemnation) of political forces.

Accountability in Action

When superintendents implement effective accountability systems, they become S.T.A.R. Leaders. This acronym represents the ability of the leader to integrate the following components:

- **S**tandards for students, teachers, and leaders

- **T**ools for teachers and leaders

- **A**ssessment and accountability systems

- **R**esults *Plus*

Standards

The role of the superintendent begins with vision, expectations, and standards. A mere recitation of state standards, however, renders the superintendent as little more than the delivery person bearing the burdens sent by people far removed from the classroom. The principle role of the superintendent in the transmission of standards is *focus*. The leader must divert the central office, curriculum specialists, and educational staff away from the practice of merely documenting standards and curriculum and lead the way to effective implementation of standards.

Without adequate focus, the transformation of standards into curriculum looks like the diagram in Figure 22.1. From state standards (which themselves are growing in number, specificity, and complexity) the district creates even more numerous sets of curriculum objectives. This exercise begins with good intentions, but rarely includes the process of discernment. The question that drives the process seems reasonable enough: "What knowledge and skills do students need to meet the standards?" From that, as the triangle shape of the diagram implies, the number of objectives for each standard expands, and the activities at the classroom level for each objective expand even more. From the perspective of a state department official or central office curriculum designer, the elegance and flow of the diagram are rational and reasonable. From the perspective of the classroom teacher and many students, however, this "triangle" approach, in which the decrees of the state flow downhill, is a prescription for disaster.

Figure 22.1

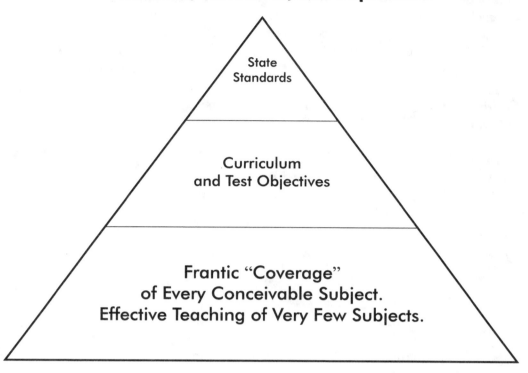

The Traditional Model of Standards, Curriculum, and Objectives

There are three central fallacies of this model. First, it assumes that the school year is longer than any school year in the world. As Marzano and his colleagues (1999) have documented, the coverage of the standards typically articulated by state departments of education would require a student to have a school career lasting 22 years rather than the usual 13.

Second, the model assumes that curriculum documents are equivalent to teacher activities. In all but the most specific programs of education, teachers use curriculum documents as guidelines, not daily scripts. Ironically, in highly prescriptive programs, such as *Success for All* and *Direct Instruction*, the teacher does not race through every conceivable academic standard, but focuses on only a few core standards in literacy.

The third fallacy of the traditional model is the presumption that teacher talk is equivalent to student learning. The curriculum leader of a school district in the Midwest displayed with satisfaction their newly "narrowed" mathematics curriculum. "It was very difficult and there were a lot of hurt feelings about the things we eliminated, but we finally have some focus," she explained. As I reviewed the documents, I found 63 separate objectives for 6th grade mathematics. With a 180-day school year (and with never a single field trip, snow day, or other diversion), students would have fewer than three days for each objective. When I gently suggested that more pruning was necessary, the response was immediate and emphatic. "We can't narrow it any more—every one of these objectives are on the state test, and if we don't cover them, then parents and the state will hammer us!" This curriculum director, though understandably agitated at the demands of voluminous state standards, failed to understand that documentation, prescription, and teacher talk were not related to student learning. The role of the superintendent and those under her leadership in the central office is not documentation, it is discernment. To illustrate the difference between these two concepts, consider the illustration in Figure 22.2. Here the traditional triangle is transformed into a diamond. The documentation does not end with the immensity of multiple objectives at the base of the triangle, but includes a filtering process that distinguishes the potential curriculum from the focused curriculum.

Figure 22.2

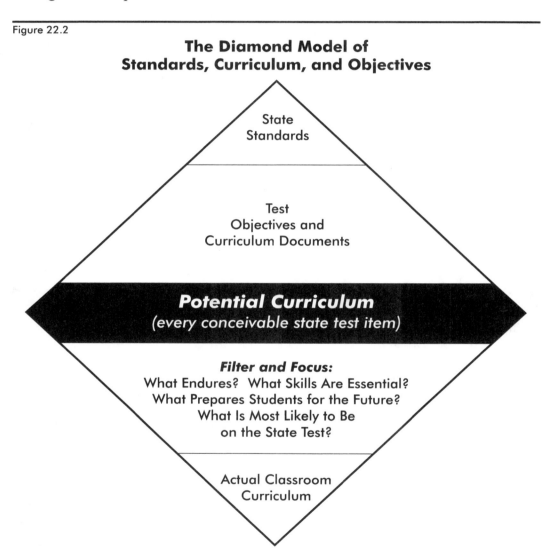

The Diamond Model of Standards, Curriculum, and Objectives

State Standards

Test Objectives and Curriculum Documents

Potential Curriculum
(every conceivable state test item)

Filter and Focus:
What Endures? What Skills Are Essential?
What Prepares Students for the Future?
What Is Most Likely to Be
on the State Test?

Actual Classroom Curriculum

The change from the triangle to the diamond is no less than the change from mind-numbing documentation of bureaucratic imperatives to a focus on student learning. As an example, apply the model above to sixth grade mathematics. Rather than 63 objectives (a modest number, compared to the many curriculum documents that exceed one hundred objectives for students of this age), let me propose the following requirements:

1. Perform number operations, with and without calculators

2. Draw in two-dimensional scale

3. Create and draw inferences from tables, charts, and graphs

4. Measure in different units (English and metric)

5. Given a story problem, draw a picture to illustrate it and solve it accurately

6. Perform fraction and decimal operations

7. Apply the properties of a triangle and rectangle

Careful readers of state standards will note with alarm several grave omissions, including the rhombus, trapezoid, and probability. Despite these omissions, I have interviewed hundreds of middle and high school math educators and asked them whether they would accept, however reluctantly, a student who had mastered these seven areas of curriculum rather than received superficial exposure to scores of state and local curriculum objectives. Secondary mathematics teachers assure me with one voice that they would be no less than ecstatic to have students with these seven skills, even if they might be, as it were, rhombus-impaired. Those who have carefully analyzed state and national tests also confirm that students with a mastery of these seven items will perform proficiently on such examinations. While they may not successfully complete 100 percent of the items, they will certainly have enough mathematical reasoning and skill to eliminate many wrong answers and think through the problems with sufficient care to score far better than their counterparts whose mathematical education was laden with coverage rather than learning.

S.T.A.R. Leaders do not preside over a documentation factory. S.T.A.R. Leaders provide focus and discernment. They lead a process in which standards are not mindless tools, but are guides to effective teaching and learning.

Tools for Teachers and Leaders

The tools for teachers and leaders in the S.T.A.R. model include transformational professional development, models of effective teaching and assessment, collaboration among professional colleagues, effective communication with parents and students, and highly visible tracking of progress. The leadership tool over which the superintendent can exercise direct influence is the organization of the central office to promote student success. Let us briefly consider just some of these tools.

Transformational Staff Development

Transformational staff development is premised on the notion that seminars, workshops, and meetings share the purpose of improved student achievement. These expensive and time-consuming exercises are not justified by mere popularity or the excitement generated by the latest fad. Rather, they are justified only by their impact on professional practice, which improves student learning. Guskey's insights on evaluating professional development (1999) provide an insightful echo of the "Dr. Fox" studies decades earlier. "Dr. Fox" was an actor who, wearing a lab coat and armed with a few medical terms, delivered an entertaining but vacuous lecture to medical students, who, presumably, would see through the ruse. The next speaker was a real physician who provided essential information the students needed. The popular but ineffective Dr. Fox received significantly higher ratings from the students.

Traditional staff development programs in schools reject the rigor of Guskey and embrace the folly of Dr. Fox by valuing entertainment over effectiveness. Challenge, rigor, and work give way to popularity, reassurance, and evangelical zeal. Transformational professional development, by contrast, focuses on reflection (often using real student work, teacher-created assessments, and practical insights). Typical staff development is infrequent, but occurs in multi-hour (often multi-day) chunks in an airy hotel. Transformational staff development occurs weekly or more frequently, with the sounds of students and colleagues only footsteps away. Typical staff development provides heavy notebooks that reside on the shelf. Transformational staff development produces practices, insights, assessments, and curriculum that are used within hours and days. The work products are not on the shelf, but on the desks of students and teachers. Chapter 6 includes more detailed information on the subject of staff development.

Models of Effective Teaching and Assessment

Models of effective teaching and assessment are essential tools in the S.T.A.R. model. If collaboration is valuable, then teachers need not speculate about what effective collaboration is, but they can see video models (Linton Professional Development, 1998b). Teachers need not ponder the theory of assessment, but can review and use models for their grade level that are relevant to their own state standards (Reeves, 1997; Gonzales, 2000).

Collaboration occurs not only with lesson planning, but when teachers have the opportunity to evaluate the work of students in other classes. Standards are little more than theoretical ideals until they are implemented through the collective action of teachers who strip the standards of their jargon and express with words and actions what "proficiency" really means. Students in such an environment understand that success is not defined by the idiosyncratic judgment of one teacher, but by the faculty's collective and consistent comparison of student work to clearly articulated standards. Time for effective collaboration is provided in these settings, not because collaborative schools have more money or longer days, but because they devote faculty meetings and staff development opportunities to collaboration rather than the typical reading of announcements and stultifying lectures. Refer to Chapter 5 for more information on accountability's effect on teaching.

Central Office Organization

Central office organization is, in most districts, the exclusive prerogative of the superintendent. It is one of the few areas in which the district leader can exercise direct authority. Unfortunately, many central offices include entrenched practices, traditions, and philosophies that focus on practice and documentation more than student achievement and effective strategies. Although a complete analysis of central office organization is beyond the scope of this book, two departments deserve special mention—curriculum and assessment (see Chapter 16 for other ways to build the central office into an accountability system). In most districts, the departments are separated on the organization chart, with the assessment office aligned with research, testing, and accountability, while the curriculum department is aligned with staff development, text book analysis, and documentation of state requirements. When the discussion turns to the divergence between curriculum and assessment, the frustration of every teacher, student, parent, and principal is palpable. Central office organizations perpetuate this frustration when organizational lines and physical distance separate curriculum and assessment. Although many people perceive the school superintendent as an immensely powerful individual, every school district leader I have interviewed expresses the common frustration that their direct influence on teaching and learning is, in fact, limited. One decision superintendents can make immediately that would have a clear and positive impact on teaching and learning is to abandon the traditional organizational division between assessment and curriculum. The people in those divisions should sit in close proximity to each other, attend common meetings, and join together to support student achievement. The superintendent can eliminate the Balkanization of the central office and forge a common commitment to student achievement from every hallway and desk within the district central office.

Superintendents frequently hesitate to use S.T.A.R. Tools because, they demur, schools must be "site-based" in their leadership. Department heads in the central office are, they insist, long-term administrators, and a reorganization could be upsetting and disruptive. If the subject were vaccinations, school violence, or even the configuration of the parking lot, the central office would doubtless exert its influence.

The tools of professional development and collaboration are no less important. When the superintendent abdicates leadership on these essential tools, resources of time and money are squandered. In this leadership vacuum, every administrator and teacher hears the rhetoric of standards and focus, but sees the reality of diffusion and chaos. When the superintendent asserts leadership from the central office to the buildings and the classrooms, the rewards far outweigh the risks.

Assessment and Accountability Systems

The "A" in S.T.A.R. Leadership stands for assessment and accountability. The role of the superintendent is far more than merely reporting results to the board. After all, most board members can read the latest test scores in the newspaper or on the Internet long before those scores appear on a board agenda. The function of the district leader is not merely to report the data, but to analyze, interpret, and most importantly, use the information from the accountability and assessment systems to inform policy and leadership decisions.

The first priority of the superintendent must be a single-minded focus on accuracy. While the Accountability Task Force, research department, assessment department, and other central office support staff play important roles in preparing the data, the accuracy of the data depends not merely on handling it carefully, but on senior policy level decisions. In a number of states, the "official" reports of state test scores are rendered inaccurate by rules at the state level that, when passively accepted at the district level, lead to significant distortions. Use of distorted data by boards and superintendents can lead to ill-informed policies, poorly designed curricula, unfair personnel decisions, and inappropriate public perceptions. Examples of data distortions encouraged or mandated by state policies that can be corrected by district-level analysis and change are described in the paragraphs below. In each case, the research department could faithfully follow state guidelines and provide inaccurate and distorted information. It is the superintendent's responsibility to deliberately change the reporting protocols and thus provide leaders and policy makers with more accurate information. It is also the superintendent's responsibility to take the inevitable criticism that accompanies such a decision. People will ask, "Why does the district report differ from the state report?" The superintendent must emphatically reply, "Because it is more accurate." Some opportunities for constructive intervention by the superintendent include:

- **Reporting "all student" data with controls for special education and grade level.**

  Educators frequently wish to include special education students as well as those students who have not progressed to the tested grade level. This inclusion stems from a desire for diagnostic information, or because their professional judgment leads them to provide opportunities for "maximum inclusion" of these students in all aspects of school life, including state tests. Such reasonable decisions can have unintended consequences, however. Schools that have progressive inclusion programs can show lower test scores that the "all student" data fail to explain. Properly done, the report will contain one column that includes all students, and a second column that only includes students in regular education and those who took the test without adaptations.

High schools that include students who do not have sufficient credit to be a "10th grader" in the state 10th grade tests do so to create opportunities for those students to become familiar with an important test. By having unprepared students take the test, however, the school sacrifices today's image for tomorrow's success. Worse yet, the school signals that revisions in 9th and 10th grade curricula may be required when, in fact, the students who brought the average test scores down were not in the 9th and 10th grade curriculum. Properly done, the report will contain one column that includes all students, and a second column that only includes students who were, in fact, 10th grade students at the time they took the test.

- **Reporting "all student" data with controls for student mobility.**

In a growing number of school systems, mobility has been recognized as having a significant impact on student achievement. Even without the research associating mobility and school change with diminished student performance (Sanders, 1998), the dictates of simple fairness would lead one to conclude that it is inappropriate to make decisions about the professional future of a teacher based on the tests scores of students who were not in that teacher's class for more than a few weeks. The frequent embrace of "all student" data is accompanied by sneers and incredulity: "What is there about the word 'all' that you don't understand?" and "Aren't you accountable for *all* of our children?" In fact, our responsibility is to all children, and part of that responsibility is the use of accurate data. Only controls for student mobility provide such accuracy. Properly done, the report will contain one column that includes all students, and a second column that only includes students who were continuously enrolled in the school for at least one year.

In addition to the responsibility for accuracy in reporting (more information on this can be found in Chapter 15), the superintendent bears a responsibility for assessments that accurately reflect the work of teachers throughout the year. While the clarion call for accountability may, in the minds of the public, be equivalent to a recitation of test scores, the superintendent knows better: real accountability is comprehensive, and, as such, includes intermediate indicators and assessments that are more timely, more accurate, more objective, and far more related to the real curriculum than those established by the state. The superintendent thus adds perspective to the accountability and assessment discussion. The "big lie" of school assessment is that there are the "real" assessments—high stakes state tests—and the other assessments, those silly exercises, papers, exams, and projects done by the ne'er-do-well teachers in the classroom. The superintendent reinforces that derogatory stereotype every time the assessment discussion is focused exclusively on a single test instrument. Just as most superintendents would hesitate to equate the success of their leadership with their score on the entrance examination to their graduate school, schools cannot be evaluated with a single number. The leader can either accept or destroy that stereotype.

Results *Plus*

School leaders are fond of focusing on "results" and, thus, it is not surprising that a best-selling book (Schmoker's *Results: The Key to Continuous School Improvement*, 1999), a periodical (National Staff Development Council's *Results*), and numerous columns, articles, products, and books seek to capitalize on this appealing term. While the focus on results is important—indeed, an integral part of effective accountability—there is a trend to superficiality in equating "results" with an annual examination of test scores. Part of the appeal of this path lies in the implication that the rough-and-tumble world of business is focused on results and, thus, effective schools must follow suit. That is a premise that deserves closer examination. When I have had the opportunity to speak to business groups, I frequently ask members of the audience if the stereotypes I have heard about them (often from people purporting to speak for "the business community") are accurate: do they manage for results?

"Preposterous," the real business people reply with one voice. "Of course we want results, but if we looked at our results—sales, expenses, profits, inventories, employee turnover, and so on—the way schools do, we'd be out of business. A focus on results is not an annual snapshot of a financial statement any more than the results of a school are represented in an annual test score. A real focus on results includes the daily grind of analyzing what we're doing, where we're going, and how we can get better. If "results" is an annual score and that were our only focus, we'd be finished."

Careful readers who examine more than the title page of the work from Schmoker and the National Staff Development Council understand that a constructive focus on "results" is not such a superficial analysis. The subtitle of Schmoker's book is revealing in its reference to "continuous improvement." The interval for examination, he argues, is not measured in years, but in days and weeks. Moreover, an examination of the underlying causes of results is critical. The discussion on results provides focus; the substantive follow-up to the discussion is methods—curriculum, time allocation, assessment techniques, student engagement—all the elements that transform good intentions into reality. Although it is less parsimonious than the single word "results," a more appropriate focus for superintendents is the "R" of the S.T.A.R. Leadership model: Results *Plus*. The *Plus* in the phrase includes not only scores, but the strategies for effectiveness, the context, and the "antecedents of excellence" which are at the heart of a comprehensive accountability system.

Conclusion

When educational analysis is reduced to sound bites and headlines in a media war, analytical depth is the first casualty. Accuracy, meaning, and relevance soon join the triage room as the least likely survivors. When the superintendent leads with a commitment to Standards, Tools, Assessment and Accountability, and Results *Plus*, then the tide of battle can be turned. Victory is far from certain, but at least the field is fair and the view is not obscured by superficiality and error.

The superintendent's time is limited and precious. Every investment of time and every decision made have wide-ranging consequences. Use this chart to help the superintendent focus time on those areas most likely to improve student achievement:

S.T.A.R.	Leadership Objective	Information We Have Now	Information We Need for Better Leadership and Policy	Possible Decisions of Superintendent to Improve Achievement and Equity
Standards	Focus and Clarity			
Standards	Move from "Potential Curriculum" to the "Learning Curriculum"			
Tools for Teachers and Leaders	Transformational Professional Development—Focused on Achievement and Student Success			
Tools for Teachers and Leaders	Curriculum That Is Meaningful and Focused			
Tools for Teachers and Leaders	Models of Effective Teaching and Assessment			
Tools for Teachers and Leaders	Collaboration Opportunities for Leaders and Teachers			
Tools for Teachers and Leaders	Central Office Organization and Support for Achievement			

S.T.A.R.	Leadership Objective	Information We Have Now	Information We Need for Better Leadership and Policy	Possible Decisions of Superintendent to Improve Achievement and Equity
Assessment and Accountability	Comprehensive Accountability System			
Assessment and Accountability	Assessments Beyond High-Stakes State Tests That Provide Intermediate Feedback and Constructive Assistance to Students and Teachers			
Results *Plus*	Broad Focus Beyond Test Scores, Including Strategies and "Antecedents of Excellence"			

CHAPTER

State Accountability Systems

The State of State Accountability Systems: Testing *Uber Alles*

When state policy makers utter the phrase "educational accountability," what they really mean is testing—lots of it. As of this printing, 48 states are currently administering statewide tests (Jerald, 2000; Mathers, 1999). Testing sounds tough, but in many instances it is superficial and unrelated to either the curriculum of the schools or the standards that the state espouses. Putting the most charitable construction on the matter, the January 2000 "Quality Counts" report of *Education Week* enthusiastically reported:

> The number of states that administer student assessments matched to their standards in at least one subject climbed from 35 in 1997-98 to 41 this school year. The number of states that test whether students are meeting standards in all four of the key academic subjects rose from 17 to 21 during that period. (p. 63)

Consider this: 49 of the 50 states have adopted standards (the lone resister, Iowa, is not as iconoclastic as it may appear, since every Iowa school district has adopted its own academic content standards); 48 states have statewide testing programs. However, the inference that standards and testing programs comprise accountability is a conclusion that would not sustain the "standards" of logic and reason in any school. Less than half the states have tests linked to four academic content standards. While 37 states offer at least one "performance item," such demands are typically only a fraction of the total test items prescribed by the state.

The gap between nominal accountability and substantive assessment has not stanched the enthusiasm for associating accountability with rewards, punishment, and headlines. Without a hint of irony, political leaders demand from the schools what they dare not require of themselves: a coherent linkage between expectations, performance, and public reporting. Not a single state embraces an accountability system that includes proper cause variables, such as teaching and assessment practices and instruction strategies. If test scores are linked to any "causes," the association is made to demographic characteristics, as if ethnicity and poverty were the "causes" of test scores. Despite the overwhelming evidence that ethnicity,

Accountability in Action

poverty, and other demographic variables are less important than teacher quality and certification (Sanders, 1998; Haycock, 1998; Jerald, 2000), the most frequent effort to "analyze" test scores at the state level is an association between those scores and demographic characteristics. It appears that state policy makers find it more convenient to blame students, parents, and their ancestors than the adults who bear responsibility for certification, teacher quality, curriculum, assessment, and leadership in the schools and districts.

Some states, such as California, provide some flexibility in the accountability system, allowing districts to provide context and explanation. The door is open, however slightly, to a constructive and comprehensive accountability system. Nevertheless, the state reports themselves uniformly rely upon the effects of student achievement rather than the causes. Effective and ineffective accountability systems are analogous to an autopsy or a physical. The autopsy reports how the patient died; the physical helps to provide some understanding about how the patient might improve. At the state level, accountability systems do not even reach the level of autopsy. State accountability reports are, at best, an incomplete death certificate. The litany of standards not met and test scores below expectations are reported; the time and date of the patient death is reported; but the causes are unknown and the opportunities for improvement remain an unwritten mystery, omitted in state reports. The brief analyses that accompany state accountability reports include such astonishing claims that state test scores are a function of student ethnicity (Lawrence, 1999). Scores declined, one analysis claimed, because "minority populations have shown increases" and "78 percent of our fourth graders were Caucasian in 1998 as compared to 82 percent in 1994." It is difficult to put a benign spin on such observations when they are made in this context: "Changing demographics in Utah may provide important information in explaining some of the changes in fourth grade performance." Indeed, the word "may" is the only redeeming feature of this report. The failure to consider teacher qualification, certification, curriculum, leadership, and local assessment practices makes clear that, at the state level at least, accountability is more related to what is easy to measure (skin color) than what is important (teaching, assessment, and leadership).

Unintended Consequences of State Policy

Giving state policy makers the benefit of the doubt, one might assume that the intention of their plunge into testing as a surrogate for accountability is the improvement of student achievement. Texas provides an interesting case study of the law of unintended consequences. Even as students and teachers focus on the state tests, scores on national indicators of student performance have declined (Bracey, 1999).

The most striking example of unintended consequences, however, comes from the state of California. Two initiatives—class size reduction and the imperative for "above average" performance on the Stanford-9 tests—have dominated educational discussions in that state. Class size reduction is a laudable effort, but the shortage of qualified educators has resulted in the expenditure of hundreds of millions of dollars to provide a higher ratio, not of teachers to students, but of people of admirable intent but limited professional qualifications to students. Rather than helping poor children in California, this policy has drastically elevated the percentage of unqualified teachers without certification or preparation serving children in the poorest areas of the state. The focus on the Stanford-9, a multiple choice test, leads California schools to disregard the writing standards of the state that are honored more in the breach than in the observance. In a recent address to a statewide education conference in California, I ran a gauntlet of the sponsors of the event. The vast majority of the sponsors were test-preparation organizations who sell sample test items closely resembling the Stanford-9. None of them promote student writing. The state accountability policy sends bitterly conflicting messages, somewhat like placing the Statue of Liberty with its message of welcome on the California-Mexico border, surrounded by barbed wire and armed guards.

Beyond Test Terror

There is a better way. State governments can move beyond the superficiality of tests and the misleading conclusions and misguided policies that result from an exclusive reliance on tests. While comprehensive accountability systems described in this book are beyond the scope of most state governments, the ideal need not be the enemy of progress. At the very least, state policy makers can consider these modest and balanced proposals for progress:

- Devote no resources of state money, student time, teacher emotion, and systemic stress to any test that does not meet the simple criteria of fairness, clear relationship to state academic standards, and utility by teachers.

- Include in any accountability report causes as well as effects. Such a report of causes must include real causes—such as teacher quality and certification, educational resources, and local curriculum—rather than demonstrably false causes, such as ethnic identity.

- Use accountability as an instrument of information, analysis, and insight, rather than humiliation, embarrassment, and threats.

- Use test scores to diagnose student needs and curriculum deficiencies rather than a means of punishing students who have been systematically denied adequate teaching and curricular resources.

- Use accountability to hold state policy makers, legislators, and executives accountable. Settle for nothing less than a greater number of standards for the adults who created the system than the number of standards for the children who must live with that system.

Conclusion

The 10th Amendment to the United States Constitution provides that those powers not given to the national government are reserved to the states. This is the source of our national tradition of local control of education. It is the states and local school districts—not any other level of government—that will ultimately define what educational accountability really means. Fortunately, states have every incentive to make wise choices. Whether motivated by educational excellence and equity or by the political imperative of conserving taxpayers' money, legislators and governors have much to gain from comprehensive accountability. Citizens and legislators of every political persuasion gain as they become confident that their resources are spent wisely. Chief Executives gain as they improve understanding of the antecedents of excellence. Governors do not raise student achievement with rhetoric and exhortation; they do not improve test scores with threats and intimidation. Governors can, through effective educational strategies informed by comprehensive accountability, influence leadership, teaching practices and resources that, in turn, lead to sustained improvements in student achievement. The vast majority of state accountability efforts are misleading, superficial, and frequently counterproductive. This state of affairs leads to many calls for abandoning even the most reasonable state initiatives. The reasoned middle ground is educational accountability that is fair, comprehensive, meaningful, and useful.

Questions for Discussion

1. Describe your state's educational accountability system.

2. How is the state accountability system enforced? What tests, rewards, and sanctions are linked to the accountability system?

3. What other state incentives for education exist? To what extent are they linked, not linked, or contradictory to the official state accountability system?

CHAPTER

The Accountability Imperative

If two philosophers were to debate whether or not they should be governed by the law of gravity, most people would regard the conversation as the idle speculation of pedants who do not understand that the existence of gravity is not a choice over which we exert any control. When administrators and teachers debate whether to adopt an accountability system, they present the odd spectacle of the futile conversation of philosophers pondering their acceptance of gravity. As the review of state accountability systems makes clear, the choice is not *whether* to have an educational accountability system, but rather what *kind* of accountability system each district will have. Will the superintendent and board accept, by default, the accountability system of the state, with its fragmentary and frequently counter-productive emphasis on a few widely-spaced tests? Or will leaders and policy makers embrace an accountability system that is comprehensive, constructive, and that includes not only the required state tests, but also a host of other assessments, including those at the classroom and building level? Will school leaders accept the fiction that accountability is nothing more than a litany of test scores, or will they search for the antecedents of excellence that give insight into effective strategies? In sum, accountability is not a choice; it is an imperative.

The gulf between the present state of educational accountability and the ideal of comprehensive, fair, and effective systems is wide, but it is not a chasm that defies crossing. Our despair that is created by stultifying tests and counterproductive accountability laws can be tempered by the optimism that is engendered by creative, innovative, and extraordinary educational leaders at the national, state, and local level. Since I began writing this book, I have traveled more than half a million miles, visiting schools throughout the world. In the course of those travels, every stereotype I had was shattered, every preconception challenged. Despite my optimistic nature and search for the silver lining in every cloud, the continuing theme of these travels and the research that accompanied my visits was clear: accountability systems throughout the nation are poorly developed, frequently destructive, and often counterproductive. The trend toward more standards and testing are associated with the term "accountability," but legislative and administrative policies fall far short of the legitimate intent of board members, governors, and legislators.

Rather than close this book with a Jeremiad, lamenting the failures of prevailing educational accountability systems, I shall leave these pages with images of hope. Some of these images are national figures, others are largely unknown outside of

Accountability in Action

their communities. All of them provide a glimpse of the future of educational accountability as a force for progress rather than a source of terror, a method of improvement rather than a ploy for politics, a source of insight rather than a fountain of contempt. The models, from national organizations to classroom teachers, form the foundation for effective educational accountability of the future.

- Kati Haycock and her colleagues at the Education Trust have marshaled impressive evidence that children of poverty are not to blame for their educational condition. With cold statistics, political courage, and deep conviction, Haycock and the Education Trust challenge liberals and conservatives, defenders and critics of the educational establishment, teachers and parents, professors and students. Defying simplistic solutions, the Trust offers free and abundant information to any policy maker and leader willing to read it on their web site, www.edtrust.org. Accountability is not a mundane policy matter, but the source of rich research and profound insights.

- Barbara Horton was instrumental in the formation of the accountability system of Milwaukee Public Schools in 1995 and 1996. Her leadership, dynamism and steadfast courage laid the groundwork for the 90/90/90 Schools, where poverty, minority enrollment, and high achievement consistently coexist. Journalists and casual observers who elevate prejudgment over evidence and claim that poor and minority children are incapable of superior achievement must take their case to Ms. Horton's court. After leading one of the nation's largest school systems, Ms. Horton turned her leadership attention to the creation of a small school supported by her church serving some of her city's most disadvantaged students. Leadership, she teaches us, is not a function of the size of the organization, but the commitment of the leader's heart. Accountability is a way of life, not a bureaucratic nuisance.

- Dan Lawson leads one of the most troubled groups of schools in one of the nation's most troubled school systems—Los Angeles Unified School District. Dr. Lawson is a career administrator who routinely works with students, examines student work, attends professional development programs, and provides unending encouragement to the champion educators and administrators that he serves. While other California leaders stared with bewilderment at the array of legislative mandates stemming from the capital, Dan gave focus, clarity, and leadership to the efforts of his school to improve achievement. While none of the children in his district have won the lottery or changed their ethnicity, a very large number of them have improved their academic achievement. Accountability is not a threat in Dr. Lawson's schools; it is a tool used to improve student learning.

- Joyce Bales suffers from a peculiar brand of myopia—she is unable to see the disadvantages the others have historically used to create convenient stereotypes for the students she serves in Southeast Colorado. She is unwilling to hear history as an excuse. She is constitutionally prevented from seeing the first effort of a student, teacher, or school as its last effort. Students in her district, rich in Latino heritage and challenged by economic disadvantage, consistently perform at a higher level than suburban districts in her state that have neither ethnic diversity nor economic challenge. Dr. Bales shares her insights not only with the district that she leads, but with a new generation of teacher education students at the University of Southern Colorado. For her, accountability is a source of encouragement and sustenance, not an impediment or a threat.

- Chris Wright is too impatient to wait for the state accountability report. If the purpose of accountability is to improve student achievement, Dr. Wright reasons, we had better get the information in a timely and accurate manner. She gathers accountability data from classrooms and schools every month, using it not as a source of humiliation and embarrassment but as a source of celebration, peace, and progress. She knows that children are not defined by last year's test scores, but that they are improving by the day.

- Tim McElhatton works in a research department, providing data not only for board reports and administrative documents, but information to support individual principals and teachers. As with most central office employees, he rarely receives recognition or credit. Nevertheless, his efforts link accountability with impact. He provides credibility, fairness, common sense, and good judgment in an environment that is too frequently plagued by politics and suspicion.

- Terry Thompson uses accountability information not only to improve school and district policies, but also to improve the lives of individual students. Recognizing that there are no quick fixes for students who are years behind their peers in reading, he provides one of the most extensive and effective intervention programs in the nation. Rather than intermittent pullout programs, students receive a year or more of assistance with reading and mathematics at the secondary level. Dr. Thompson accepts the political grief that accompanies tough choices, but stands fast in pursuit of the principle that accountability information is of little value if it is not used to help the children he serves.

- Ray Simon leads a state department of education that offers some of the nation's most challenging, innovative, and comprehensive reforms. His results speak for themselves, with schools from the Arkansas Delta to the Ozarks, from the most complex urban areas to the most remote rural schools achieving extraordinary results and consistent improvement. Mr. Simon's colleagues will not tolerate accountability as a mystery laden with bureaucratic obfuscation. From his "refrigerator curriculum" to his common sense approach to accountability and assessment, he brings political leaders, parents, teachers, and school administrators together in a common commitment to success.

These everyday heroes are the future of effective educational accountability. Though they represent vastly different political viewpoints and professional backgrounds, these women and men share a common commitment to excellence. Although the brief stories shared here are a fraction of the ordinary heroics of policy makers, leaders, and teachers, the stories are elusive. Headlines are more likely to be dominated by our failures than our successes. At The Leadership and Learning Center, we will continue to identify, document, and share the best models of educational accountability and assessment. Readers are invited to share their insights, stories, and vignettes of success through the Center's web site at . www.LeadandLearn.com. Assessments, research, and accountability information can be downloaded without cost. Readers without Internet access can get the same documents free of charge by calling (866) 399-6019.

None of the educational heroes described in this chapter follow a cookie-cutter approach to accountability. None of them share a common job description, legislative burden, or testing regime. What they have in common, however, is far more important than their differences. All of them have in common a commitment to fairness, accuracy, and comprehensiveness in their views of accountability. Most importantly, all of them have transformed educational accountability into a force for improved student achievement. They realize the central purpose of this enterprise is neither a bureaucratic mandate nor a political agenda, but the compelling imperative of improved student learning.

References

Alaska Department of Education and Early Development. (1997). *Standards for Alaska's Administrators*. [Brochure]. Juneau, AK: Author.

Alaska Department of Education and Early Development. (1997). *Standards for Alaska's Teachers*. [Brochure]. Juneau, AK: Author.

Benjamin, G.R. (1998). *Japanese Lessons: A Year in a Japanese High School Through the Eyes of an American Anthropologist and Her Children*. New York, NY: NYU Press.

Berliner, D.C. & Biddle, B.J. (1996). *The Manufactured Crisis: Myths, Fraud, and the Attack on America's Public Schools*. Reading, MA: Addison-Wesley Publishing Company.

Blackford, L.B. (1999, December 8). Education Secretary Lauds Kentucky School Reform. Lexington Herald-Leader. [On line] Available: www.kentuckyconnect.com/heraldleader/news/120899/statedocs/08rileybox.htm.

Bracey, G. (1998, October). The Eighth Bracey Report on the Condition of Public Education. *Phi Delta Kappan*, *80* (2), 112-131.

Bracey, G. (1999, October). The Ninth Bracey Report on the Condition of Public Education. *Phi Delta Kappan*, *81* (2), 147-168.

Brown, F. (1999, December 9). Owens: Shut Worst Schools, Require Tests. *The Denver Post*. [On line] Available: www.denverpost.com/news/news1209a.htm.

Bruinius, H. (1999, December 14). School Cheating Up as Stakes Rise. *The Christian Science Monitor*. [On line] Available: www.csmonitor.com.

Bryant, A., Seamon, H., Bushweller, K., Hardy, L., & Zakariya, S.B. (Eds.). (1998, December). School Leaders Focus on Standards and Achievement. *The American School Board Journal*, *185*(12), A13-15.

Bryant, A., Seamon, H., Bushweller, K., Hardy, L., & Zakariya, S.B. (Eds.). (1998, December). Education Vital Signs. *The American School Board Journal*, *185*(12), A22-27.

Buchbinder, J. (1999, November/December). The Arts Step Out from the Wings. *Harvard Education Letter*, *15*(6).

Carter, S. C. (1999). *No Excuses: Seven Principals of Low-Income Schools Who Set the Standard for High Achievement*. Washington, D.C.: The Heritage Foundation.

Chawla, S. & Renesch, J. (Eds.). (1995). *Learning Organizations: Developing Cultures for Tomorrow's Workplace*. Portland, OR: Productivity Press.

The Christian Science Monitor (1999, December 10). How to Use School Tests. *The Christian Science Monitor* [On line] Available: www.csmonitor.com/durable.1999/12/10/p10s2.htm.

Colorado Department of Education. (1999, September). Accountability in Colorado Education. *Colorado Department of Education* [On line]. Available: www.cde.state.co.us/cdeedserv/account.htm.

Council of Chief State School Officers. (1999, April 1). *State Educational Accountability Systems: Alabama*. Washington, D.C.: Author.

Council of Chief State School Officers. (1999, April 1). *State Educational Accountability Systems: Connecticut*. Washington, D.C.: Author.

Daley, B. & Vigue, D.I. (1999, December 8). Some School Districts Surge in Test Results. *The Boston Globe*.

Darling-Hammond, L. (1997). *The Right to Learn*. San Francisco, CA: Jossey-Bass.

Darling-Hammond, L. & Sykes, G. (Eds.). (1998). *Teaching as the Learning Profession: Handbook of Policy and Procedure*. San Francisco, CA: Jossey-Bass.

Drummond, S. (Ed.). (1999, January). Quality Counts '99 [Special Issue]. *Education Week, 18*(17).

Edwards, V.B. (Ed.). (1999, January 11). Quality Counts '99: Rewarding Results, Punishing Failure. *Education Week, 18*(17).

Englekemeyer, S.W. & Brown, S.C. (1998, October). Powerful Partnerships: A Shared Responsibility for Learning. *AAHE Bulletin, 51*(2), 10-12.

FairTest Examiner. (1998, Spring). Weak Tests Drive Math, Science Curricula, *FairTest Examiner, 12*(2).

Ferguson, R.F. (1991). Paying for Public Education: New Evidence on How and Why Money Matters. *Harvard Journal on Legislation, 28*, 465-498.

Finn, C.E., Jr., Petrilli, M.J., & Vanourek, G. (1998, July). The State of State Standards. *Fordham Report, 2*(5).

Flexner, S.B. (Ed.). (1987). *The Random House Dictionary of the English Language*. (2nd Ed.). New York, NY: Random House.

Foersterling, F. & Morgenstern, M. (2002). Accuracy of self-assessment and task performance: Does it pay to know the truth? *Journal of Educational Psychology, 94(3),* 576-585

French, D. (1998, November). The State's Role in Shaping a Progressive Vision of Public Education. *Phi Delta Kappan, 80*(3), 184-194.

Gerstner, L.V. (2000, January 3). Don't Dumb Down Educational Standards. *USA Today,* p 19A.

Gonzales, R. (2000, January). IPAS Fills a Variety of Assessment Needs. *Focus on Achievement, 1*(1), 2.

Goodlad, J.I. (1994). *Educational Renewal: Better Teachers, Better Schools.* San Francisco, CA: Jossey-Bass.

Goodlad, J.I. (1991). *A Place Called School: Prospects for the Future.* New York, NY: McGraw-Hill.

Groves, M. & Colvin, R.L. (1999, December 10). High School Exit Exam for State Hits Roadblock. *Los Angeles Times* [On line] Available: www.latimes.com/archives.

Guskey, T.R. (1999). *Evaluating Professional Development.* Thousand Oaks, CA: Corwin Press.

Harrington-Lucker, D. (1998, June). States Raise the Bar. *American School Board Journal, 185*(6), 16-21.

Haycock, K. (1998). *Dispelling the Myth.* Washington, D.C.: The Education Trust.

Haycock, K. (1998, Summer). Good Teaching Matters: How Well-Qualified Teachers Can Close the Gap. *Thinking K-16, A Publication of The Education Trust, 3*(2), 1-16.

Haycock, K. (2001). *Dispelling the Myth, Revisited.* Washington, D.C.: The Education Trust.

Haycock, K., Barth, P., Jackson, H., Mora, K., Ruiz, P., Robinson, S., & Wilkins, A. (Eds.). (1999). *Dispelling the Myth: High Poverty Schools Exceeding Expectations.* Washington, D.C.: The Education Trust.

Henry, T. (2000, January 26). Superintendents in Demand: Schools Struggling with Loss of Leadership from the Top. *USA Today,* p 1A.

Herrnstein, R.J. & Murray, C. (1994). *The Bell Curve: Intelligence and Class Structure in American Life.* New York, NY: The Free Press.

Hirsch, E.D., Jr. (1996). *The Schools We Need: And Why We Don't Have Them.* New York, NY: Doubleday.

Howard, R. (Ed.). (1993). *The Learning Imperative: Managing People for Continuous Innovation.* Boston, MA: Harvard Business School Publishing Corp.

Jerald, C.D. (2000, January 19). The State of the States. *Education Week, 19* (19), 22.

Jones, R. (1998, April). What Works? *The American School Board Journal, 185*(4), 28-32.

Klentschy, M., Garrison, L., & Amaral, O. (2000). Valle Imperale Project in Science (VIPS), National Science Foundation Grant #ESI-9731274

Kohn, A. (1999). *The Schools Our Children Deserve: Moving Beyond Traditional Classrooms and "Tougher Standards."* Boston, MA: Houghton Mifflin.

Ladd, H.F. (Ed.). (1996). *Holding Schools Accountable: Performance-based Reform in Education.* Washington, D.C.: The Brookings Institution.

Lawrence, B.J. (1999). *Performance of Utah Fourth and Eighth Grade Students in the 1998 National Assessment of Reading.* Utah State Office of Education.

Linton Professional Development Corporation. (Producer and Director). (1998a). *Standards that Work, Volume 802.* [Videotape]. (Available from The LPD Video Journal of Education; Salt Lake City, UT; 1-800-572-1153; Facsimile—1-888-566-6888; Web site—www.teachstream.com/index.jsp)

Linton Professional Development Corporation. (Producer and Director). (1998b). *Assessments and Scoring Guides Based on Standards, Volume 803.* [Videotape.] (Available from The LPD Video Journal of Education)

Marzano, R.J (2003). *What Works in Schools: Translating Research into Action.* Alexandria, VA: ASCD.

Marzano, R.J. & Kendall, J.S. (1996). *Designing Standards-based Districts, Schools, and Classrooms.* Alexandria, VA: Association for Supervision and Curriculum Development.

Marzano, R.J & Kendall, J.S. (1999, January). *Awash in a Sea of Standards.* Aurora, CO: Mid-continent Regional Educational Laboratory.

Marzano, R.J., Pollock, J.E., & Pickering, D.J. (2001). *Classroom Instruction that Works*. Alexandria, VA: ASCD.

Mathers, J.K. (1999). *Education Accountability Systems in 50 States*. Denver, CO: Education Commission of the States.

Merriam Webster's Collegiate Dictionary. (10th ed.) (1998). Springfield, MA: Merriam Webster.

Milwaukee Public Schools. (1998). *1997-98 Accountability Report*. Milwaukee, WI: Author.

Mitchell, R. (1992). *Testing for Learning: How New Approaches to Evaluation Can Improve American Schools*. New York, NY: The Free Press.

Murphy Commission Education Workgroup. (1998). *Arkansas' Public Schools...A Thirty Year $20 Billion Taxpayer Investment Yields an Unprecedented Crisis in Academic Performance*. Little Rock, AR: The Murphy Commission: An Arkansas Policy Foundation Initiative.

Murphy, J. & Schiller, J. (1992). *Transforming America's Schools: An Administrator's Call to Action*. Chicago, IL: Open Court Publications.

Murray, D. & Herrnstein, R. (1994). *The Bell Curve*. New York: Simon & Schuster.

Neill, M. (1998, Winter). High-Stakes Tests Do Not Improve Student Learning. *FairTest Examiner*, *12*, (1).

Neill, M. (1998, Winter). Assessment in Milwaukee Public Schools. *FairTest Examiner*, *12*(1).

Neill, M. (1998, Winter). Test Scores Do Not Equal Merit: Executive Summary. *FairTest Examiner*, *12*(1).

Ohanian, S. (1999). *One Size Fits Few: The Folly of Educational Standards*. New York, NY: Heinemann.

Orwell, G. (1949). *Nineteen Eighty-four*. New York, NY: Harcourt, Brace.

Perkins, D. (1992). *Smart Schools: Better Thinking and Learning for Every Child*. New York, NY: The Free Press.

Perkins, D. (1995). *Outsmarting IQ: The Emerging Science of Learnable Intelligence*. New York, NY: Free Press.

Peters, T. & Waterman, R.H. (1982). *In Search of Excellence*. New York: Warner Business.

Peters, T. & Waterman, R.H. (1988). *In Search of Excellence: Lessons from America's Best-run Companies*. New York, NY: Warner Books.

Popham, W.J. (1997, September). The Standards Movement and the Emperor's New Clothes. *NASSP Bulletin, 81*(590).

Popham, W.J. (1999, March). Why Standardized Tests Don't Measure Educational Quality. *Educational Leadership, 56*(6), 8-15.

Potter, E.C. (Ed.). (1998, April). Arts Education: The New Basic. *NASSP Bulletin, (82)*.

Public Schools Accountability Act of 1999, 1999 California State Legislature. Chapter 3, Sections 52050-52058 (1999).

Reeves, D.B. (1997). *Making Standards Work: How To Implement Standards-Based Assessments in the Classroom, School, and District*. Denver, CO: Advanced Learning Centers.

Reeves, D.B. (1997, June). Defending Performance Assessment Without Being Defensive. *School Administrator Magazine, 54*(6), 35-36.

Reeves, D.B. (1998, January/February). Practical Performance Assessment for Busy Teachers. *Learning Magazine, 26*(4), 58-60.

Reeves, D.B. (1998, March). Responding to the Rhetoric of the Radical Right. *School Administrator Magazine, 55*(3), 37.

Reeves, D.B. (1998, October). Holding Principals Accountable: Seven Considerations For Effectively Evaluating Your Site Administrators. *School Administrator Magazine, 55*(9), 6-12.

Reeves, D.B. (1999). *The 90/90/90 Schools: High Poverty, High Minority Enrollment, AND High Achievement*. [Conference Handout] Denver, CO: The Leadership and Learning Center.

Reeves, D. B. (2000, March/April). Effective Accountability: Clear Answers for Common Sense Questions. *Thrust for Educational Leadership, 129*(4).

Reeves, D.B. (2000, December). *Accountability in Action: A Blueprint for Learning Organizations*. Denver, CO: Advanced Learning Press.

Reeves, D.B. (2001). *Holistic Accountability: Serving Students, Schools, and Community*. Thousand Oaks, California: Corwin Press.

Rothman, R. (1995). *Measuring Up: Standards, Assessment, and School Reform.* San Francisco, CA: Jossey-Bass.

Sanders, W.L. (1998, December). Value-Added Assessment. *AASA School Administrator, 55*(11).

Scherer, M.M. (Ed.). (1999, March). Using Standards and Assessments. *Educational Leadership, 56*(6).

Schmoker, M. & Marzano, R.J. (1999, March). Realizing the Promise of Standards-based Education. *Educational Leadership, 56*(6), 17-21.

Schmoker, M.J. (1999). *Results: The Key to Continuous School Improvement.* (2nd ed.) Alexandria, VA: Association for Supervision and Curriculum Development.

Schmoker, M. (2001). *The Results Fieldbook.* Alexandria, Virginia: Association for Supervision and Curriculum Development (ASCD).

Schulte, B. (1999, December 15). Kindergarten Gets Tougher. *The Washington Post.*

Simpson, J.O. (2003, January). Beating the odds. *American School Board Journal, 190*, 43-47.

Simpson, J.A. & Weiner, E.S. (Eds.). (1989). *Oxford English Dictionary* (2nd Ed.). Oxford: Clarendon Press.

Slavin, R.E. & Olatokunbo, S.F. (1998). *Show Me the Evidence!: Proven and Promising Programs for America's Schools.* Thousand Oaks, CA: Corwin Press.

Slavin, R.E. (1994). *Educational Psychology: Theory and Practice.* (4th ed.). Needham Heights, MA: Allyn & Bacon.

Slavin, R.E. (1997, December/ 1998, January). Can Education Reduce Social Inequity? *Educational Leadership, 5*(4), 6-12.

Strong, R., Silver, H. & Perini, M. (1999, March). Simple and Deep: What Do Japanese Haiku Have To Do With Innovative School Reform? More Than You Might Think. *Educational Leadership, 56*(6), 22-24.

Sykes, C.J. (1995). *Dumbing Down Our Kids: Why American Children Feel Good About Themselves But Can't Read, Write, or Add.* New York, NY: St. Martin's Press.

Tucker, M.S. & Coddings, J.B. (1998). *Standards For Our Schools: How to Set Them, Measure Them, and Reach Them.* San Francisco, CA: Jossey-Bass.

Van Dunk, E. (1998, February). *Choice School Accountability: A Consensus of Views in Ohio and Wisconsin.* Milwaukee, WI: Public Policy Forum.

Varner, L.K. (1999, December 14). Minorities Seek Better Access to Advanced Classes in Schools. *Seattle Times.* [On line] Available: www.seattletimes.com/news/local/html98/altskul_19991214.html.

Washburn, K. & Thornton, J. (Eds.) (1996). *Dumbing Down: Essays on the Strip-mining of American Culture.* New York, NY: W.W. Norton & Company.

Wiggins, G. (1998). *Educative Assessment.* San Francisco, CA: Jossey-Bass.

Wiggins, G. & McTighe, J. (1998). *Understanding by Design.* Alexandria, VA: Association for Supervision and Curriculum Development.

Williams, J. (1999, December 8). Promotion Policy Has Some Kids Scrambling. *Milwaukee Journal Sentinel.* [On line] Available: www.jsonline.com/news/metro/dec99/mps08120899a.asp.

Wong, H.K. (1999, April). *There Is Only One Way to Improve Student Achievement.* Paper prepared for the National Conference on Urban Education, Jersey City, NJ.

Woolfolk, A.E. (1995). *Educational Psychology.* (6th ed.). Needham Heights, MA: Allyn & Bacon.

Appendices

A P P E N D I X

Template for Accountability System Design

Comprehensive Accountability System
Your State, District, or System
Date

Template for Accountability System Design

Descriptions of Major Headings

1.0 Executive Summary

The Executive Summary provides an overview of the comprehensive accountability system. Included in this section is a brief description of the purposes, benefits, and audience for the accountability system, as well as information about tests and other measures used. The summary also includes an explanation of Tier 1, Tier 2, and Tier 3 indicators. Historical information about how accountability evolved in your state or system, including explanations of any task forces or committees that helped put the system into place, may also be included in the executive summary.

2.0 State, System, or District Accountability Structure

2.1 Introduction—Includes a more detailed description of the overall accountability system and the point system used for rewards or sanctions.

2.2 State, System, or District-wide Expectations—Delineates the state, system, or district expectations adopted for all students: achievement, graduation rates, attendance rates, teacher certification, and/or other factors that have been mandated. These expectations may be spelled out in public law, by school board mandate, or by other official sanction.

2.3 State, System, or District-level Indicators (Tier 1)—Lists and describes the specific indicators used to assess whether or not state, system, or district expectations have been achieved. These are Tier I indicators. A chart or table may also be included to provide a visual summary of information included in this section.

2.4 School-selected Indicators (Tier 2)—Describes and gives examples of how schools select Tier II indicators either for an entire school or for specific populations within schools. Information about a menu system for selecting Tier II indicators (if one is used) is included in this section.

2.5 School Narratives (Tier 3)—Explains the narrative section of the accountability system. This section includes information about the length of the narrative as well as general guidelines for what kind of information should be addressed.

3.0 School Performance Report

3.1 <u>Introduction</u>—Describes the length and scope of any school performance reports or "report cards" that the accountability system will create. Such reports are prepared for and distributed to interested parties in order to inform them about individual school results. A brief description of what kinds of data will be used, what kinds of comparisons will be made, and what measures will serve as baseline data is included.

3.2 <u>Evaluating Progress, Tier I Indicators</u>—Details how school progress on Tier I indicators will be measured, as well as which student populations will be included in or excluded from such measures. A chart or table may also be included to provide a visual summary of information included in this section.

3.3 <u>Evaluating Progress, Tier II Indicators</u>—Explains how school progress on Tier II indicators will be measured. A chart or table may also be included to provide a visual summary of information included in this section.

4.0 Professional Development Plan

4.1 <u>Introduction</u>—Provides an overview of the kinds of professional development that will be put in place for accountability system users.

4.2 <u>Teacher Development</u>—Focuses on any specific professional development for teachers that will help them understand and use the accountability system to improve classroom teaching and learning.

4.3 <u>District-sponsored Staff Development for Principals and Staff</u>—Describes any specific district-sponsored professional development for administrators and staff members that will help them understand and use the accountability system.

4.4 <u>State or System Staff Development</u>—Outlines the professional development opportunities offered to familiarize state or system personnel with the accountability system.

5.0 Communication Plan

5.1 <u>Introduction</u>—Describes how accountability system results will be communicated to various stakeholders.

5.2 <u>School Report</u>—Explains who is responsible for preparing the school portion of the accountability report and how these results will be communicated to administrators, teachers, students, parents, and others.

5.3 <u>Community Report</u>—Details who will prepare an accountability report for the larger community, what should be included in this report, and how this information will be communicated to the media, community and business members, and others. In some cases, the school report may also serve as the community report.

5.4 <u>State or System Report</u>—Explains who will prepare an accountability report for individuals at the state or system level. Guidelines for what should be included in such a report, as well as how this information will be disseminated is included in this section.

5.5 <u>Policy Recommendations</u>—Describes how, to whom, and by whom policy recommendations based on accountability system information will be developed and disseminated.

6.0 Rewards and Sanctions

6.1 <u>Introduction</u>—Contains an overview of how schools and/or school districts will be rewarded for improvement and what steps will be taken to help under-performing schools.

6.2 <u>System, District, or other Incentives</u>—Outlines in more specific detail the system, district, or other incentives that have been put in place to recognize school improvement or to sanction under-performing schools. A chart or table may also be included to provide a visual summary of information included in this section.

6.3 <u>Relief from Sanctions</u>—Specifies what steps under-performing schools need to take in order to get relief from sanctions.

7.0 Timeline

The timeline is a document used for internal purposes. It divides accountability system design into steps and/or phases. The timeline maps out which system design activities will be undertaken, the date by which they will be completed, and the person responsible for completing them.

APPENDIX

Sample Accountability Reports

There are several components that should be included in a comprehensive accountability report. Once you have an accountability system in place, creating the report is as simple as assessing the progress made toward all of your indicators and then reporting that progress. However, it may be helpful to work from an existing structure or example. The following pages provide examples of the components and a framework for the reports.

The information in these sample reports is taken from actual schools and assimilated to form a comprehensive report. As such, they should not be taken as prototypes for the "perfect" report. Instead, they are intended to provide an example of how these schools blended qualitative and quantitative indicators to provide useful, concise information for their stakeholders and decision makers.

Although the design of educational accountability systems may vary from one locale to the next, every effective system contains several key components. The theme of effective accountability system design is clear: accountability is more than test scores! An effective accountability system should have five elements: system-wide indicators, school-based indicators, demographic information, qualitative descriptions of the school environment, and clear guidance about the application of data (see Chapter 11 for an in-depth discussion of each of these topics).

The purpose of the accountability report is to provide useful information in these areas to assess performance and to make decisions based on data. Based on the system established, the report should clearly communicate to all educational stakeholders the progress of the students, schools, and district.

An effective framework for a comprehensive accountability system involves three tiers.

- Tier 1 is made up of system-wide indicators

- Tier 2 consists of school-based indicators

- Tier 3 is a narrative description of the schools' successes and challenges

The Tier 1 and Tier 2 data must have clear and understandable explanations for the numbers reported. Test scores should include information about how the tests are scored and when the tests are administered—both grade level and time of year. In addition, the report should include demographic and statistical data by school, such as enrollment, and a breakdown by ethnicity, socioeconomic level, etc.

An essential element of a comprehensive accountability report is the narrative description in Tier 3. Many schools and school systems include numbers and statistics, but few think to provide a context for those numbers. Including a narrative in your report provides your readers with the background information they need to interpret the numbers.

The following sample accountability reports include one for each school level: elementary school, middle school, and high school. Notice that although each report is made at the school level, each school's progress toward system-wide indicators is reported.

Wellington Elementary School

Annual Accountability Report
June 1999

General Information

Address . . . . 1495 S. 3rd St.

Phone 487-8723

Principal . . . . Thomas Greene

Enrollment

Total 365

Kindergarten 65

1st grade 67

2nd grade 54

3rd grade 59

4th grade 62

5th grade 58

Demographics

Female 53%

Male 47%

African American 74%

Hispanic 2%

White 24%

Regular Education 91%

Special Education 9%

LEP 0%

Free/Reduced Lunch 49%

System-wide Indicators (Tier 1)

Indicator	System Goal	System Score 98-99	School Score 97-98	School Score 98-99	% Change
% of students who scored proficient or higher on State Criterion-Referenced Test in Reading	80%	74%	68%	72%	5.8%
% of students who scored proficient or higher on State Criterion-Referenced Test in Mathematics	55%	52%	40%	50%	25%
% of students with attendance rates of 90% or higher	85%	87%	84%	76%	–9.5%
% of students who have been in school since September 1998 who scored proficient or higher on district fourth-grade, 4-point scoring guide for writing	80%	71%	62%	64%	3%
% of African-American students who perform at or above their grade level in reading	85%	70%	66%	75%	13.6%

System score = average of all elementary schools

Wellington Elementary School

Annual Accountability Report
June 1999, Page 2

School-Based Indicators (Tier 2)

Indicator	School Score 97-98	School Score 98-99	% Change
Increase number of parent volunteer hours	652 hours	704 hours	7.9%
Increase number of community service projects undertaken by the school	3 projects	5 projects	66%
Increase number of computers available for student use at all grade levels	30 computers	40 computers	33%
Increase number of students who participate in school-sponsored conflict resolution/reduction workshops	142 students	204 students	43%
Increase the number of students performing at or above expected grade level or age on a teacher-made language arts assessment	165 students	212 students	28%
Increase the number of students who read 8 books and share something they learned orally, artistically, musically, or by doing multi-media presentation	60 students	134 students	123%
Increase the number of writing samples scored by someone other than the student's classroom teacher	56 writing samples	115 writing samples	105%

School Narrative (Tier 3)

The 1998-1999 school year was a success in many respects for Wellington Elementary. The school was also presented with some challenges. Our academic performance based on the state fourth grade test improved in the areas of reading and math.

- Reading—A new reading program was implemented during the 1998-99 school year in the third and fourth grades. Every student in the third and fourth grades participated in this program for approximately 5 hours per week from January through May 1999. In this program, teacher-made performance assessments for reading were given every two weeks. These assessments included multiple methods of demonstrating learning.

- Mathematics—Wellington began an intervention program for students with low performance in mathematics. The students attended tutor sessions with a certified teacher for 45 minutes once a week. In addition, the new computers we received gave more students the opportunity to practice their math skills on the *Math Lab* program. The program was so much fun that the students were asking to practice on it during the lunch period.

- <u>Parent involvement</u>—Parents were encouraged to participate in many activities. The fourth and fifth grade teachers held a special night for student arts and crafts with help from many parents. The Parent Teacher Association at Wellington held two fundraisers this year to raise money for the resource center. Our school is attempting to improve the attendance rates by increasing parent involvement.

- <u>Conflict resolution</u>—We hired a new school counselor this year, Dr. Marcia Wembley, who organized weekly conflict resolution workshops. Students were required to attend their first workshop, and subsequent participation was on a volunteer basis. Our hope is that this will help them grow into better and more peaceful citizens.

- <u>Writing</u>—Our teachers came to consensus on what proficiency is for writing at the 3rd, 4th, and 5th grade levels. During a staff meeting in March, teachers traded student writing samples to score based on the district's 4-point scoring guide for writing.

Greenleaf Middle School

Annual Accountability Report
June 1999

General Information

Address . . . . 132 Schoolhouse Way

Phone 486-0846

Principal . . . . Sharon Mozier Jones

Enrollment

Total 813

6th grade 265

7th grade 301

8th grade 247

Demographics

Female 54%

Male 46%

African American 36%

Native American 2%

Hispanic 14%

White 48%

Regular Education 86%

Special Education 11%

LEP 3%

Free/Reduced Lunch 43%

System-wide Indicators (Tier 1)

Indicator	System Goal	System Score 98-99	School Score 97-98	School Score 98-99	% Change
% of students who scored proficient or higher on Grade 8 State Criterion-Referenced Test in Language Arts (Number of students tested = 254)	65%	42%	45%	41%	−8.9%
% of students who scored proficient or higher on Grade 8 State Criterion-Referenced Test in Mathematics (Number of students tested = 241)	40%	43%	35%	41%	17%
% of students who scored proficient or higher on Grade 7 State Criterion-Referenced Test in Science (Number of students tested = 201)	50%	58%	60%	62%	3.3%
% of students with attendance rates of 90% or higher	85%	83%	89%	92%	3.4%

Greenleaf Middle School

Annual Accountability Report
June 1999, Page 2

School-Based Indicators (Tier 2)

Indicator	School Score 97-98	School Score 98-99	% Change
Increase the percentage of students who meet or exceed the district standard on the district writing performance assessment	52%	45%	–13.5%
Increase the percentage of students directly involved in the performing arts	10%	15%	50%
Increase the percentage of parents who attend parent-teacher conferences	46%	42%	–8.7%
Reduce to zero the number of incidents involving violence, drugs, alcohol, and gangs	18 incidents	14 incidents	–22%
Increase the percentage of middle-school trained and licensed teachers	47%	62%	31%
Increase the percentage of students who engage in direct interaction with community/business partners on science projects	13%	25%	92%
Increase the percentage of students enrolled in pre-algebra and/or algebra courses	26%	31%	19%

School Narrative (Tier 3)

I am proud to report that the 1998-99 school year was a very good one for Greenleaf Middle School.

- Our increase in proficient or higher State Math scores is due in part to the hiring of two teachers, Mr. Ludwig and Mrs. Ramirez, who are licensed in teaching mathematics at the middle school level. Their understanding of their field and patience with their students made a huge difference in the students' understanding of and enthusiasm for math.

- I cannot, unfortunately, report such good scores in state and district language arts. Last year, we agreed to get rid of our existing language program, *Language is Power*, in favor of a new one, *Newman's Reading and Writing*. I fear that the decision was not the wisest, as the new program did not aid the children in understanding the material as well as they have in past years. We will look again for a new program this summer.

- With regard to the decrease in parents attending parent teacher conferences, a change of staff in our main office caused several notices for said conferences not to be mailed. As a result, fewer parents were informed of the fall conferences this year than last year. We have agreed to monitor the main office more closely and to aim for lower personnel turnover in the future.

- While violence and substance abuse were down this year from last, none of us can let down our guard. I believe that part of the decrease has to do with a particularly troublesome group of eighth graders who left after the 97-98 school year to go to high school.

- We added a new music teacher to the department this year, Miss Long, whose expertise in and enthusiasm for jazz is contagious. After her choir's first in-school performance, students lined up to ask to participate in her after-school choir.

Bainbridge High School

Annual Accountability Report
June 1999

General Information

Address . . . . 2636 Foundation Rd.

Phone 485-9673

Principal . . . . Jeanine Howard

Enrollment

Total 1,758

9th grade 512

10th grade 478

11th grade 416

12th grade 352

Demographics

Female 49%

Male 51%

African American 58%

Native American 3%

Hispanic 8%

White 31%

Regular Education 89%

Special Education 7%

LEP 4%

System-wide Indicators (Tier 1)

Indicator	System Goal	System Score 98-99	School Score 97-98	School Score 98-99	% Change
% of students who scored proficient or higher on 10th grade State Criterion-Referenced Test in Language Arts	80%	67%	72%	70%	−2.8%
% of students who scored proficient or higher on 10th grade State Criterion-Referenced Test in Mathematics	70%	65%	64%	72%	12.5%
% of students who scored proficient or higher on State Criterion-Referenced Test in Science	65%	66%	57%	67%	17.5%
% of students with attendance rates of 90% or higher	75%	72%	74%	73%	−1.4%
Percentage of 9th grade students meeting Algebra requirements	80%	67%	56%	61%	9%

Bainbridge High School

School-Based Indicators (Tier 2)

Indicator	School Score 97-98	School Score 98-99	% Change
Increase the number of career-oriented projects and activities	9	15	66%
Increase the percentage of students who successfully meet standards in college preparatory classes based on standards-based performance assessments	30%	35%	16%
Increase the percentage of students who pass the High School Competency Examination required for graduation on the first trial	46%	52%	13%
Increase the percentage of high school graduates who enroll in a four-year college or university	33%	43%	30%
Decrease the number of violent incidents in the school	39	30	–23%
Increase the percentage of students who score proficient or higher in writing, as demonstrated by student portfolios	65%	70%	7.7%

School Narrative (Tier 3)

Overall, the 1998-99 school year was one of great academic progress for Bainbridge High School. Many of our school-based indicators were structured so that, once met successfully, they helped us achieve other indicators. An excellent example of this was our goal for more students to meet standards in the college prep classes. A change in personnel and curriculum seemed to help, as did making some of the study guides and materials available online. And since these classes were mainly math and science oriented, students who had taken them did better on the state test in those subjects.

I believe that the college prep courses also helped more students to successfully complete the High School Competency Examination. During this exam, we also strived to make the environment much less stressful than it has been in recent years, offering more frequent breaks and making available an assortment of snacks to help test takers keep their energy up.

Our exciting increase in the number of four-year college-bound students is due to the forward thinking of the senior class counselor, Ms. Dickinson. Ms. D. was finally approved this year to set up three computers with internet access in her office, so that students could come in to research and apply for colleges, scholarships, and grants. Students became aware of the availability and ease with which they could plan their futures, and did so accordingly.

I would like to credit the school board for planning this year's school calendar so that the breaks were more evenly distributed and we never had to go too long without one. I have noticed that, the longer kids have to go without a break, the more irritable and short-fused they become. Giving students a chance to rest their bodies and minds helped them avoid potential physical conflicts.

I also believe that the new schedule was responsible in part for the better GPA of the kids who were present at least 90 percent of the time. They were better able to concentrate on their studies.

A P P E N D I X

Sample System-Wide Accountability Indicators

Academic Performance

Standardized Tests

1. Percentage of ___ grade students who have been enrolled since (specify time period) who score at or above the "proficient" level on the District ___ grade reading (or other subject area) test.

2. Percentage of ___ grade students who score at or above the proficient level on the (specify test), as compared with the same students' scores from the previous year.

3. Percentage of regular education students who have been in school since (specify time period) who score at or above the "proficient" level on the reading (or other subject area) sub-test of the (specify test).

4. Percentage of regular education students who have been in school since (specify time period) who score at or above the "proficient" level on the reading (or other subject area) sub-test of the (specify test), as compared with the same students' scores from the previous year.

5. Percentage of students performing at or above the state standard in (specify subject area) on the (specify test).

6. Percentage of students performing at or above the national percentile rank for the mean normal curve equivalent on the (specify test) reading (or other subject area) sub-test.

7. Percentage of students performing at or above the proficient level on the district criterion-referenced reading (or other subject area) test.

8. Percentage of students who read at or above grade or age level by the end of grade 3 before being promoted to grade 4 as measured by the (specify test).

9. Percentage of special education students who participate in state and district assessments with no accommodations, with appropriate accommodations, or with an alternative assessment consistent with the individualized educational plan (IEP).

10. Percentage of participation by special education students in state and district testing, as compared with the percentage of students who participated the previous school year.

11. Percentage of students who meet or exceed grade-level standards in reading, writing, mathematics, and science by ___ (specify time frame).

Locally Created Tests/Assessments

1. Percentage of students who have been in school since (specify time period) whose two ratings totaled 6 or more on the district 4-point rubric for writing assessment.

2. Percentage of students who score at or above the proficient level on four out of five school-based writing assessments, as compared with the same students' scores from the previous year.

3. Percentage of ___ grade students who have been in school since (specify time period) who receive a score of proficient or higher on the District science performance assessment.

4. Percentage of ___ grade students with attendance rates of 90 percent or more and who have been in school since (specify time period) who score at or above the proficient level on the District performance assessment in (specify subject area).

5. Percentage of students who achieve a passing score on the Eighth-Grade Proficiency Examination required for continuation to high school.

6. Percentage of students who achieve a passing score on the Eighth-Grade Proficiency Examination required for continuation to high school on the first trial.

7. Percentage of students who achieve a passing score on the Eighth-Grade Proficiency Examination required for continuation to high school, as compared with the percentage of eighth-graders who passed the examination the previous year.

8. Percentage of high school seniors who pass the High School Competency Assessment required for graduation.

9. Percentage of high school seniors who demonstrate proficiency based on the district's writing assessments required for graduation. The district goal is ___ percent.

10. Percentage of high school seniors who scored at or above the proficient level on the District (specify subject area) assessment, as compared with scores of seniors from the previous year. The district goal is ___ percent.

Locally-Created Performance Tasks

1. Percentage of students who demonstrate mastery of written and spoken expression by writing, presenting, and defending a clearly reasoned, persuasively argued research paper.

2. Through participation in a group project that benefits the community, percentage of students who demonstrate the capacity to analyze a social issue from multiple points of view and to interact as a constructive member of a team.

Teacher Observation

1. Percentage of students who demonstrate an understanding of scientific inquiry and its application to real-life situations.

School Records

1. Percentage of students expected to show proficiency in first-year algebra by the end of the eighth grade.

2. Percentage of students who demonstrate mastery of mathematical proficiency equivalent to three years of study beyond Algebra One.

3. Percentage of students who demonstrate a high level of proficiency in science, equivalent to three years of high school study to include the physical, biological, and chemical sciences.

4. Percentage of students who meet or exceed standards in core subject areas: English, mathematics, science, and social studies.

Student Engagement Indicators

School Records

Attendance

1. Percentage of students with attendance rates of ___ percent or higher.

2. Percentage of students whose attendance rates meet or exceed district or school goals, as compared with the attendance rate from the previous year.

Grade and School Completion

1. Percentage of elementary school students who meet the standards needed for promotion to the next grade level.

2. Percentage of students who complete eighth grade and go on to high school.

3. Percentage of high school students who graduate from 12th grade.

4. Percentage of students who persist and do not drop out of school.

Grade Point Average

1. Percentage of students with attendance rates of ___ percent or higher who attain a grade point average of at least ___ .

2. Increase in school'ₔ overall grade point average, as compared with the grade point average from the previous year.

Teacher Effectiveness Indicators

Teacher Observation

Time on Task

1. Percentage of students who participate in __ hours of (specify subject area) instruction per week.

School Records

Teacher Qualifications

1. Percentage of school's students taught by a teacher licensed in the appropriate grade level or subject area.

School Effectiveness Indicators

School Records

Class Size

1. Percentage of self-contained elementary school classrooms that achieve an average class size of __ to __ for kindergarten; __ to __ for grades one through three; and __ to __ for grades three to five.

2. Percentage of non-self-contained elementary school classrooms that achieve an average class size of __ to __ for kindergarten; __ to __ for grades one through three; and __ to __ for grades three to five.

3. Percentage of middle school classrooms that achieve a student-teacher ratio of between __ to __ by (specify time period).

4. Percentage of high school classrooms that achieve a student-teacher ratio of between __ to __ by (specify time period).

Equity Indicators

1. Percentage of (specify target group) students who meet or exceed District standards in (specify subject area) as measured by the (specify test).

2. Percentage of (specify target group) students who earn at least __ hours of credit in mathematics and science (or other subject area).

3. Percentage of (specify target group) students who achieve high school graduation rates at or above (specify percentage).

4. Percentage of (specify target group) students who enroll in Advanced Placement courses.

5. Decrease in percentage of (specify target group) students who are suspended or expelled from school.

6. Decrease in percentage of (specify target group) students who receive disciplinary referrals.

Stakeholder Satisfaction Indicators

1. Percentage of parents who report that they are satisfied or very satisfied with their children's schools on a parent satisfaction survey.

2. Percentage of teachers who report that they are satisfied or very satisfied with their ability to help all children succeed at high levels on a teacher satisfaction survey.

3. Percentage of students who report that they are satisfied or very satisfied with the quality of the learning at their schools on a student satisfaction survey.

Safety Indicators

1. Number of violent acts committed against students by (target date).

2. Number of violent acts committed against teachers and staff by (target date).

3. Number of incidents involving violence, weapons, drugs, and/or alcohol.

APPENDIX

Sample School-Based Accountability Indicators

Elementary Schools

Reading

1. Increase the percentage of students (specify a particular group) who score at or above the state standard on the grade 3 (or other grade level) norm-referenced reading comprehension test.

2. Increase the percentage of students (specify a particular group) who meet or exceed the district goal for norm-referenced reading scores.

3. Increase the percentage of students who are at or above grade level as measured by informal or formal criterion-referenced reading assessments.

4. Increase the percentage of students who are reading at or above grade level as measured by the district norm-referenced reading test.

5. Increase the percentage of students who score at or above the 50th percentile on the district norm-referenced reading test.

6. Increase the percentage of students (specify a particular group) performing at or above expected grade or age level in reading using the Test of Early Reading Ability (or other diagnostic instrument).

7. Increase the percentage of students (specify a particular group) performing at or above expected grade or age level in reading using the Durrell Analysis of Reading Difficulty (or other reading test).

8. Increase the percentage of students (specify a particular group) performing at or above expected grade or age level in reading on the Gillingham Child Phonics Proficiency Scales (or other reading test).

9. Increase the percentage of students who score at or above age or grade level on the Pre-reading Expectancy Screening Scale (or other reading test).

10. Increase the percentage of students performing at or above expected grade or age level on a teacher-made language arts assessment.

11. Increase the percentage of students who are able to read and pronounce basic vocabulary words for reading, as reported by teacher observation.

12. Increase the percentage of students who are able to use letter/sound relationships to phonetically decode words while reading.

13. Increase the percentage of students who are able to use context clues to decode unfamiliar words.

14. Increase the percentage of students who are at or above grade level as measured by reading readiness scores.

15. Decrease the number of "at-risk" students reading one year or more below grade level.

16. Increase the percentage of students who complete satisfactory book reports.

17. Increase the percentage of students who successfully complete the Junior Great Books program.

18. Increase the number of students who read ___ (specify number) of books and share something they learned orally, artistically, musically, or by doing a multi-media presentation.

19. Increase the amount of material available for student reading in classrooms and/or the school library/media center.

20. Increase the number of students involved in project-based reading assignments.

Writing

1. Increase the percentage of students (specify a particular group) who meet or exceed the district goal on a district writing performance assessment.

2. Increase the percentage of students who score at or above the 50th percentile on the district norm-referenced writing test.

3. Increase the percentage of students who score at or above the "proficient" level on a Test of Early Written Language (or other writing test).

4. Increase the percentage of students who publish their own books and achieve a score of "proficient" or better.

5. Increase the percentage of students performing at or above expected grade or age level in writing as demonstrated through student portfolios.

6. Increase the percentage of students who use word processing to satisfactorily complete writing assignments.

7. Increase the percentage of students involved in writing portfolio conferences, based on portfolio guidelines.

8. Increase the number of students involved in project-based writing assignments.

9. Increase the percentage of classes that use writing performance assessment portfolios.

10. Increase the number of writing samples scored by someone other than the child's classroom teacher.

Language

1. Increase the percentage of students (specify a particular group) performing at or above expected grade or age level in language as reported by their teacher.

2. Increase the percentage of students (specify a particular group) performing at or above expected grade or age level in language using performance assessments.

3. Increase the percentage of students who speak a language other than English as their primary language (specify a particular group) who score at the "proficient" or higher level on a norm-referenced English proficiency test.

4. Increase the percentage of students who speak a language other than English as a primary language (specify a particular group) who score at the "proficient" or higher level on a criterion-referenced English proficiency test.

5. Increase the percentage of students who meet the standard on a (specify language) version of a school-selected reading test.

6. Increase the number of students involved in project-based language assignments.

7. Increase the percentage of students who score at or above the "proficient" level on a Test of Children's Language (or other test instrument).

8. Increase the percentage of students who score at or above the "proficient" level on the district language proficiency test.

9. Increase the percentage of students who score at or above the "proficient" level on the district English proficiency test.

Speaking

1. Increase the percentage of students who achieve a score of "proficient" or higher on an oral communication performance assessment.

2. Increase the number of students involved in project-based public speaking assignments.

3. Increase the percentage of students who achieve a score of "proficient" or higher on a public speaking performance assessment.

4. Increase the percentage of students who achieve a score of "proficient" or higher on a teacher-made public speaking assessment.

Mathematics Achievement

1. Increase the percentage of students (specify a particular group) who score at or above the "proficient" level on a grade 4 (or other grade) norm-referenced mathematics assessment.

2. Increase the percentage of students (specify a particular group) performing at or above the expected grade or age level in mathematics using the Slosson-Diagnostic Math Screener (or other diagnostic test).

3. Increase the percentage of students (specify a particular group) performing at or above the expected grade or age level in mathematics using the Test of Early Written Language (or other assessment instrument).

4. Increase the percentage of students performing at or above the expected grade or age level in mathematics using the Sequential Assessment of Mathematics Inventory (or other assessment instrument).

5. Increase the percentage of students who achieve a score of "proficient" or higher on a mathematics performance assessment.

6. Increase the percentage of students who achieve a score of "proficient" or higher on a teacher-made computation test.

7. Increase the percentage of students who achieve a score of "proficient" or higher on a mathematical problem-solving test.

8. Increase the percentage of students who achieve a "proficient" or higher score on a calculator proficiency performance assessment.

9. Increase the percentage of students who achieve a score of "proficient" or higher on a performance assessment that evaluates their ability to use computer-generated charts and graphs to solve real-world math problems.

10. Increase the percentage of students who correctly use manipulatives in mathematics as observed by the teacher.

11. Increase the percentage of students who achieve a score of "proficient" or higher on a problem-solving performance assessment.

12. Increase the percentage of students involved in projects using mathematical principles in collaboration with community/business partners, and who achieve a score of "proficient" or higher on a school-based performance assessment.

13. Increase the percentage of students who meet or exceed the district goal (50th percentile or higher) on the grade 5 (or other grade) norm-referenced mathematics test.

14. Increase the percentage of students who score at or above the 50th percentile on the grade 5 norm-referenced math test, compared with the same students' grade 4 norm-referenced math scores.

15. Increase the percentage of students who are at or above grade level as measured by a mathematics readiness test.

16. Increase the percentage of students (specify a particular group) performing at or above expected grade/age level in mathematics as demonstrated through student portfolios.

17. Increase the percentage of students (specify a particular group) performing at or above grade level in mathematics.

18. Increase the percentage of classes that use mathematics performance assessment portfolios.

Science Achievement

1. Increase the percentage of students who participate in a science fair.

2. Increase the percentage of students (specify a particular group) who receive a "proficient" or higher score on a district science performance assessment.

3. Increase the percentage of students who achieve a score of "proficient" or higher on a district science performance assessment.

4. Increase the percentage of students who achieve a score of "proficient" or higher on a scientific problem solving performance assessment.

5. Increase the number of hours of science instruction facilitated in science laboratories and/or classrooms.

6. Increase the percentage of students who use manipulatives in science as observed by the teacher.

7. Increase the percentage of students who achieve a score of "proficient" or higher on a teacher-constructed test of scientific knowledge and skills.

8. Increase the number of science activities that involve community/business partnerships.

9. Increase the percentage of students who achieve a score of "proficient" or higher on the science sub-test of a norm-referenced test.

10. Increase the number of hours of science instruction provided by certified science teachers.

11. Increase the amount of laboratory and other equipment available for science experiments.

12. Increase the number of outdoor field experiments and/or visits to science museums and scientific points of interest.

13. Increase participation in collaborative university/college-sponsored science programs and projects.

14. Increase the percentage of students who score "proficient" or higher on writing-to-learn science performance assessments.

15. Increase the percentage of students (specify a particular group) who can use the scientific method to solve real-world science problems or issues.

16. Increase the percentage of students involved in community or school-based projects that involve environmental issues and concerns.

17. Increase the percentage of students who use computers to access and use information from science-related Internet web sites.

Arts

1. Increase the percentage of students who participate in art classes/instruction.

2. Increase the percentage of students who participate in music performances.

3. Increase the percentage of students who participate in dance performances.

4. Increase the percentage of students who complete art projects for public display or presentation.

5. Increase the number of art-related activities that involve community/business partners.

6. Increase the percentage of students who achieve a score of "proficient" or higher on an art portfolio.

7. Increase the percentage of students who achieve a score of "proficient" or higher on a music performance.

Study Skills

1. Increase the percentage of students who achieve a score of "proficient" or higher on a time management performance assessment.

2. Increase the percentage of students who prepare and regularly use a study schedule, as reported by the teacher.

3. Increase the percentage of students who demonstrate their ability to use effective reading habits.

4. Increase the percentage of students who take notes while they read to improve their overall comprehension.

5. Increase the percentage of students who demonstrate their ability to take effective classroom notes from lectures and/or whole-group activities.

6. Increase the percentage of students who demonstrate effective test-taking strategies.

7. Increase the percentage of students who demonstrate their ability to use SQ3R (Survey, Question, Read, Recite, Review) or other "before/during/after" strategies to read textbooks effectively, as measured by reading performance assessments.

8. Increase the percentage of students who achieve a score of "proficient" or higher on a teacher-made study skills performance assessment.

Technology

1. Increase the number of classrooms wired/equipped for technology (computers, etc.).

2. Increase the number of computers available for student use at all grade levels.

3. Increase the percentage of computer-proficient students who demonstrate all of the skills listed on a school-wide computer assessment checklist.

4. Increase the total percentage of assessments administered using computers.

5. Increase the number of instructional days on which students use the computer as part of planned instruction.

6. Increase the percentage of students who successfully complete a keyboarding performance assessment.

7. Increase the number of students who increase their keyboarding speed from ___ words per minute to ___ words per minute.

8. Increase the percentage of students who score "proficient" or higher on a computer usage performance assessment.

9. Increase the percentage of students who demonstrate their ability to log on to, access, and download information from Internet web sites.

10. Increase the percentage of students using the Internet, electronic data searches, etc. for research.

11. Increase the percentage of students who complete a technology portfolio with a score of "proficient" or higher.

12. Increase the number of multimedia projects that students complete using technology.

13. Increase the number of word-processed products included in writing portfolios.

Other

1. Increase the number of classrooms using project-based learning to integrate math, science, communication (reading, writing, language, speaking) and the arts.

School/Community Service

1. Increase the number of hours that students volunteer in the community.

2. Increase the number of business/community partnership activities that link classroom learning with real-world issues and problems.

3. Increase the number of community service or career awareness projects undertaken by the school.

4. Increase the percentage of students who participate in student government.

5. Increase the number of students who achieve a score of "proficient" or higher on a social studies or global awareness assessment.

6. Increase the number of adult mentor and tutor contacts with students.

7. Increase the percentage of students (specify a particular group or age/grade level) who participate in school-to-work activities.

8. Increase the percentage of students who use academics to operate student-run school businesses.

Parental Involvement

1. Increase the percentage of parents who participate in parent-teacher conferences.

2. Increase the number of parent volunteer hours.

3. Increase the number of parent activities offered at the school.

4. Increase the number of parents who log on to the school web site to access information about their children's performance.

5. Increase the number of parents who use the school's Parent Resource Room.

6. Increase the number of parents who attend school or district-sponsored workshops.

7. Increase the number of parents who attend Back-to-School Nights.

8. Increase the number of parents who pick up their children's report cards at the school.

Safety and Climate

1. Increase the percentage of students who ride the school bus without bus complaints.

2. Increase the percentage of students who receive "good bus rider" incentive awards.

3. Increase the percentage of students who do not receive lunchroom complaints.

4. Increase the percentage of students who receive "good lunchroom behavior" incentive awards.

5. Increase the percentage of students who receive positive school recognition for following school rules.

6. Increase the percentage of students who achieve a score of "proficient" or higher on a peer mediation performance assessment.

7. Increase the number of students who participate in school-sponsored conflict resolution/reduction workshops.

School Completion

1. Increase the percentage of students (specify a particular group) who remain enrolled from grade to grade, controlled for student mobility.

2. Increase the percentage of students who demonstrate their mastery of requisite standards by being promoted to the next grade.

Middle School

Language Arts

1. Increase the percentage of students (specify a particular group) who meet or exceed the district standard on a district writing performance assessment.

2. Increase the percentage of students who are reading at or above grade level on a school-selected reading test.

3. Increase the number of students who achieve a score of "proficient" or higher on written book reports as demonstrated by student portfolios.

4. Increase the percentage of students participating in debate, drama, newspaper, or other communication-related extracurricular activities.

5. Increase the percentage of students (specify a particular group) who meet or exceed the district goal on a norm-referenced grade 8 reading assessment.

6. Increase the percentage of students who successfully pass the reading portion of the Middle School Proficiency examination.

7. Increase the percentage of students who meet or exceed the district goal on a norm-referenced grade 8 writing assessment.

8. Increase the percentage of students who successfully pass the writing portion of the Middle School Proficiency examination.

9. Increase the number of project-based language arts activities.

10. Increase the percentage of students who achieve a score of "proficient" or higher on a school-based oral communication performance assessment.

Mathematics Achievement

1. Increase the percentage of grade 8 students (specify a particular group) who score at or above the "proficient" level on a norm-referenced mathematics test, comparing spring of _____ to spring of _____.

2. Increase the percentage of students who receive a score of "proficient" or higher on a mathematics performance assessment.

3. Increase the percentage of students who participate in community/business projects that involve mathematical principles and problems.

4. Increase the percentage of students who use computer-generated charts and graphs to solve real-world math problems.

5. Increase the percentage of students who achieve a score of "proficient" or higher on a problem solving performance assessment.

6. Increase the percentage of students who achieve a score of "proficient" or higher on a mathematical computation performance assessment.

7. Increase the percentage of students who achieve a score of "proficient" or higher on a teacher-made mathematics assessment.

8. Increase the percentage of students who correctly use manipulatives in mathematics as observed by the teacher.

9. Increase the percentage of students who achieve a score of "proficient" or higher on a calculator proficiency performance assessment.

10. Increase the percentage of students who achieve a score of "proficient" or higher on a scientific calculator proficiency performance assessment.

11. Increase the percentage of students enrolled in pre-algebra and/or algebra courses.

12. Increase the percentage of students who successfully complete the mathematics portion of the Middle School Proficiency examination.

13. Increase the percentage of students "at-risk of failure" who participate in a mathematics intervention designed to improve their performance.

14. Increase the percentage of students taking higher-level mathematics courses.

Science Achievement

1. Increase the percentage of students who achieve a score at or above the district goal on a norm-referenced science test.

2. Increase the percentage of students (specify a particular group) who achieve a score of "proficient" or higher on a science performance assessment.

3. Increase the percentage of students who achieve a score of "proficient" or higher on a science performance assessment.

4. Increase the percentage of students who enter a science fair.

5. Increase the percentage of students who engage in direct interaction with community/ business partners on science projects.

6. Increase the percentage of students who achieve a score of "proficient" or higher on a teacher-made science assessment.

7. Increase the percentage of students who correctly use science manipulatives as observed by the teacher.

8. Increase the number of students taught by a teacher with a science certification or endorsement.

9. Increase the number of science instructional hours taught in a laboratory or science classroom.

10. Increase the amount of laboratory and other equipment available for science experiments.

School/Community Service

1. Increase the percentage of students participating in school-approved community service activities.

2. Increase the percentage of students and/or student families served by school-based service organizations.

3. Increase the number of business partnership activities where students have an opportunity to use classroom learning to solve business and/or community problems.

4. Increase the number of students who participate in student government.

5. Increase the percentage of students participating in academic extracurricular activities, including debate, forensics, chess, math, drama, space, technology, or any other extracurricular activity approved by the school that encourages the thinking and communication skills of students.

6. Increase the percentage of students who participate in school-to-work activities.

7. Increase the number of students who serve as volunteer tutors and/or mentors for other students.

8. Increase the number of business people who speak to students about the connection between school and work.

9. Increase the number of students who participate in high school transition activities, such as visits to high schools, shadowing programs that allow middle school students to shadow high school students, participation in high school information fairs, etc.

10. Increase the number of students who participate in service learning projects that integrate academics with community service.

11. Increase the percentage of students who operate student-run businesses within the school.

Arts

1. Increase the percentage of students directly involved in the performing arts.

2. Increase the percentage of students directly involved in public displays of visual arts.

3. Increase the percentage of students involved in extracurricular art activities.

4. Increase the number of class sessions in which the arts are explicitly integrated into academics.

5. Increase the number of academic performance assessments that successfully integrate the arts.

Technology

1. Increase the number of computers available for student use at all grade levels.

2. Increase the percentage of students involved in technology-related extracurricular activities. These may include a computer club, audio-visual club, video production club, and/or other school-approved technology activities.

3. Increase the percentage of students successfully completing a school-based computer-assisted instruction program.

4. Increase the average grades in computer classes.

5. Increase the percentage of students who complete a technology portfolio with a score of "proficient" or higher.

6. Increase the percentage of students using the Internet, electronic data searches, etc. for research.

7. Increase the amount of instructional time in which students use computers as a tool to meet academic standards.

8. Increase the number of students who can design Internet web pages.

9. Increase the number of students who use a computer to word-process, edit, and revise writing assignments.

Parental Involvement

1. Increase the number of hours that parents volunteer in the school.

2. Increase the percentage of parents who attend parent-teacher conferences.

3. Increase the number of parents who attend school activities.

4. Increase the number of parent activities offered by the school.

5. Increase the number of home visitations made by school personnel.

6. Increase the number of parents who volunteer to speak to classes about life skills and/or careers.

School Safety

1. Increase the percentage of students who achieve a score of "proficient" or higher on a peer mediation performance assessment.

2. Increase the percentage of students who ride the school bus without discipline complaints.

3. Increase the percentage of students who do not receive lunchroom complaints.

4. Increase the percentage of students who receive recognition for following classroom and school rules.

5. Increase the number of student contact days without student fighting.

6. Reduce to zero the number of incidents involving violence, drugs, alcohol, and gangs.

Graduation Rates

1. Increase the percentage of students who pass the Middle School Proficiency examination the first time they take it.

2. Increase the percentage of students who demonstrate their mastery of middle school academic standards by matriculating to high school.

Dropout Rates

1. Decrease the number of students who drop out of middle school.

2. Increase the percentage of students who successfully complete middle school, controlled for student mobility.

3. Increase the number of students identified as "at risk of failing" who persist because of individualized intervention plans.

Teacher Qualifications

1. Increase the percentage of middle-school trained and licensed teachers.

High School

English/Language Arts

1. Increase the percentage of students (specify a particular group) who score at or above the "proficient" level on a district norm-referenced reading assessment, comparing spring of ___ to spring of ___.

2. Increase the percentage of students who are reading at or above grade level on a school or district-selected reading test.

3. Increase the percentage of students who meet or exceed the district goal on a norm-referenced writing test.

4. Increase the percentage of students who score at or above the "proficient" level on a district norm-referenced writing assessment, comparing spring of ___ to spring of ___.

5. Increase the percentage of students (specify a particular group) who score "proficient" or better on a district writing assessment.

6. Increase the percentage of students who achieve a score of "proficient" or better in writing, as demonstrated by student portfolios.

7. Increase the percentage of students who meet standards in English courses.

8. Increase the percentage of students who can fill out a job application correctly, as scored by a teacher or business partner.

9. Increase the percentage of students who can prepare a resume, as scored by a teacher or business partner.

10. Increase the percentage of students who score "proficient" or higher on a school-based oral presentation assessment.

11. Increase the percentage of students who successfully complete an Advanced Placement English course.

12. Increase the percentage of students who achieve a score of "proficient" or higher on a school-based oral communication performance assessment.

13. Increase the percentage of students who demonstrate proficiency in their oral communication skills as measured by scored videotaped presentations.

14. Increase the percentage of students who can successfully role-play a job interview as reported by a teacher or business partner.

Mathematics Achievement

1. Increase the percentage of (specify a particular group) students who score "proficient" or higher on a mathematics performance assessment.

2. Increase the percentage of students who receive a score of "proficient" or higher on a school-based calculator proficiency assessment.

3. Increase the percentage of students who receive a score of "proficient" or higher on a school-based scientific calculator proficiency assessment.

4. Increase the percentage of students who meet or exceed district goals on a norm-referenced mathematics test.

5. Increase the percentage of students who meet or exceed district goals on a norm-referenced mathematical problem-solving test.

6. Increase the percentage of students who can use a graphing calculator as measured by a performance assessment.

7. Increase the percentage of students who are involved in projects using mathematical principles in collaboration with community/business partners.

8. Increase the percentage of students who score "proficient" or higher on a school-based math performance assessment.

9. Increase the percentage of students who score "proficient" or higher on a budget preparation performance assessment.

10. Increase the percentage of students who can demonstrate their ability to successfully balance a checkbook, as reported by the teacher.

11. Increase the percentage of students who achieve a score of "proficient" or higher on a performance assessment that requires them to do comparison shopping at a store.

12. Increase the percentage of students who achieve a score of "proficient" or higher on a performance assessment that requires them to demonstrate life skills, such as researching and locating an affordable apartment, writing checks to pay bills, calculating interest on a savings account, etc.

13. Increase the percentage of students who have successfully completed a class in algebra or higher-level mathematics.

Science Achievement

1. Increase the percentage of students who take advanced science courses.

2. Increase the percentage of students who successfully complete advanced science courses.

3. Increase the percentage of students who achieve a score of "proficient" or higher on a school-based science performance assessment.

4. Increase the percentage of students (specify a particular group) who achieve a score of "proficient" or higher on a district performance assessment.

5. Increase the percentage of students who meet or exceed the district goal on a norm-referenced science sub-test.

6. Increase the percentage of students who follow laboratory safety guidelines as observed by a teacher.

7. Increase the percentage of students who participate with community/business partners on science projects.

School/Community Service

1. Increase the percentage of students who satisfactorily participate in contests designed to enhance community involvement and awareness.

2. Increase the number of hours that students volunteer in community service projects.

3. Increase the number of district business partner activities.

4. Increase the percentage of students who achieve a score of "proficient" or higher on a school-based time management performance assessment.

5. Increase the percentage of students who achieve a score of "proficient" or higher on a school-based peer mediation performance assessment.

6. Increase the percentage of students who participate in academic extracurricular activities that improve the thinking and communication skills of students. Examples of these might include activities that involve debate, forensics, chess, math, drama, space, or technology.

7. Increase the number of students who serve as volunteer tutors and/or mentors for younger (or other population) students.

8. Increase the number of career-oriented projects and activities.

9. Increase the number of students who participate in a school-sponsored job-shadowing program.

10. Increase the number of students who successfully complete service learning projects that integrate academics with community service.

11. Increase the percentage of students who operate and/or work in student-run businesses on campus.

Arts

1. Increase the percentage of students who successfully complete an art performance assessment.

2. Increase the percentage of students who submit and achieve a score of "proficient" or higher on Advanced Placement Art portfolios.

3. Increase the number of students who participate in arts-related extracurricular activities (band, orchestra, dance, choir, drama).

4. Increase the number of performance assessments that successfully integrate academics with the arts.

Technology

1. Increase the number of computers available for student use at all grade levels.

2. Increase the amount of computer laboratory time available to all students.

3. Increase the percentage of students who score "proficient" or higher on a district technology rubric that includes assessment of knowledge of the Internet, word processing, electronic data search skills, and other related computer skills.

4. Increase the number of parents and/or community volunteers trained as technology tutors.

5. Increase the number of students who satisfactorily complete computer courses.

6. Increase the number of students who achieve a score of "proficient" or higher on a performance assessment that requires them to download and read information from their school's Internet web pages.

Parent and Alumni Involvement

1. Increase the number of parents who attend school events.

2. Increase the number of parents who participate on advisory boards.

3. Increase the percentage of parents and guardians who successfully complete parenting classes.

4. Increase the number of alumni actively serving as mentors to students in a school-based mentoring program.

Type of Courses Taken

1. Increase the percentage of students who enroll in college preparatory classes.

2. Increase the percentage of students who successfully meet standards in college preparatory classes.

3. Increase the percentage of students who enroll in advanced placement courses.

4. Increase the percentage of students who successfully complete advanced placement courses.

5. Increase the percentage of students who pass an advanced placement exit examination.

6. Increase the number of students enrolled in Pre-International Baccalaureate classes.

7. Increase the number of students enrolled in International Baccalaureate classes.

8. Increase the percentage of students who successfully complete job training courses.

9. Increase the percentage of students successfully completing upper-level mathematics courses.

10. Increase the percentage of students successfully completing upper-level science courses.

11. Increase the percentage of students who enroll in college/university courses while still in high school.

12. Increase the percentage of students who successfully complete college/university courses while still in high school.

13. Increase the percentage of students (specify target group) who enroll in college/university courses while still in high school.

14. Increase the percentage of students (specify target group) who successfully complete college/university courses while still in high school.

Graduation Rates

1. Increase the percentage of students who earn a high school diploma.

2. Increase the percentage of students who pass the High School Competency Examination required for graduation.

3. Increase the percentage of students who pass the High School Competency Examination required for graduation on the first trial.

4. Increase the percentage of students who pass the (specify proficiency sub-test) of the High School Competency Examination required for graduation.

5. Increase the percentage of students who pass the (specify proficiency sub-test) of the High School Competency Examination required for graduation.

Post-High School Plans

1. Increase the percentage of high school graduates who enroll in a post-secondary vocational training program.

2. Increase the percentage of high school graduates who enroll in a community or junior college.

3. Increased the percentage of high school graduates who enroll in a four-year college or university.

4. Increase the percentage of high school graduates who secure full-time employment.

5. Increase the number of students who participate in college fairs.

Dropout Rate

1. Decrease the annual dropout rate from ____ to ____ (specify percentages).

2. Increase the annual persistence rate, adjusted for mobility, from ___ to ____ (specify percentages).

3. Increase the longitudinal persistence rate from ___ to ___ (specify percentages).

General Menu (all grade levels)

Attendance

1. Increase attendance for (specify a particular group) students.

2. Increase average daily attendance from 85 to 90 percent (or other percentages).

3. Decrease the percentage of students with attendance rates below 90 (or other) percent.

4. Increase the percentage of students who attend school on assessment/testing days.

5. Increase the average number of days that high-mobility populations spend in the same school.

6. Decrease the number of truancies.

7. Decrease the habitual truancy rate from __ to __ (specify percentages) by ___ (specify timeframe).

8. Increase the stability rate from ___ to ___ (specify percentages) by ___ (specify timeframe).

9. Decrease the number of in-school suspensions.

10. Decrease the number of out-of-school suspensions.

11. Decrease the number of expulsions.

12. Increase the percentage of students who arrive at school on time.

13. Increase the percentage of students who arrive at class on time.

Benchmarks

1. Increase the percentage of students who meet (specify grade level) benchmarks in (specify subject area).

Class Size

1. Decrease class size in (specify grade or area) by __ (specify percentage).

2. Reduce class size from __ students per class to __ students per class by (specify time frame).

3. Increase the number of paraprofessionals assigned to (specify grade or area).

Equity

1. Reduce the percentage gap between (specify population) and (specify population) on the district (specify subject area) assessment.

2. Close the gap between males and females on the (specify assessment tool) by ___ percent.

3. Increase the number of (specify population) who meet or exceed the district goal on the (specify assessment tool).

4. Increase the percentage of students (specify population) who perform at or above age or grade level as assessed by the (specify assessment tool).

5. Decrease the gap between (specify population) and (specify population) who score at or above the national average on (specify assessment tool).

Honors

1. Increase the number/percentage of students who make the honor roll.

2. Increase the number/percentage of students who participate in school-sponsored academic honor programs.

3. Increase the percentage of students (specify target group) that improve their grade point average from ___ to ___ fall to spring semester.

4. Increase the percentage of students (specify target group) that achieve a grade point average of (specify GPA) or higher.

5. Increase the grade point average of students with a ____ (specify percentage) attendance rate.

Instructional Strategies

1. Increase the percentage of time students spend on hands-on activities throughout the school year.

2. Increase the number of teachers who use rubrics (scoring guides) to assess student performance.

3. Increase the number of classroom activities that require students to use higher-order thinking skills.

4. Increase the percentage of time that students spend involved in collaborative learning activities.

5. Increase the percentage of instructional time spent in student-centered rather than teacher-centered activities.

6. Increase the number of classrooms where learning centers are used.

7. Decrease the amount of time spent in whole-group instruction.

8. Increase the amount of time students spend assessing their own work products, using rubrics written in student-friendly language.

9. Increase the percentage of time students spend defining, solving, and communicating about solutions to real-world problems.

10. Increase the percentage of instructional time spent in problem/inquiry-based learning.

11. Increase the percentage of teachers who use computerized grade and attendance reports.

12. Increase the percentage of teachers who use computers as routine parts of instruction.

13. Increase the percentage of instructional time spent in cross-discipline (and/or cross-grade) learning activities.

14. Increase the percentage of instructional time spent on student learning needs identified by analyzing student performance data.

Parental Involvement

1. Increase the number of after-school activities offered for parents.

2. Increase the number of telephone calls received from parents about their children's performance during specified "teacher telephone/office hours."

3. Increase the percentage of parents who have signed agreements that outline how they and the school will collaborate to make sure children achieve.

4. Increase the number/frequency of school-initiated contacts made with parents.

5. Increase the number of parents who participate on school advisory councils and/or committees.

6. Increase the number of parents who attend site-based decision-making team meetings.

7. Increase the number of parents who participate in school fundraising activities.

8. Increase the number of parents who assume leadership roles in school activities.

Qualifications of Teachers

1. Increase the percentage of teachers licensed for (specify subject area or grade level).

2. Increase the percentage of new teachers hired in the district who meet state licensure standards.

3. Increase the percentage of teachers who meet national licensure standards.

4. Increase the number of teachers participating in induction programs for new teachers.

5. Increase the percentage of middle and high school teachers who hold a degree in the subject they teach.

6. Increase the percentage of teachers who receive training in (specify area).

7. Increase the percentage of teachers who apply professional development activities and/or information on (specify area) in their classrooms.

8. Increase the number of teachers who participate in collaborative scoring of student performance assessments.

9. Increase the number of teachers who exchange student papers with one another.

10. Increase the number of teachers who mentor/coach one another in (specify area).

11. Increase the number of teachers who participate in sessions where they share teaching/learning resources, strategies, methods, etc. with other teachers.

12. Increase the percentage of professional development time devoted to meeting needs identified by analyzing student performance data.

13. Increase the number of teachers who participate in computer training.

Retention

1. Reduce the number of (specify a grade level) students who are retained.

2. Increase the number of retained students who participate in intervention activities designed to improve their performance.

School Safety

1. Reduce the number of students sent to the office for discipline-related reasons.

2. Increase the percentage/number of students recognized for following classroom and/or school rules.

3. Increase the percentage/number of students who are trained peer mediators.

Science

1. Increase the percentage of students able to use the scientific method to conduct and explain a scientific experiment.

Special Education

1. Increase the percentage of special education students who participate in district and school assessment programs.

2. Increase the number of adaptations available to special education students.

3. Increase the number of testing adaptations available to special education students that allow them to participate in district assessment plans.

4. Increase the number of performance assessments integrated into individualized educational plans.

5. Increase the number of special education students who participate in district performance assessments.

6. Increase the number of parents who participate in IEP (individualized educational plan) staffings.

7. Increase the percentage of special education students who demonstrate improvement in (specify subject area) on a district norm-referenced test from spring of __ to spring of __.

8. Increase the percentage of special education students who demonstrate improvement in (specify subject area) on a district or school-selected criterion-referenced test from _____ to _____ (specify time period).

Writing

1. Increase the amount of writing instructional time that students spend in self-assessment of their own writing, using rubrics written in student-friendly language.

2. Increase the amount of writing instructional time that students spend in peer editing groups, using rubrics written in student-friendly language.

3. Increase the amount of writing instructional time that students spend editing and correcting their own writing and explaining (orally or in writing) why they made specific corrections.

4. Increase the percentage of students who write a research paper of (specify length) and achieve a score of "proficient" or higher as measured by a rubric/scoring guide.

5. Increase the number of students involved in writing projects that require them to send (mail, e-mail) their writing to and receive a response from someone else.

6. Increase the number of times per (specify timeframe) students use computers to create and publish their own work.

7. Increase the number of students who submit their writing to school-sanctioned writing contests.

APPENDIX

Accountability System Checklist

Accountability Practice	Exemplary	Proficient	Progressing	Remarks
1. The system has an accountability plan that measures student achievement against explicit standards, not on comparisons among students and/or schools.				
2. A way to monitor the "antecedents of excellence," that is, the strategies that schools use to achieve high standards, is built into the accountability system. The monitoring system is based on more than just test scores.				
3. The system explicitly authorizes teachers to modify the curriculum in quantity and emphasis so that students meet rigorous standards in the core academic areas of math, science, language arts, and social studies.				
4. The system has established an assessment task force to monitor the implementation of effective and fair assessments throughout the year.				
5. The accountability system has system-wide indicators (Tier 1 measures), and the data sources and achievement criteria for each indicator have been identified.				
6. The system uses multiple assessment methods for system-wide indicators. It never relies on only one indicator or assessment method to represent student achievement.				
7. The accountability system has school-based indicators (Tier 2 measures), and the data sources, methods of calculation, and criteria for success have been identified.				
8. The accountability system includes narratives (Tier 3 measures) that describe each school's demographics, challenges, and successes for the school year.				
9. The system reports comprehensive, user-friendly student achievement results to the public throughout the year.				

Accountability Practice	Exemplary	Proficient	Progressing	Remarks
10. There is a clearly identified senior leader at the system level who is responsible for standards, assessment, and accountability, and who clearly communicates accountability information to all stakeholders.				
11. A clearly defined point or other method has been built into the system, in order to reward improvement and/or identify schools in need of additional assistance.				
12. Evaluations of schools and building leaders are based on student achievement, not on competition with one another or on norm-referenced measures.				
13. Teachers use a variety of assessment techniques in the classroom.				
14. Teachers can easily enter and retrieve information from the accountability system and regularly share this information with students and parents.				
15. Every system stakeholder knows for what and to whom he/she is being held accountable.				
16. The accountability system provides a mechanism for integrating other plans, such as school improvement, accreditation, and strategic plans.				
17. Students can explain what "proficient" work means for each assignment.				
18. Teachers give students explicit expectations (a scoring guide/rubric) for "proficient" work before students begin work on an assignment.				

Accountability Practice	Exemplary	Proficient	Progressing	Remarks
19. Accountability information is used to make professional development decisions.				
20. Other accountability practices appropriate for your system:				

A P P E N D I X

List of Worksheets

Number	Name	Page

APPENDIX

Internet Addresses for External Accountability Research

This appendix contains web addresses and phone numbers for the Departments of Education in all fifty states. In conducting their external study of other accountability systems, Task Force members may find that the internet is a good place to go for the most current information on educational policy. Most of these sites contain information on the accountability system that a state has in place, although they are not necessarily titled as such. A careful look at the testing, rewards, sanctions, and success indicators mentioned on the site will provide a clue as to how that state holds its stakeholders accountable.

State	Web Sites	Department	Telephone Numbers
Alabama	www.alsde.edu	Dept. of Education	(334) 242-9700
Alaska	www.eed.state.ak.us /standards/	Dept. of Education	(907) 465-2800
Arizona	www.ade.state.az.us	School & Student Accountability	(602) 542-3111
Arkansas	arkedu.state.ar.us	Dept. of Education	(501) 682-4475
California	www.cde.ca.gov/be/st/ss /index.asp	Accountability Assistance	(916) 657-3745
Colorado	www.cde.state.co.us	Dept. of Education	(303) 866-6600
Connecticut	www.state.ct.us/sde/	Dept. of Education	(860) 566-5677
Delaware	www.doe.state.de.us	Dept. of Education	(302) 739-4601
District of Columbia	www.k12.dc.us	Office of Accountability	(202) 541-6338
Florida	www.firn.edu/doe/index.html	Dept. of Education	(850) 488-9968
Georgia	www.glc.k12.ga.us/	Dept. of Education	(404) 656-2800
Hawaii	http://doe.k12.hi.us/	Planning and Evaluation	(808) 733-4008
Idaho	www.idahoboardofed.org/saa/	School Accountability	(208) 332-6800

Accountability in Action

State	Web Sites	Department	Telephone Numbers
Illinois	www.isbe.state.il.us/ils	Quality Assurance Office	(217) 782-2948
Indiana	http://.doe.state.in.us/standards/welcome.html	Dept. of Education	(317) 232-0808
Iowa	www.state.ia.us/educate	Dept. of Education	(515) 281-5294
Kansas	www.ksde.org/assessment	Dept. of Education	(785) 296-3201
Kentucky	www.education.ky.gov/	Director, Assessment/ Accountability Communications	(502) 564-3421
Louisiana	www.doe.state.la.us	Dept. of Education	(504) 342-3602
Maine	www.state.me.us/education/	Educational Assessment Coordinator	(207) 287-5996
Maryland	http://mdk12.org/mspp/vsc/index.html	Dept. of Education	(888) 246-0016
Massachusetts	www.doe.mass.edu	State Testing	(617) 388-3300 ext. 327
Michigan	www.michigan.gov/mde	Dept. of Education	(517) 373-3900
Minnesota	http://children.state.mn.us/html/mde_home.htm	Educational Effectiveness Program	(612) 296-1429
Mississippi	www.mde.k12.ms.us/	Office of Student Assessment	(601) 359-3052
Missouri	www.dese.state.mo.us/standards/	School Improvement Program	(573) 751-4426
Montana	www.opi.state.mt.us/	Dept. of Education	(406) 444-3680
Nebraska	www.nde.state.ne.us/AcadStand.htmo	Dept. of Education	(402) 471-2295
Nevada	www.nde.state.nv.us/sca/standards/index.html	Dept. of Education	(702) 687-9200
New Hampshire	www.ed.state.nh.us/	Educational Improvement Assessment Program	(603) 271-2298
New Jersey	www.state.nj.us/njded/cccs/index.html	Dept. of Education	(609) 292-4469
New Mexico	http://164.64.166.11/cilt/standards/	Assessment/Evaluation Unit	(505) 827-6524
New York	www.nysed.gov	Dept. of Education	(518) 474-3852
North Carolina	www.dpi.state.nc.us/curriculum/		
North Dakota	www.dpi.state.nd.us	Dept. of Education	(701) 328-2260

State	Web Sites	Department	Telephone Numbers
Ohio	www.ode.state.oh.us /academic_content_standards/	Dept. of Education	(877) 772-7771
Oklahoma	sde.state.ok.us	Dept. of Education	(405) 521-6205
Oregon	www.ode.state.or.us/asmt/	Dept. of Education	(503) 378-3569
Pennsylvania	www.pde.state.pa.us/	Dept. of Education	(717) 783-1831
Rhode Island	www.ridoe.net/standards /frameworks/default.htm	Dept. of Education	(401) 222-4600
South Carolina	www.myschools.com/offices /cso/	Evaluation Dept.	(803) 734-8290
South Dakota	www.state.sd.us/deca/OCTA /contentstandards/index.htm	Office of Technical Assistance	(605) 773-5229
Tennessee	www.state.tn.us/education	Dept. of Education	(615) 741-2731
Texas	www.tea.state.tx.us/teks/	Office of Accountability	(512) 463-8998
Utah	www.uen.org/core/	Statewide Testing Program	(801) 538-7810
Vermont	www.state.vt.us/educ	School Reports	(802) 828-3353
Virginia	www.pen.k12.va.us/VDOE/ Instruction/sol.html	Dept. of Education	(804) 225-2020
Washington	www.k12.wa.us /CurriculumInstruct /default.aspx	Assessment & Evaluation	(360) 753-3449
West Virginia	wvde.state.wv.us		
Wisconsin	www.dpi.state.wi.us/standards /index.html	Dept. of Public Instruction	(800) 441-4563
Wyoming	www.k12.wy.us	Assessment	(307) 777-6213

In addition to looking at the accountability web pages of other states, Task Force members can also use Internet search engines to locate external resource information. By entering terms like "educational accountability" or "school accountability" at a search engine prompt, task force members can scan articles and other resources. Some Internet web site addresses that you may find helpful in your external search for accountability information are listed below:

Subject	Web Sites
Annenberg Institute for School Reform	www.annenberginstitute.org/

Subject	Web Sites
Emerging Student Assessment Systems for School Reform	www.ed.gov/databases/ERIC_Digests/ed389959.html
Framework for Educational Accountability	http://education.umn.edu/nceo/OnlingPubs/Framework/FrameworkText.html
National Center on Educational Outcomes	http://education.umn.edu/NCEO/
NEA (National Education Association) Issues	www.nea.org/issues/
Occidental College Library	http://oasys.lib.oxy.edu/search/deducational+accountability
Western Regional Resource Center	interact.uoregon.edu/wrrc/stanassess.html
The Center for Education Reform: About Education Reform	edreform.com/reform.htm
U.S. Department of Education Publications	www.ed.gov/about/pubs/intro/index.html

Index

A

academic achievement, 105, 116, 185, 187, 195, 200-201, 205

academic challenge, 189

academic leadership, 37

academic performance, 187

academic preparation, 202

academic sanctions, 34

academic skills, 8, 188

academic standards, 27, 201, 241

access to information, 35

accountability, 33-34, 37, 61, 206, 232-235, 243, 246

accountability data, 175

accountability indicators, 46, 106, 108, 135

accountability information, 24, 98, 170

accountability plan, 56, 197

accountability principles, 9, 77, 93

accountability report, 87, 121, 141, 149, 151, 172, 174, 192, 209, 241, 263, 265, 268-269, 271-272

accountability reporting, 117, 155

accountability results, 118

accountability system, 15, 20, 26, 41, 43, 45-46, 49, 55, 57, 62, 64, 85-86, 103, 106, 108, 115-116, 119, 121-122, 129, 132-134, 144, 151, 157, 179, 194-195, 200-201, 206, 210, 212, 225-226, 231, 263

accountability system checklist, 311

accountability system design, 259-260

accountability system results, 262

accountability systems, 45, 206

Accountability Task Force, 46, 79, 83-85, 87, 90, 103-106, 130-132, 135, 139, 142-144, 148-149, 157, 160, 232

accreditation, 18

accreditation plan, 85, 94

accuracy, 93, 95, 129

achievement, 8, 37, 244-245

achievement gap, 194

action research, 197

administration, 46

administrative evaluations, 93

administrator, 8, 45, 61, 80, 86, 93, 95, 103, 105, 116, 231

adult leader, 199

adults, 210

advanced degree, 10

Alaska, 93

Alaska Department of Education, 210

alternative indications of performance, 95

Amaral, O., 206

antecedents of excellence, 95

application of data, 121

architect, 69

architecture, 87, 115, 122, 148, 157, 218

assessment, 43, 49, 55-56, 62, 142, 175, 188-189, 199, 226, 229-233, 235, 246

assessment practices, 53-54, 58, 93, 100, 240

assessments, 243

attendance, 71-72, 115

auditing, 37

average, 37

average test scores, 37-38

B

Bales, J., 244

best practices, 27, 201

bias, 132-133

bi-variate, 9, 118

block schedule, 21, 196

board, 50, 80, 98, 103, 232

board members, 7, 61, 86, 129-130, 217, 220

board of education, 84, 217

box score approach, 19

Bracey Report, 133

building-level assessment, 201

C

Carter, C., 193

categories, 133-134

cause, 8, 21-22, 101, 239

cause variables, 131

central office, 87, 98, 103, 157-158, 160, 166, 226, 228, 230-231, 245

central office accountability system, 157-158, 164

central office common goals, 158

central office departmental goals, 161

certified, 10

Chamber of Commerce, 82

classroom, 9, 50, 52, 63, 245

classroom assessment, 37, 54

classroom management, 199

classroom observation, 54

classroom strategies, 185

classroom-level assessment, 86

clear guidance about the interpretation and use of data, 115

clear specifications, 191

collaboration, 71, 187, 193, 195-196, 200-201, 207-208, 231

collaborative scoring, 196, 202

collection of data, 143

common assessments, 198, 202

common goals, 157-158

communication, 33, 35, 38, 49, 57, 87-88, 151, 175, 229, 259, 262

communications plan, 33

community, 38, 81, 84, 86, 151, 157, 210, 218, 221, 262

comparative imperative, 133

comprehensive accountability plan, 225

comprehensive accountability system, 166, 188, 193, 234, 259

computers, 172

congruence, 93-94

consensus, 89

consequences, 100

consistency, 190-191, 199

context, 23-25

Cooperating School Districts of St. Louis County, 201

core objectives, 139

cross-disciplinary integration, 200

curriculum, 16, 21-22, 24, 26, 49-50, 53, 55, 58, 62, 116, 118, 142, 173, 187-188, 190, 198, 226-228, 231, 240

curriculum standards, 190

D

data, 19-21, 49, 55-57, 71, 97, 170-171, 199, 219-221

data analysis, 198

data-driven decision-making, 220, 222

Data-Driven Decision-Making Seminars, 97-98

decision-makers, 41, 45, 129

decision-making, 41, 43

demographic data, 8, 97, 115, 117-119, 122, 141-142, 169, 263

demographic variables, 9-10, 195

departmental goals, 157, 160-161

departmental narrative, 164

diagnostic information, 189-190

diligence, 61, 63

direct authority, 231

disaggregate, 143

distinction without a difference, a, 133

district summary, 151

diversity, 93-94

Dorsey, D., 201

dropout, 115

E

economic status, 9, 118, 141

education, 7, 11, 84

Education Trust, 193-194, 244

educational accountability, 25, 33, 53, 106, 130, 151, 225, 243-245

educational accountability systems, 38

educational analysis, 8-9

educational fads, 7

educational leadership, 23, 74

educational policy, 42, 49

educational practices, 95, 186

educational programs, 15, 21-22, 45

educational reform, 7, 11

educational strategies, 97

educative assessment, 17

educators, 8, 61

effect, 21

effective accountability, 93

effective organizations, 195

effective teaching, 194

effectiveness, 41-43, 46

effects, 8

efficacy, 61-63, 100

principles, 93

professional development, 10, 20, 61-64, 95, 117, 229-231, 259, 261

professional education, 61

professional programs, 62

professional qualifications, 10

proficiency, 26, 34, 53-54, 56, 95, 100, 174, 180

proficient, 54

program, 19-20, 25, 27, 33, 38, 43, 45-46, 54, 63, 94

program analysis, 45

programs, 43, 94

promotion rates, 115

public, 23, 26, 222

public education, 56

public schools, 180

Q

qualitative descriptions, 115, 263

qualitative information, 25-26, 86, 119, 121-122, 218

quantitative information, 25-26, 86, 119, 122

R

ranking, 133-134

reading, 132, 206

Reeves, D.B., 200

reforms, 11

replicable, 193, 207

report, 259, 261-262, 264

report cards, 34, 43, 57, 85, 87

reporting, 37, 219, 222, 232-233, 239

research, 103, 106, 108, 117, 152

resources, 69

respect for diversity, 93

results, 18, 58, 104, 116, 226, 234-235

revenge of the nerds, 131

rewards, 103-104, 242, 259, 262

rigor, 16

Riverview Gardens, 54, 201, 204-205

S

S.T.A.R. Leadership, 225-226, 229, 232, 234

S.T.A.R. model, 229-230

S.T.A.R. Tools, 231

safety, 115

sanctions, 104, 242, 259, 262

Sanders, W., 16

schedule, 196

Schmoker, M.J., 18, 192

school accountability reports, 152

school achievement, 19

school board, 37-38, 43

school board members, 218, 222

school districts, 104, 227, 231

school improvement plan, 94

school leaders, 69, 73, 97-98, 100, 225

school performance, 17, 26

school systems, 8, 38, 63, 85-86, 139, 233

school year, 227

school-based, 171, 281

school-based accountability indicators, 148

school-based accountability reports, 151

school-based goals, 116, 157

school-based indicators, 115-117, 121, 130, 147-149, 152, 160, 210, 263

schools, 7, 33-34, 84, 94, 122, 230, 234, 245, 263

Schools from Milwaukee, Wisconsin, 192

schoolwork, 34

science, 206

scoring criteria, 191

scoring guide, 189

scoring rubrics, 53-54, 201-202

Simon, R., 245

Simpson, J.A., 194-195

Slavin, R., 19

social studies, 206

socioeconomic status, 118, 219

sorting, 37

Southern Regional Education Board, 74

special education, 141

specificity, 93, 96

staff development, 45-46, 64, 230-231, 261

stakeholders, 17, 19, 24, 26, 29-31, 33, 38, 42, 58, 79-82, 87, 90, 96, 115-116, 121-122, 132, 149, 263

standard deviation, 23-24

textbooks, 25
Thompson, T., 245
Tier 1, 260, 263
Tier 2, 260, 263
Tier 3, 260, 263-264
time on task, 53, 55, 57
tools, 226, 229, 235
two-column technique, 131

U

universality, 93, 98

V

values, 62
Video Journal of Education, 192

W

Wayne Township, 200, 202, 204-205
Wiggins, G., 17
Wright, C., 201, 245
writing, 16, 25, 27, 53-54, 57, 132, 148, 172, 193, 207
writing improvement, 190
writing prompt, 17
writing rubrics, 197
written responses, 189

Notes

Notes

Notes

Notes

Notes

Notes

Notes

Notes

Notes

Notes